A Pictorial Record of
BRITISH RAILWAYS
DIESEL MULTIPLE UNITS

by
Brian Golding

CHEONA PUBLICATIONS

ISBN 1 900298 00 7

Production, design and setting by
Print-Rite, The Willows, School Lane,
Stadhampton, Oxford. OX44 7TR

Printed by Alpha Print (Witney), Crawley Mill, Witney, Oxon.

This publication is bound vertically, but presented in a landscape format to accommodate the 4mm drawings on one page. This presentation also allows the book to be used easily on the modelling table.

Front cover, left : Metro Cammell Class 101 unit No. 304 in Starthclyde PTE livery at Haymarket on a suburban service from Glasgow to Edinburgh, July 1986.
Colour-Rail

Front cover, right : A BR Derby lightweight unit in original green and cream livery with whiskers, stands by at Cambridge station. *Colour-Rail*

Back cover, top : Birmingham RC & W Co. Class 118 unit P640 (shortened to two cars) with DMBS 51302 and DMS 51317 in the eye catching, special British Telecom livery at Plymouth North Road, 2nd April,1985. *Colour-Rail*

Back cover, upper left : A Metro Cammell Class 101/102 set stands in the bay as a BR Derby Class 108 unit arrives at Lincoln. In both cases the DMBS car is nearer the camera. 28th August, 1990. *G. Gamble.*

Back cover, upper right : A blue liveried BR Derby Class 127 unit composed of 2 DMBS cars arrives at Gospel Oak from Barking, May 198 *Colour-Rail.*

Back cover, lower left : Gloucester R C & W Co. Class 122 No. 55012 in Regional Railways livery shunts 55000, 55006 and a coach at Long Rock Depot, Penzance on 30th September,1993. *J.Turner.*

Back cover, lower right : Set L263 with Birmingham RC & W Co. Class 104 DMBS No. 53540 leading BR Derby Class 108 DTCL No.54495 forming the 08.20 Basingstoke to Reading service seen here at Bramley, 26th August,1993. *J.Turner.*

Published by :
Cheona Publications,
39 The Avenue,Chinnor, Oxfordshire OX9 4PD

CONTENTS

INTRODUCTION

The Modernisation Plan of the 1950's introduced Diesel and Electric traction in a wholesale replacement of the traditional steam locomotive. In the hectic pursuit of operating economies some of the early purchases proved to be less than ideal, many types of Diesel locomotive having very short operating lives. Inevitably, the scrapping of many favourite classes of locomotive meant that the Diesels were resented by many enthusiasts although most train crews welcomed their improved working conditions.

To the travelling public the new trains gave the promise of more reliability and greater comfort and speed. Mainline services were the first to experience the new forms of motive power and the first electrification schemes were announced. Commuter services were also improved with extensions to existing electrified lines and some totally new schemes. But by far the greatest impact on the pattern of services was brought about by the introduction of the Diesel Multiple Unit - DMU. These new trains quickly swept away loco - hauled commuter trains, mainline cross - country trains and countless branchline and push - pull trains.

Many railway enthusiasts, numbed by brutal elimination of many revered locomotive types, found little appealing about these newcomers. This is unfortunate because without them even more of our railway network would have perished in the Beeching era and later. Many areas only have a railway service today because of the improved efficiency provided by these first generation DMU's. Some of those lines which have now closed retained their service longer with DMU's than would otherwise have been the case.

The first British Railways DMU entered service in 1954 and the last of what has become known as the Classic or Heritage DMU was delivered as long ago as 1963. More than a quarter of a century later they were still providing a high percentage (in some cases 100%) of all passenger services.

The Classic DMU had a variety of body designs, depending upon the manufacturer and the purpose for which it was originally destined. They all conformed to the same basic specification in that power was provided by a 'bus - type diesel engine, manufactured by AEC, Leyland, Albion, or Rolls - Royce, horizontally mounted below the floor and driving through an epicyclic gearbox and cardan shaft. A variation to this standard drive system was the use of hydraulic drive on some classes of unit. This was an LMS influence resulting from their pre-1939 Leyland railbus and a three-car semi-streamlined set.

This new breed of unit was a direct and logical development of the AEC - GWR railcars built just before and during the early part of World War 2. These finished their days operating alongside the new units for a number of years.

The Southern Region took a totally different view of their requirements for Multiple Units to operate on their non-electrified lines.

With the massive re-equipment programme of their suburban EMU fleet then in progress for the replacement of older, and war - weary stock and the increased requirements resulting from major extensions to their electrified network, they opted for the Eastleigh pattern of stock. The resultant units had a larger, slower running diesel engine driving an electric generator in the same way as on contemporary diesel - electric locomotives. This was mounted above floor level in an engine room immediately behind the driver's cab. The final drive used the same type of electric motor as the EMU's then entering service. The result was a highly standardised fleet of Electric and Diesel - Electric Multiple Units with a high degree of component interchangeability. A narrow bodied version to main line standards was built to suit the Hastings line loading gauge and to the same mechanical specification as the other Southern Region units.

These DEMU's were developed relatively cheaply and quickly and have proved to be long - lived. When the first thoughts for a replacement design for the Classic DMU were being formulated BR opted for the diesel - electric format in preference to the standard DMU and the prototype Class 210 units showed more than a passing resemblance to the Southern units.

In this work, which commenced in 1979, I have produced drawings of each type of vehicle to the scale of 4mm:1ft. In some cases Works Drawings have been used to show additional detail. These are supported by photographs and a brief description. In order to keep the book to manageable proportions some of the drawings apply to more than one closely related type with the differences noted where appropriate. The choice of section headings has been made to break the subject matter into logical groupings. The later TOPS Classes are annotated against the relevant sections.

Brian Golding, Buckingham, 1995

Abbreviations used within this book

DMC	Driving Motor Composite		TC	Trailer Composite
DMS	Driving Motor Second		TS	Trailer Second
DMBC	Driving Motor Brake Composite		TF	Trailer First
DMBS	Driving Motor Brake Second		TBS	Trailer Brake Second
DTC	Driving Trailer Composite		TC(L)	Trailer Composite...........Toilet
DTS	Driving Trailer Second		TS(L)	Trailer Second...............Toilet
MBS	Motor Brake Second		TF(L)	Trailer First....................Toilet
DMBS(P)	DMBS Parcels Car		TBS(L)	Trailer Brake Second......Toilet
DMPV	Driving Motor Parcels Van		TC(K)	Trailer Composite........Kitchen
DHMC	Driving Half Motor Composite		TF(K)	Trailer First.................Kitchen
DHMBS	Driving Half Motor Brake Second			

Acknowledgements

My sincere thanks are due to all those who have assisted me in the reasearch and compilation of the drawings and finally the finished book.
In particular Frank Bonneres of Metro Cammell, J.E.Atkinson of D.Wickham & Co., Pat Brookes, Michael Foster, Geoff Gamble, Basil Hancock, Bernard Harding, Colin Judge, Joe Turner, and countless others. In addition to Metro Cammell and Wickham, I would like to record my thanks to the following organisations for their help :- Park Royal Vehicles, BR Swindon, North Norfolk Railway Co. Ltd. and the Keighley & Worth Valley Railway Preservation Society.

The 'TOTAL OPERATIONS PROCESSING SYSTEM' or TOPS scheme was a computerised control system introduced around 1970 to enable BR operations to be more efficiently organised. It produced better stock utilisation and allowed a drastic reduction in the number of 'standby' items of rolling stock.

As initially applied to the DMU fleet each type of car had its own separate class number. This was later changed so that all cars in each type of unit shared a common class number.

In the following table the various types are grouped by their later classification indicating the builder. Their original class numbers are listed against the individual car descriptions and finally, the recognised codes for these are shown.

Class	Set	Description	Type	Ref
120		**Swindon Works 3-car Cross Country sets**		122
	120/1	Driving Motor Brake Composite	DMBC	
	120/2	Driving Motor Second	DMSL	
	120/3	Driving Motor Brake First-ex DMBC	DMBF	
	179	Trailer Buffet Second (L)	TRBSL	
	179	Trailer Second (L)	TSL	
121		**Pressed Steel Co. Single Units / Trailers**		86
	121	Driving Motor Brake Second	DMBS	
	149	Driving Trailer Second	DTS	
122		**Gloucester RC& W Single Units / Trailers**		86
	122	Driving Motor Brake Second	DMBS	
	150	Driving Trailer Second	DTS	
123		**Swindon Works 4-car Inter City sets**		107
	123/1	Driving Motor Second (K)	DMSK	
	123/2	Driving Motor Brake Second	DMBS	
	182	Trailer Second (L)	TSL	
	183	Trailer Composite (K)	TCK	
124		**Swindon Works 6-car Trans Pennine sets**		106
	124/1	Driving Motor Composite	DMC	
	124/2	Motor Brake Second non-driving (K)	MBSK	
	180	Trailer Second (L)	TSL	
125		**Derby Works 3-car High Density sets (Rolls Royce powered)**		86
	125/1	Driving Motor Second	DMS	
	125/2	Driving Motor Brake Second	DMBS	
	185	Trailer Second	TS	
126		**Swindon Works 3/6 car Inter City sets**		105
	126/1	Driving Motor Second (L)	DMSL	
	126/2	Driving Motor Brake Second (L)	DMBSL	
	188	Trailer First (K)	TFK	
	189	Trailer Composite (L)	TCL	
127		**Derby Works 4-car High density sets (Rolls Royce powered)**		87
	127	Driving Motor Brake Second	DMBS	
	186	Trailer Second	TS	
128		**Gloucester RC & W Parcels Units**		133
	128	Driving Motor Parcels & Mail Van	DMPMV	
		later - Driving Motor Luggage Van	DMLV	
129		**Cravens Parcels Van**		133
	129	Driving Motor Parcels Van	DMPV	
130		**Derby Works Parcels Units**		84
	130	Converted DMBS Class 116	DMPV	
131		**Gloucester RC & W Parcels Units**		86
	131	Converted DMBS Class 122	DMPV	

Southern Region DEMU sets

Class	Set	Description	Ref
201	6S	6-car (short) Hastings sets	147
202	6L	6-car (long) Hastings sets	147
203	6B	6-car (long) Hastings Buffet sets	148
204	3T	3-car High Density sets	
		(formed from 2-car 205 and DTS ex-206 sets)	156
205	2H/3H	2- & 3- car High Density Hampshire sets	156
206	3R	3-car 'Tadpole' sets	165
207	3D	3-car High Density Oxted Line sets	161

As the TOPS numbering system spread through the fleet those DMU's in the 50XXX and 56XXX series were re-numbered 53XXX and 54XXX respectively to avoid clashing with Class 50 and Class 56 locomotives.

Coupling Codes for DMU's for Multiple Operation of Sets

1. RED TRIANGLE	Original Derby Lightweight 2-car	79XXX series	
	Class 127 BR Derby 4-car units		
2. YELLOW DIAMOND	Original Derby Lightweight 1/2/4-car	79XXX series	
	Original Metro Cammell 2-car	79XXX series	
	Class 129 Cravens Single Parcels cars		
3. BLUE SQUARE	All other DMU Classes not in 1,2,4 & 5		
4. WHITE CIRCLE	Class 126 BR Swindon Inter City 3/6-car	79XXX series	
5. ORANGE STAR	Class 125 BR Derby 3-car units		

The BLUE SQUARE code is regarded as the 'standard coupling code' for the DMU fleet and classes with this code may be coupled together and operated as one unit, being controlled from the leading cab.

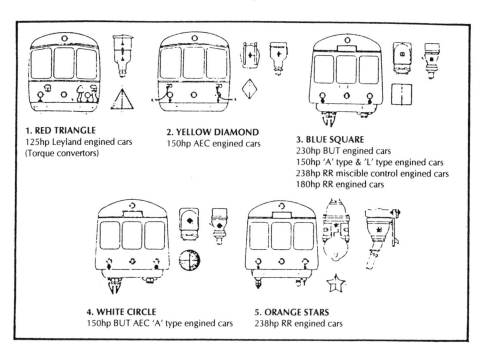

1. RED TRIANGLE
125hp Leyland engined cars
(Torque convertors)

2. YELLOW DIAMOND
150hp AEC engined cars

3. BLUE SQUARE
230hp BUT engined cars
150hp 'A' type & 'L' type engined cars
238hp RR miscible control engined cars
180hp RR engined cars

4. WHITE CIRCLE
150hp BUT AEC 'A' type engined cars

5. ORANGE STARS
238hp RR engined cars

Pressed Steel Class 121 car in green livery at Radley, Oxon (Western Region) with the Abingdon branch service.
J.Turner.

Refurbished Pressed Steel Class 117 unit L420 (Nos.51358, 59510 and 51400) leaves Ealing Broadway with the 12.58pm Oxford to Paddington service, 28th August, 1979.
C.Gamble.

Gloucester C & W Co. Class 122 cars No. 55011 (nearest camera) and 55004 in blue and grey livery with yellow ends, standing in the Stratford-on-Avon service bay at Leamington Spa, 22nd July, 1985.
C.Gamble.

Pressed Steel Class 121 car L131 (No. 55031) in NSE livery, at Bletchley, on a service from Bedford, 30th April 1993.
J.Turner.

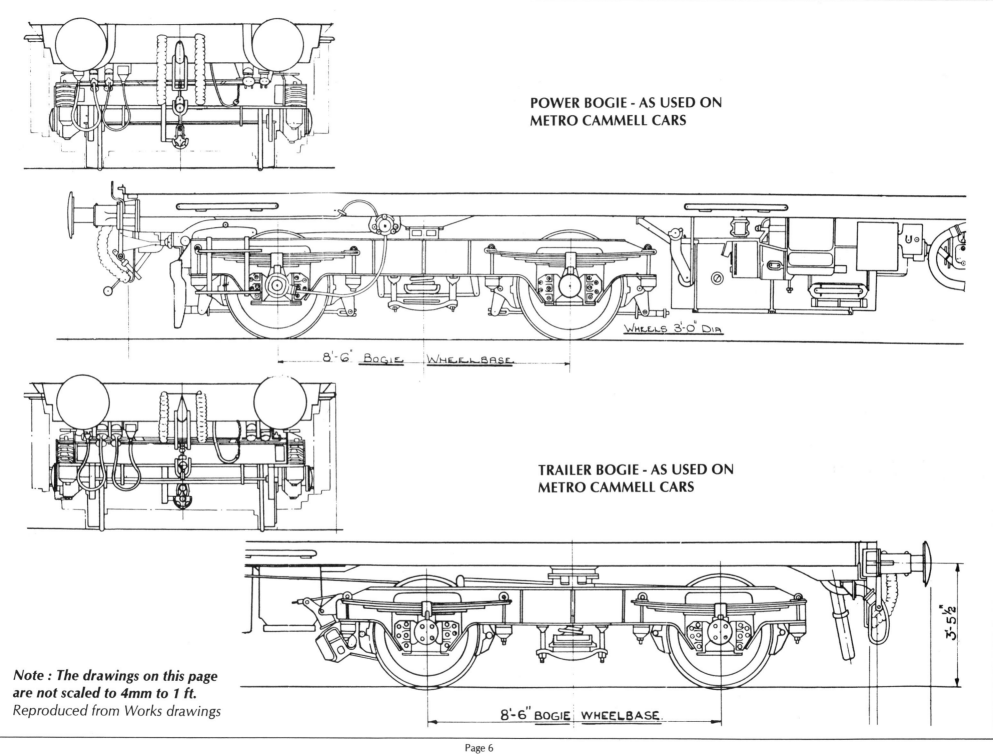

**POWER BOGIE - AS USED ON
METRO CAMMELL CARS**

WHEELS 3'-0" DIA

8'-6" BOGIE WHEELBASE

**TRAILER BOGIE - AS USED ON
METRO CAMMELL CARS**

3'-5½"

*Note : The drawings on this page
are not scaled to 4mm to 1 ft.*
Reproduced from Works drawings

8'-6" BOGIE WHEELBASE

A BR Derby Class 115 unit in NSE revised livery at Marylebone station with a Parcels unit at the buffer stops on the adjacent road.
P.Watson.

L404 – a Class 117 Pressed Steel suburban unit (cars No. 51337, 59489 and 51379) is seen at Aldermarston with a Reading – Newbury – Bedwyn service, 17th May, 1989.
B.Denton, Milepost 92½.

Birmingham RC & W Co. Class 118 unit T318, with car No. 51331 leading, arrives at Leamington Spa from Birmingham, 8th February, 1990.
J.Turner.

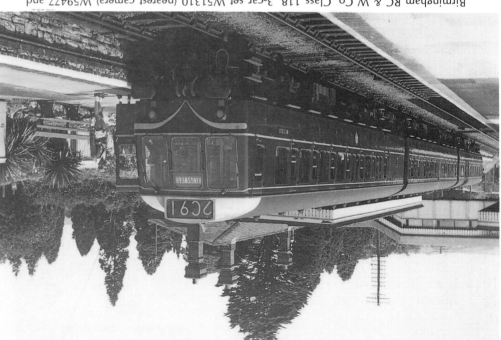

Birmingham RC & W Co. Class 118, 3-car set W51310 (nearest camera) W59477 and W51325 in green and cream livery with whiskers, stands at Brent with a Kingswear train on 21st June, 1961.
J.H.Meredith.

A Swindon Class 124, 6-car set in original green and cream livery. Note the characteristic end to the DMC and the 4-digit headcode box in use.   *The late R. Mack.*
Swindon Class 126 DMS car No. SC51021, with headcode boxes and corridor connection still in situ, in all blue livery with yellow end, 1973 at Ayr shed.
Cheona Collection.

Swindon Class 124 'Trans Pennine' unit with DMC No. E51956 leading, in the final livery carried - blue and grey with yellow end. Seen calling at Scunthorpe on a service to Cleethorpes, 1st July, 1982.   *Merchant Navy Loco. Preservation Society Ltd.*
Swindon Class 123 unit (DMS No. W52098 leading) in green livery with headcode boxes still in use but corridor connection boarded over.   *Cheona Collection.*

A Metro Cammell Class 101/2 with DMBS nearest the camera in green and cream livery in the up fast platform at Millers Dale with a train from Buxton, 16th August, 1959.

J.R.Morten.

A BR Derby Class 114 DTCL coupled to a DMBS stands by at Wolverhampton in green and cream livery, with yellow whiskers. *The late M. Gregory.*

BR Derby Class 108 with car No. M51947 nearest the camera seen here in blue and grey livery with the all yellow end at Worcester Shrub Hill on 23rd April, 1992.

G.Gamble.

Cravens units at Accrington. A DMBS of the Rolls Royce-engined Class 113 with hydraulic transmission and four digit headcode box in the roof dome. On the left a Class 105 with the more typical Cravens end. Both units appear in green and cream livery with yellow end panels. *Cheona collection.*

CHAPTER ONE

BR Derby - Early Lightweight Units

The first type of DMU to be introduced was the lightweight Low-Density unit designed and built by the BR works at Derby. These had a common seating layout comprising - entrance vestibule (on the driving cars this area accommodated the cab), a two-bay seating area, a central entrance vestibule, a three-and-a-half-bay seating area, a further entrance vestibule, a two-and-a-half-bay seating area incorporating a single lavatory (this last section accommodated the guard's / luggage area on brake cars - except on some four car sets which we deal with later). A further variant was a batch of five Driving Motor Composite cars for the North Eastern Region 4-car sets which had the first class accommodation in the centre of the vehicle. On these cars the window arrangement in this portion was completely different from the rest of the series.

Derby Works produced the first of these sets in 1954 using new lightweight materials with body styling in line with the newly introduced standard locomotive hauled coaches (now referred to as Mark 1 stock). These units may be regarded as the logical development of the GWR Railcars, the later versions of which had already demonstrated the practicality of multiple unit operation. These pioneer units replaced steam hauled trains on branch and feeder lines. First introduced on the London Midland, North Eastern and Eastern Regions in 1954, they set the pattern for the future. In the manner of any early development of a project, there were a number of different patterns of vehicle and set formations, largely dictated by regional and service requirements, with a number of car types appearing in more than one type of set. This makes a logical order of coverage difficult but hopefully we can avoid confusion.

The early units were very distinctive with their 'Glasshouse' or 'Cathedral' cab fronts and Mark 1 bodyside profiles. In fact, careful observation will show that the large side windows were placed lower than in the Mark 1 coaching stock. This characteristic was perpetuated in the later Derby Lightweight units of Class 108 (see later). The front ends proved to be too weak in service and did not conform to the later impact resistance specification and they were considerably altered for the Class 108 units.

Mechanically these units were compatible with each other and the pioneer Metro-Cammell units (see Chapter Two) . To avoid the possibility of any attempt to couple these with any non-compatible stock they were coded 'Yellow Diamond'. This was intended to be the BR standard although some of the early sets were to 'White Circle' and 'Red Triangle' codes and eventually, as the control systems evolved, the 'Blue Square' pattern was adopted as the Standard and most of the later series· of cars conformed to it. The early cars were, therefore, not compatible with the later and more numerous units.

In order to try and keep matters as clear as possible these cars are dealt with in their original formations with reference made to the appropriate drawings.

a) North Eastern Region Two-car Power Twin Sets

There were eight of these sets which differed from the rest of the early units being fitted with hydro-mechanical transmission and branded 'Red Triangle' thus being incompatible with any of the other early sets. Each car was powered by two BUT Leyland 'Bus-type 125 bhp horizontally mounted diesel engines driving through Lysholm-Smith (Leyland) torque converters to the final drive. The bodies were 57' 6" long and each car weighed 26 tons.

Driving Motor Brake Second - DMBS
Seats :	61 second class.
Nos.	E79000 - 7 (Lot No. 30084)
Drawing :	*Fig.1, fig.2.* Seating Plan : *Fig.19.*
	End views. *Fig.4 & fig.8.*

Driving Motor Composite with Lavatory - DMCL
Seats :	16 first class, 53 second class
Nos.	E79500 - 7 (Lot No. 30085)
Drawing :	*Fig.11, fig.12.* Seating Plan : *Fig.17,*with front section to *fig.10.*

b) London Midland Region and Eastern Region two-car sets

Within this group there were actually five variations and here it is easier to describe the individual types of car and then to deal with the formations of the five sub groups. Each of the power cars was equipped with two BUT (AEC) 'Bus-type 150 bhp horizontal diesel engines with mechanical transmission by cardan shaft to a four - speed epicyclic gearbox and a further cardan shaft to the final drive. Bodies were 57' 6" long, power cars weighed 27 tons and trailers 21 tons.

Driving Motor Brake second - DMBS
There were three different types of DMBS in this group of units having 61, 56 and 52 seats respectively, which for convenience are denoted **a, b** and **c.**

Type a - 61 seats
These were the first type to be built and are depicted in *fig.1, fig.2* and seating plan *fig.19.*   In this design there was a two-row saloon in the rear section reducing the size of the brake van. This saloon had a large window on each side and thus *fig.2* is correct and it is necessary to substitute this for the small window in *fig.1.*

Type b - 56 seats

This type was developed as an alternative to the above and had a slightly larger brake van and a single row of seats in the rear section. The windows in this half saloon were smaller and a further small window was situated in the brake van. Whilst the same drawings apply in this case *fig.1* is correct and for the right hand side *fig.2* has to be altered to include the two small windows in place of the single large one. The seating plan is *fig.1*.

Type c - 52 seats

This possibly was the most successful arrangement with the brake van occupying the whole of the rear section. The two small windows were retained and the comments regarding drawings *fig.1* and *fig.2* for *type b,* apply here also. Seating plan for this type is *fig.3*.

Driving Motor Composite with Lavatory - DMCL

For clarity these are included in the same type notation.

Type d

These cars had seating for 12 first class passengers and a total of 53 second class in the centre and rear sections.

The lavatory was in the standard position in the rear section. *Fig.11* shows the left hand side, *fig.12* shows the right hand side of the chassis and *fig.13* of the body. The seating plan is *fig.17*.

Driving Trailer Composite with Lavatory - DTCL

These cars were similar to the DMCL except, of course, that they were unpowered. There were two variants in this sub group:-

Type e

These trailer cars provided first class accommodation for 9 passengers in the front section and, like the DMCL above, for 53 second class in the centre and rear, *fig.13* shows the right hand side of these cars whilst the left hand side of the body is as *fig.11* without the exhaust stacks and power car underframe detail. Seating plan is *fig.17* with front portion to *fig.15*.

Type f

These were virtually identical to *type e* but had 16 first class seats instead of 9. The comments about the drawings are the same as for *type e* and the seating plan can be arrived at by taking *fig.17* and superimposing *fig.10* over the front section.

Formations

1). London Midland Region two-car Power - twin sets.

There were 5 of these sets formed as follows:-

DMBS *Type a* Nos. M79184 - 88 (Lot No. 30324)
DMCL *Type d* Nos. M79189 - 93 (Lot No. 30325)
(*Note* : M79191 - 93 later converted to DTCL and renumbered M79633 - 5)

2). London Midland Region two-car sets.

DMBS *Type a* Nos. M79008 - 20 (Lot No. 30123)
DTCL *Type e* Nos. M79600 - 12 (Lot No. 30124)

3). Eastern Region two-car sets.

DMBS *Type b* Nos. E79021 - 33 (Lot No. 30126)
Nos. E79034 - 46 (Lot No. 30177)
DTCL *Type f* Nos. E79250 - 62 (Lot No. 30178)
Nos. E79613 - 25 (Lot No. 30127)

4). London Midland Region two-car sets.

These 41 sets represent the final production design and as such they set the pattern for the later Derby sets.

DMBS *Type c* Nos. M79118 - 36 /41 - 49 / 69 - 81.
DTCL *Type e* Nos. M79639 - 57 / 62 - 84.

These cars ran in the following set formations :

M79118 - 26 (Lot No. 30235)   M79639 - 47 (Lot No. 30326)
M79127 - 36 (Lot No. 30240)   M79648 - 57 (Lot No. 30241)
M79683 (Lot No. 30322)

Note : M79649 converted to an Inspection Saloon before 1964 but not renumbered or transferred to Departmental stock until 1964.

M79141 (Lot No. 30246)   M79662 (Lot No. 30247)
M79142 (Lot No. 30246)   M79684 (Lot No. 30322)
M79143 - 9 (Lot No. 30201)   M79663 - 9 (Lot No. 30202)
M79169 - 70 (Lot No. 30321)   M79670 - 1 (Lot No. 30322)
M79171 - 81 (Lot No. 30321)   M79672 - 82 (Lot No. 30322)

5). North Eastern Region two-car sets.

The North Eastern Region had 4 sets which were virtually identical to the London Midland Region units just described, but they had 16 first class seats.

DMBS *Type c* Nos. E79137 - 40 (Lot No. 30240)
DTCL *Type f* Nos. E79658 - 61 (Lot No. 30241)

c). North Eastern Region four-car sets

There were 5 of these sets for services in the North East. They introduced a new formation which was repeated in later designs from Derby, Metro-Cammell, and BRCW. In these units the brake van was situated in one of the trailer cars. Mechanically they were the same as the LMR/ER two-car sets and were compatible for multiple operation. As mentioned in the introduction to this chapter, the Driving Motor Composite cars had the first class accommodation in the centre and the windows in this section were unique.

Driving Motor Second - DMS

This design had no lavatory, but the body design was the same as the DMCL previously described. One feature of the four-car units was 2 + 2 seating in the second class saloons giving more comfort than the

Gloucester RC & W Co. Class 119 DMSL No. W51105 in green and cream livery with whiskers seen at Bridport.
Cheona collection.
Swindon Class 120 unit DMBC No. W50696 smartly turned out in green and cream livery with whiskers at Swindon, 27th September, 1959.
Merchant Navy Loco Preservation Society Ltd.

Gloucester RC & W Co. Class 119 set L594 in revised NSE livery arrives at Wokingham with the 12.05 Reading to Redhill service. Car No. 51073 leads 59435 and 51104, 3rd September, 1993.
J. Turner.
Swindon Class 120 in blue and grey livery and yellow ends, with DMBC No. M53705 nearest the camera is followed by a Class 101 trailer. Photographed at Leicester station on 2nd June, 1983.
Merchant Navy Loco. Preservation Society Ltd.

normal 2 + 3 arrangement.

Seats: 64 second
Nos.   E79150 - 54   (Lot No. 30193)
Drawing   *Fig.11*, LHS (chassis only): *fig.12*, RHS.
                Seating Plan as *Fig. 14*

Trailer Brake Second with Lavatory - TBSL

In this design the brake van was accommodated in the front section enabling the lavatory to be in its normal position in the rear section. Seating was again 2 + 2.

Seats: 45 second.
Nos.   E79325 - 29. (Lot No. 30194)
Drawing   *Fig. 20, fig 21* and *fig 22.*

Trailer Second with Lavatory - TSL

This followed the standard pattern with an entrance vestibule at the front in place of the cab of a driving car. 2 + 2 seating was provided and the lavatory was in the rear section.

Seats: 61 second.
Nos.   E79400 - 04.   (Lot No. 30195)
Drawing   *Fig.23, fig.24* and *fig.25.*

Driving Motor Composite - DMC

These cars differed from all others in the series in having the first class accommodation located in the centre section.
Like the DMS, no lavatory was provided.

Seats: 20 first, 36 second.
Nos.   E79508 - 12   (Lot No. 30192)
Drawing   *Fig.11* shows LHS and *fig.12* RHS (chassis only).
                Seating plan is arrived at by superimposing *fig.16* over centre section of *fig.14.*

d). London Midland Region Single car units

Finally, we come to the two single car units introduced in 1956 for the Bletchley - Banbury branch. Basically they were a *type c* DMBS with a driving cab at each end. It is typical of the way in which this early series was developed that these two cars were not identical. The first one , M79900, had a large window on both sides in the brake van whereas M79901 had a single small one on each side.

Seats: 52 second.
Nos.   M79900   (Lot No. 30380)
                M79901   (Lot No. 30387)
Drawing :   *Fig.26* (LHS M79900). *Fig. 27* (RHS M79901). *Fig. 28.*

Pressed Steel Class 121 single car No. W55033 in blue and grey livery at Rhymney on a Cardiff service, 8th August,1983. The unit has been fitted with a Gloucester C & W Co. dome from a Class 119 or 122 but the exhaust pipes have been left as they were.

G.Gamble.

General

The end elevations of the whole series are shown in *figs.4 -9* and can be summarised as follows.

Fig. 4   Cab end of all Driving cars (except brake end of M79900/01).
Fig. 5   Cab end at brake end of M79900/01.
Fig. 6   Brake end of TBSL.
Fig. 7   Brake end of all DMBS (except M79900/01).
Fig. 8   Both ends of TSL, non-brake end of TBSL and inner end of DTCL.
Fig. 9   Inner end of all non-brake power cars.

The above descriptions cover the development of this series of pioneer units. When first introduced all cars carried the standard multiple unit green livery with two cream lines along the bodyside - one at the waist and one at the cantrail level. Later two whiskers were added to the cab ends until these were replaced by yellow warning panels below the cab windows. Withdrawals were well under way by the time the Rail Blue livery was introduced in the latter half of the 1960's. However, the later survivors most certainly carried the blue livery with all-over yellow cab ends and at least one of the single units ended its service in this style. Seating material was of a green patterned type in second class and blue patterned in first class. The earliest cars had one-piece cab windows on each side, the horizontal bars shown on the drawings appear on the later builds. Swing links were removed from the bogie sides in an attempt to improve the riding qualities at speed - however without much effect.

Two cars of this type were converted to Battery - Electric operation at Cowlairs Works in 1958 and were renumbered 79998 and 79999.

Class 127 BR Derby suburban unit 920 with cars No. 55966 and 55967 in green livery and cream whiskers on a yellow end. This was a special conversion for the conveyance of newspapers. Birmingham New Street, May 1987.   *P.Watson.*

Class 128 Gloucester RC & W Co. Parcels Car No. 55993 in the same livery as the top right photograph. Note : the removal of corridor connection and split headcode boxes. Crewe station.   *Brian Golding.*

Class 127 BR Derby suburban unit 915 with cars No. 55975 and 55976 in blue livery with red and white waistband, yellow end and white lettering. This was a special conversion for 'Express Parcels', seen here at Birmingham New Street in May, 1987.
                                                                        P.Watson.

Class 128 Gloucester RC & W Co. Parcels Car No. W55992 in all blue livery with yellow ends at Reading on 24th May, 1975.   *C.Reid.*

Class 205, 1959-built set No. 1102 in green livery and yellow end panel with DMBSO nearest the camera. Southampton, 1967. *Cheona collection.*

Berks and Hants 3H, Class 205 unit in blue and grey livery with black triangle on the yellow end panel which warns platform staff that the train has no luggage accommodation at the rear. March, 1986. *P.Watson.*

Class 204, Berks and Hants 2-car set No. 1121 in Rail Blue with yellow ends at Southampton. *Cheona collection.*

Class 203, No. 203001 in restored green livery with yellow end awaits departure from Charing Cross in October, 1988. *P.Watson.*

Blue Pullman DMBS of a Western Region set in the final livery of light grey and blue, with yellow ends and white lettering. *P.Watson.*

Metro Cammell Class III (on the left) - cars No. E50170, 59072, 59079 and 50149 bound for Darlington and a similar class on the right (still bearing its headcode box) forming the 10.13 to Middlesbrough. Both units are in Rail Blue with all yellow ends and were photographed at Whitby, 24th July, 1980. *G.Gamble.*

No. E 79963, one of five Waggon und Maschinenbau railbuses built for BR and the one fitted with an AEC engine for comparison tests. North Norfolk in 1960.
Cheona collection.

Gloucester RC & W Co., Class 100, 2-car set on a service to Stafford from Wolverhampton. Livery is green and cream with the DMBS nearest the camera.
The late M.Gregory.

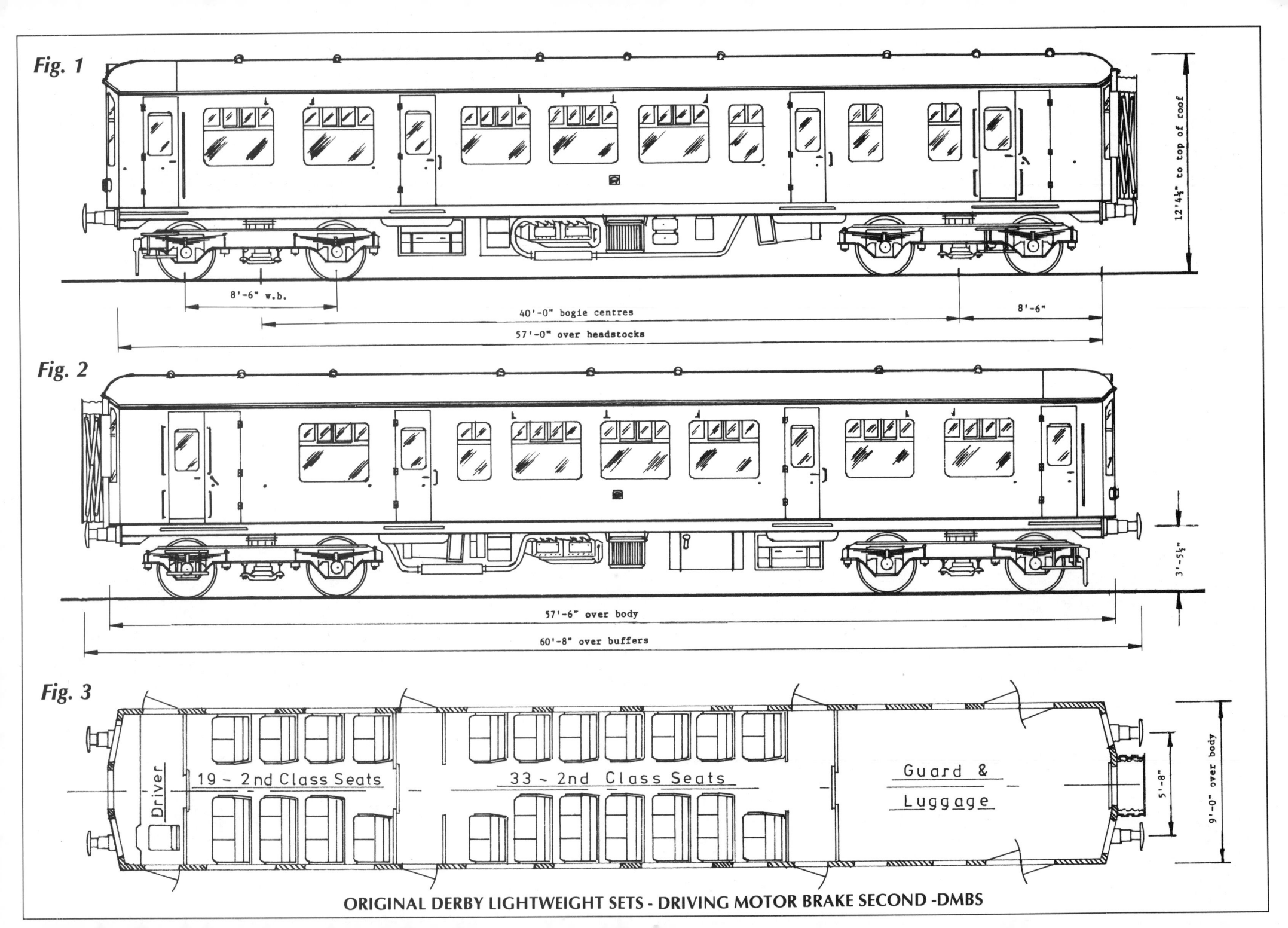

Fig. 1

12'4½" to top of roof

8'-6" w.b.

40'-0" bogie centres

57'-0" over headstocks

8'-6"

Fig. 2

57'-6" over body

60'-8" over buffers

3'-5½"

Fig. 3

Driver

19 - 2nd Class Seats

33 - 2nd Class Seats

Guard & Luggage

9'-0" over body

5'-8"

ORIGINAL DERBY LIGHTWEIGHT SETS - DRIVING MOTOR BRAKE SECOND -DMBS

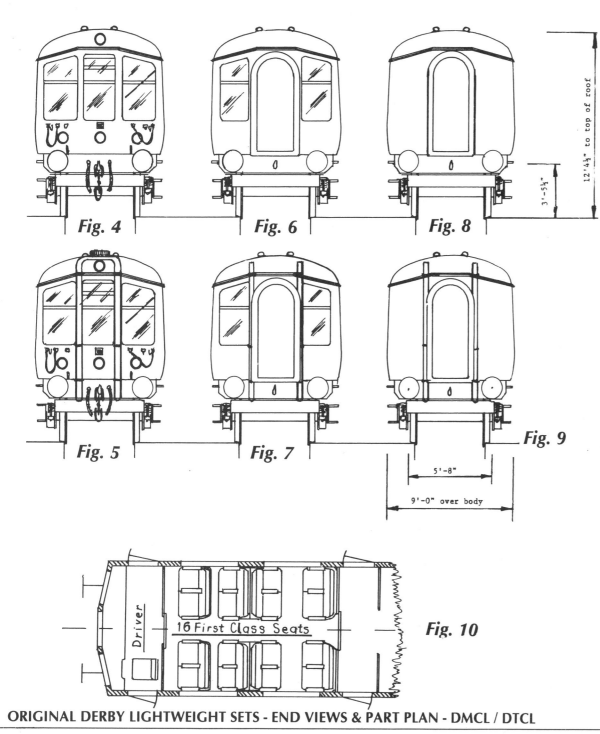

Fig. 4

Fig. 6

Fig. 8

12'4½" to top of roof

3'-5¼"

Fig. 5

Fig. 7

Fig. 9

5'-8"

9'-0" over body

Driver

16 First Class Seats

Fig. 10

ORIGINAL DERBY LIGHTWEIGHT SETS - END VIEWS & PART PLAN - DMCL / DTCL

A DTCL leads this 2-car Derby lightweight unit on a service to Carlisle. Green and cream livery with whiskers. Note the safety bars fitted to the droplights on the passenger doors.   *M.Smith/Kelland collection.*

A Derby lightweight unit at Blaenau Festiniog on a service to Llandudno Junction. The livery is as the picture above.   *R.S.Carpenter.*

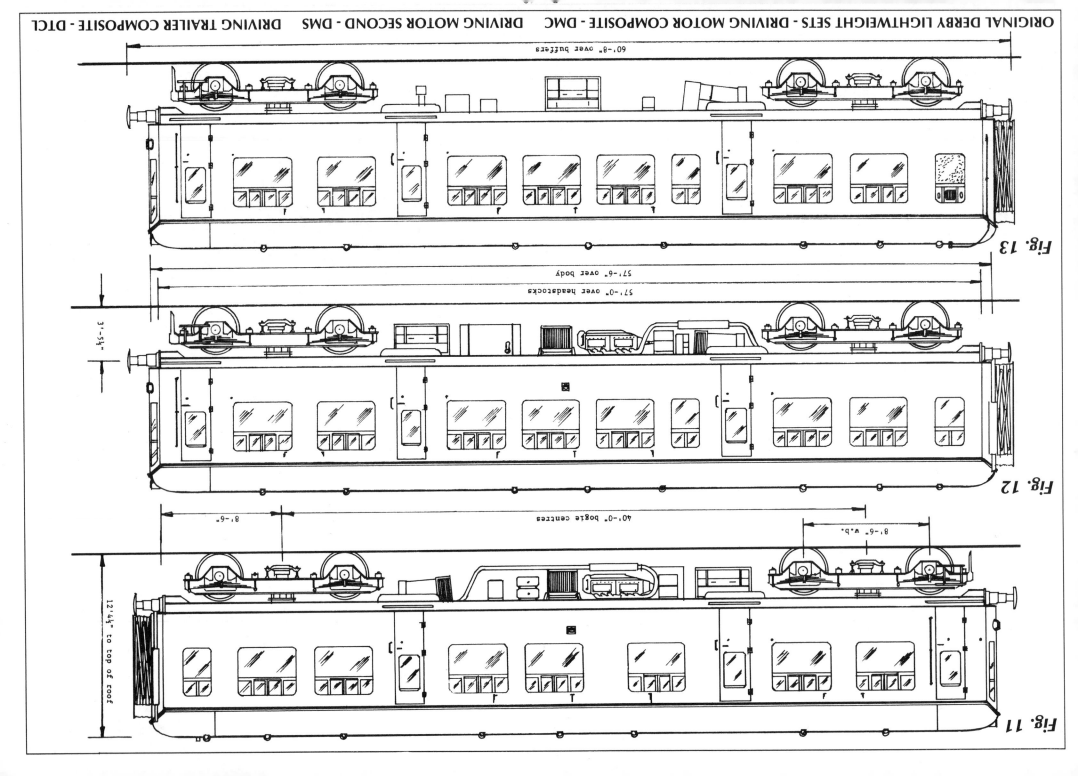

ORIGINAL DERBY LIGHTWEIGHT SETS - DRIVING MOTOR COMPOSITE - DMC   DRIVING MOTOR SECOND - DMS   DRIVING TRAILER COMPOSITE - DTCL

Fig. 13

60'-8" over buffers

57'-6" over body

57'-0" over headstocks

3'-5¼"

Fig. 12

40'-0" bogie centres

8'-6"

8'-6" w.b.

12'-4¼" to top of roof

Fig. 11

Fig. 14

16 Second Class Seats   28 Second Class Seats   20 Second Class Seats

Driver

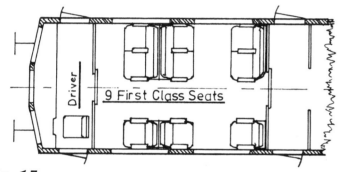

Fig. 15

9 First Class Seats

Driver

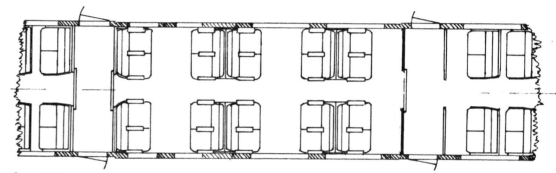

Fig. 16

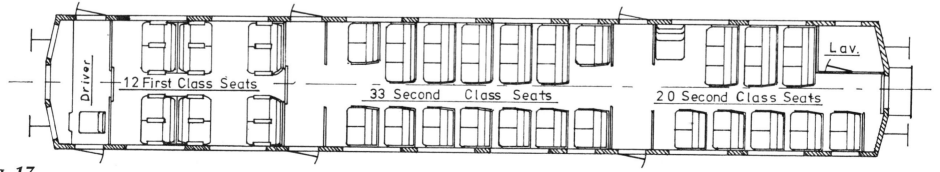

Fig. 17

Driver

12 First Class Seats   33 Second Class Seats   20 Second Class Seats

Lav.

ORIGINAL DERBY LIGHTWEIGHT SETS - SEATING PLANS

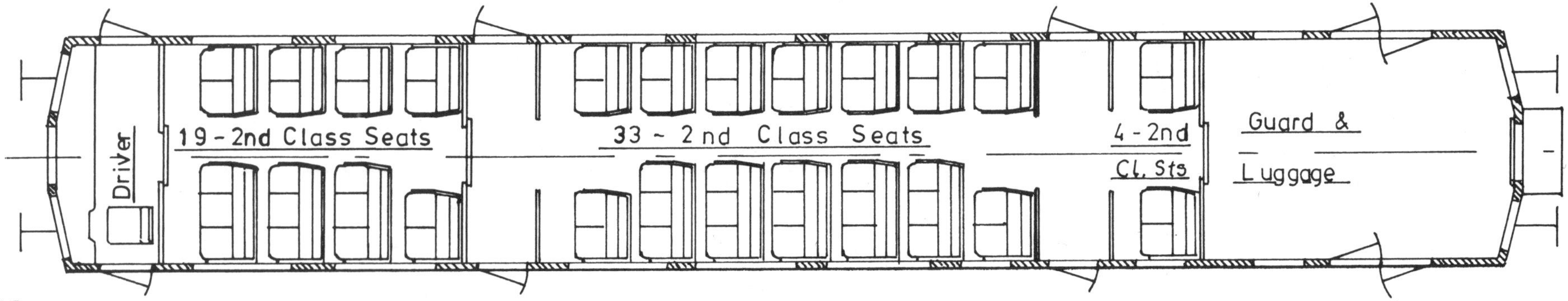

Fig. 18

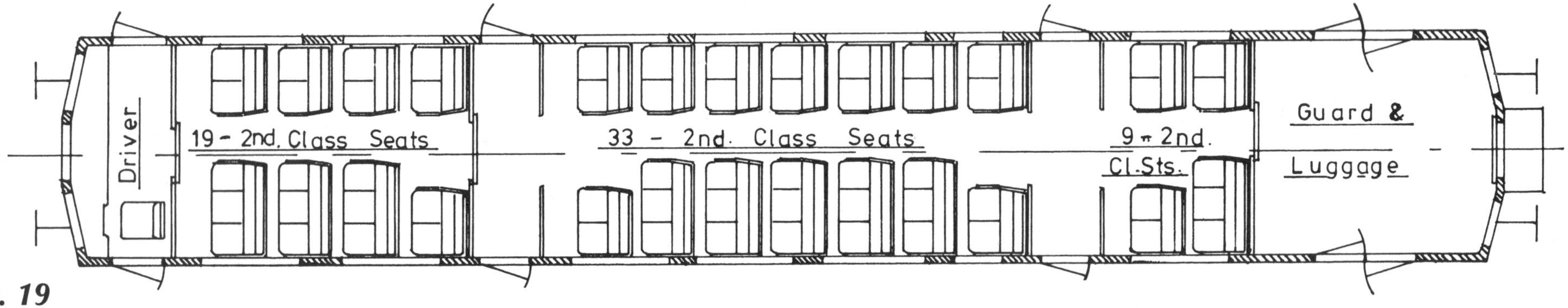

Driver | 19 – 2nd Class Seats | 33 – 2nd Class Seats | 4 – 2nd Cl. Sts | Guard & Luggage

Fig. 19

Driver | 19 – 2nd. Class Seats | 33 – 2nd. Class Seats | 9 – 2nd. Cl. Sts. | Guard & Luggage

ORIGINAL DERBY LIGHTWEIGHT SETS - SEATING PLANS

Derby lightweight units passing Castle Bromwich, May 1955, in green and cream livery with DMCL car leading. This was a British Industries Fair Special and was the first use of DMU's in the Birmingham area. Note roofboards below the cantrail along the sides of the car.

R.S.Carpenter.

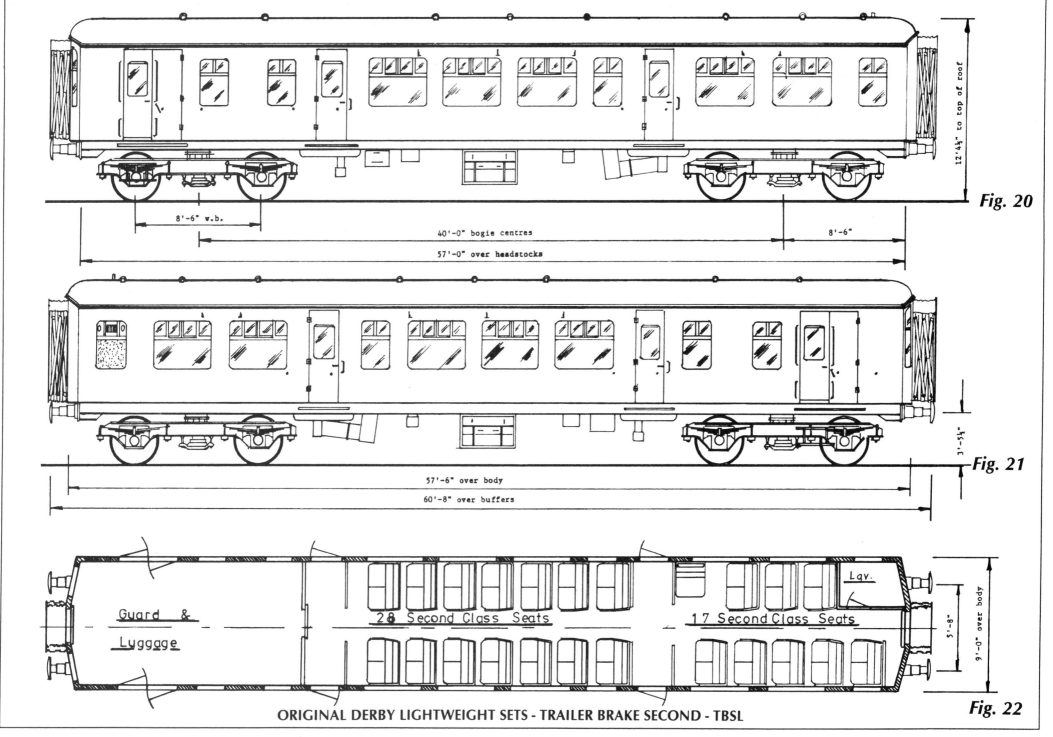

12'4½" to top of roof

8'-6" w.b.

40'-0" bogie centres

8'-6"

57'-0" over headstocks

Fig. 20

3'-5¼"

57'-6" over body

60'-8" over buffers

Fig. 21

Guard & Luggage

28 Second Class Seats

17 Second Class Seats

Lav.

5'-8"

9'-0" over body

Fig. 22

ORIGINAL DERBY LIGHTWEIGHT SETS - TRAILER BRAKE SECOND - TBSL

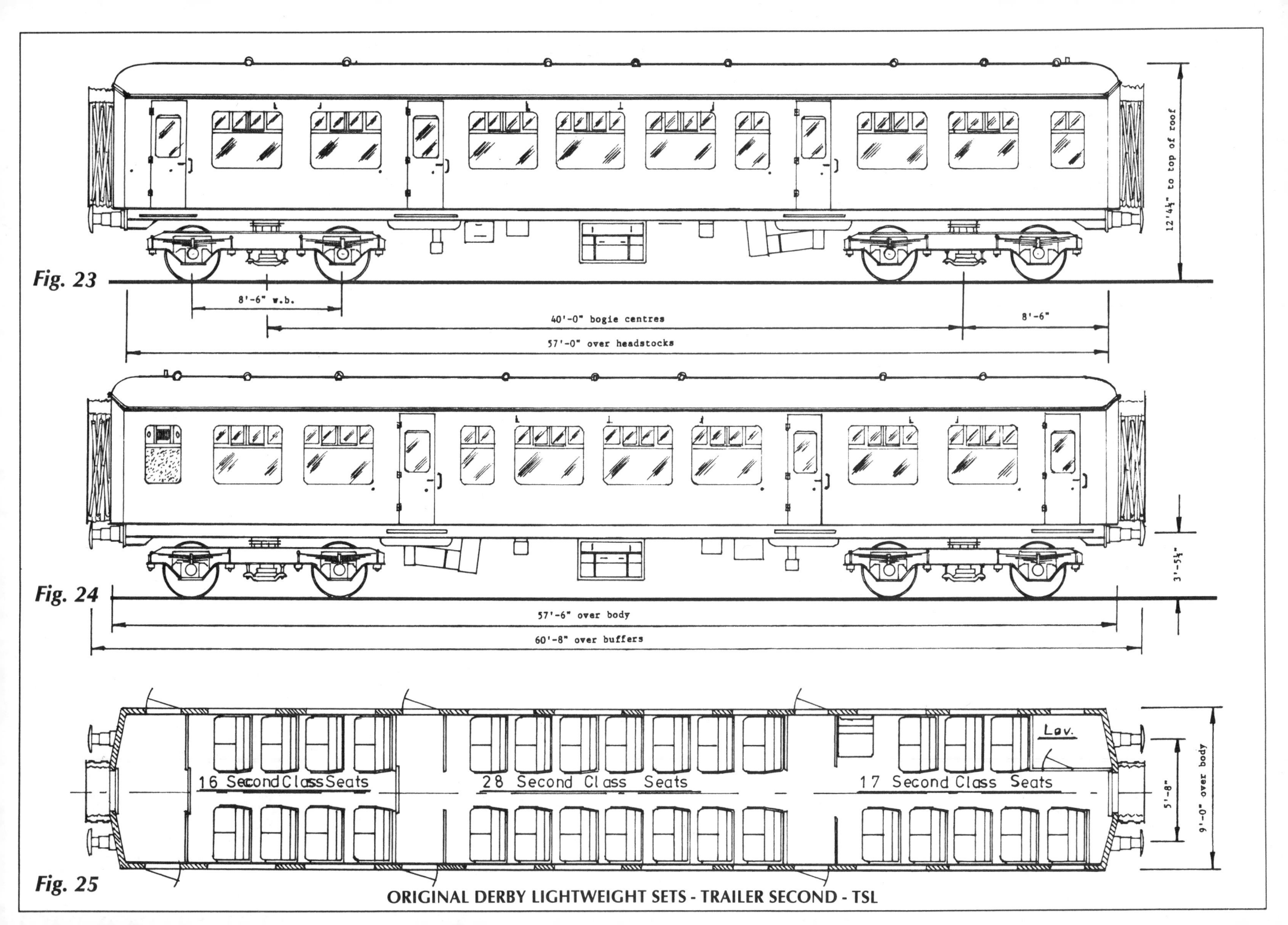

Fig. 23

12'4¼" to top of roof

8'-6" w.b.

40'-0" bogie centres

8'-6"

57'-0" over headstocks

Fig. 24

3'-5¼"

57'-6" over body

60'-8" over buffers

Fig. 25

16 Second Class Seats   28 Second Class Seats   17 Second Class Seats   Lav.

5'-8"

9'-0" over body

ORIGINAL DERBY LIGHTWEIGHT SETS - TRAILER SECOND - TSL

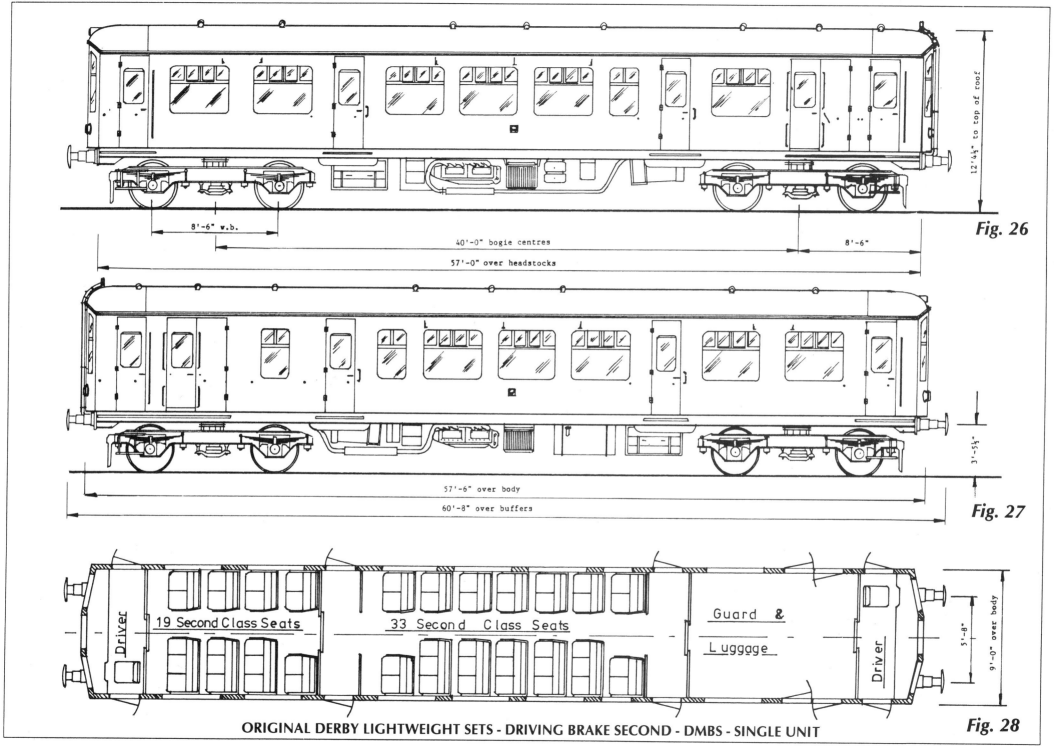

Fig. 26

12'4½" to top of roof

8'-6" v.b.

40'-0" bogie centres

8'-6"

57'-0" over headstocks

Fig. 27

57'-6" over body

60'-8" over buffers

3'-5½"

Driver

19 Second Class Seats

33 Second Class Seats

Guard & Luggage

Driver

5'-8"

9'-0" over body

ORIGINAL DERBY LIGHTWEIGHT SETS - DRIVING BRAKE SECOND - DMBS - SINGLE UNIT

Fig. 28

CHAPTER TWO

Metro-Cammell - Early Lightweight Units

The Metro-Cammell interpretation of the basic BR specification for DMU's first appeared with the introduction of their early lightweight sets at about the same time as the Derby units. The basic bodyshell followed the same layout as the Derby designs, but featured a very distinctive window pattern, being much shallower and set in a prominent, polished aluminium frame. The side doors were more or less the standard BR pattern, but the most noticeable feature of the sides was the lack of a rain gutter, the side panels being carried up over the normal cantrail in a smooth arc and short gutters were placed above each door. The cab ends were also unique since they were virtually devoid of the usual dome in the end of the roof. This early series had an extended front skirt below the buffer beams although this was not repeated on the later series. (Classes 101 & 110).

The original paint finish was again refreshingly different from the normal style. The basic colour was the standard multiple unit green, but instead of the two cream lines favoured by Derby, the Metro-Cammell sets had three. The top one followed the normal line just above the side windows, but the middle one passed along the bodyside level with the base of the sliding ventilators in the large windows. At the front end it swept down diagonally around the front corner of the body to run across the front immediately under the cab windows. The third line ran right round the car approximately 2" from the bottom of the sides. Initially they had the two whiskers below the cab windows until this was replaced by the yellow warning panel.

There were 36 two-car sets, 29 all second-class for the Eastern Region and 7 DMBS + DTCL combinations for the London Midland Region. Power cars were each fitted with two AEC 'Bus type diesel engines of 150 bhp with the same mechanical transmission arrangements as described for the Derby units. Bodies were 57' 0" long, the power cars weighing 26.5 tons and the trailers 25 tons.

Driving Motor Brake Second - DMBS

Seats:	56 second (Eastern Region)
	52 second (London Midland Region)
Nos.	E79047 - 75 (Lot No. 30190)
	M79076 - 82 (Lot No. 30190)
Drawings:	*Fig.29*, *fig.30* and *fig.36* (Eastern Region)
	Fig.29, *fig.30* and *fig.31* (London Midland Region)
	End views, *fig.33* and *fig.34*.

Driving Trailer Second with Lavatory - DTSL

Seats:	72 second.
Nos.	E79263 - 91 (Lot No. 30191)
Drawings:	*Fig.37*, *fig.38* and *fig.32*.
	End views *fig.33* and *fig.35*.

Driving Trailer Composite with Lavatory - DTCL

Seats:	12 first, 53 second.
Nos.	M79626 - 32 (Lot No. 30191)
Drawing:	*Fig.37*, *fig.38* and *fig.39*.
	End views *fig.33* and *fig.35*.

These units were coupling code 'Yellow Diamond' and were fully compatible with the contemporary Derby lightweight units. All have long since been withdrawn from service.

The Eastern Region units were used on various East Anglian branches whilst the Midland Region used theirs on the Bury - Bacup route. The original Tri-ang two-car '00' model was based on this type.

A Middlesbrough-bound Class 101/2 Metro Cammell unit in green and cream livery, with DMCL nearest the camera, calls at Ryhope. *Cheona collection.*

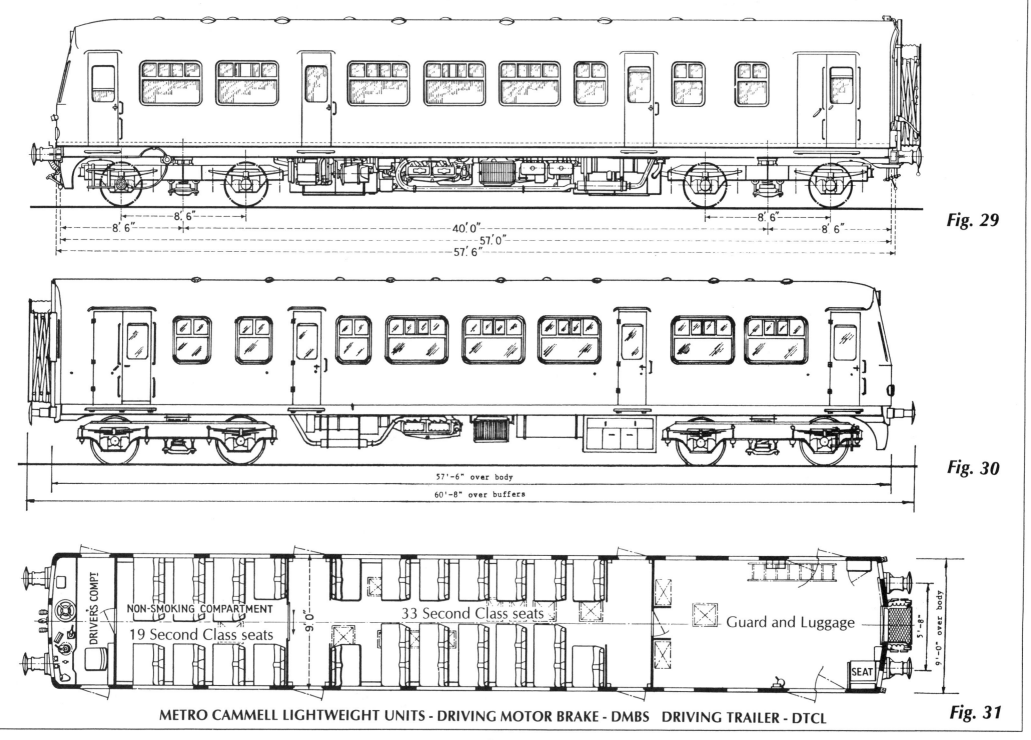

Fig. 29

Fig. 30

57'-6" over body

60'-8" over buffers

8' 6"
8' 6"
40' 0"
57' 0"
57' 6"
8' 6"
8' 6"

DRIVER'S COMPT

NON-SMOKING COMPARTMENT

9'-0"

19 Second Class seats

33 Second Class seats

Guard and Luggage

SEAT

5'-8"

9'-0" over body

METRO CAMMELL LIGHTWEIGHT UNITS - DRIVING MOTOR BRAKE - DMBS   DRIVING TRAILER - DTCL

Fig. 31

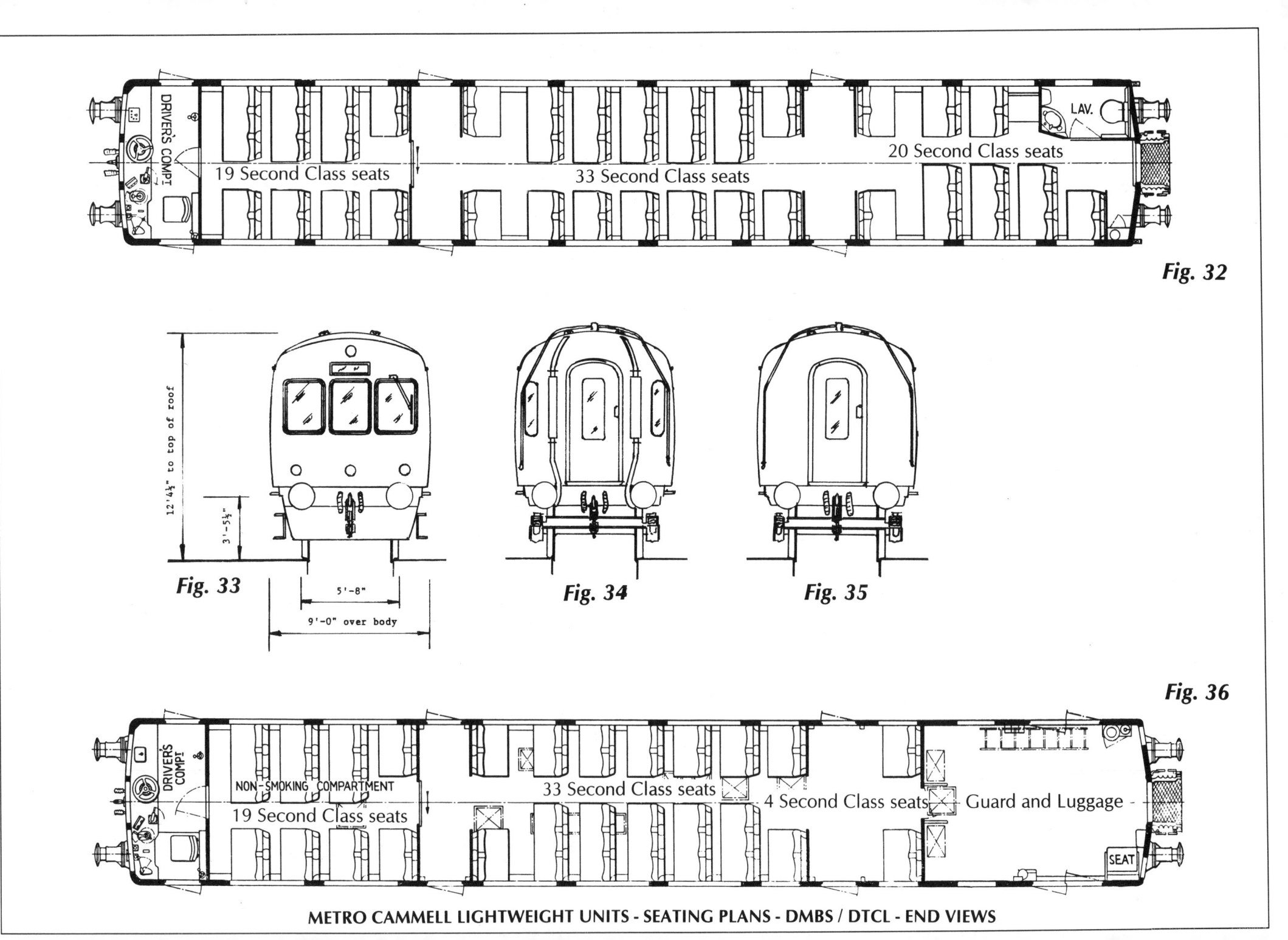

Fig. 32

DRIVER'S COMPT

19 Second Class seats

33 Second Class seats

20 Second Class seats

LAV.

Fig. 33

12'·4½" to top of roof

3'·5½"

5'·8"

9'·0" over body

Fig. 34

Fig. 35

Fig. 36

DRIVER'S COMPT

NON-SMOKING COMPARTMENT

19 Second Class seats

33 Second Class seats

4 Second Class seats

Guard and Luggage

SEAT

METRO CAMMELL LIGHTWEIGHT UNITS - SEATING PLANS - DMBS / DTCL - END VIEWS

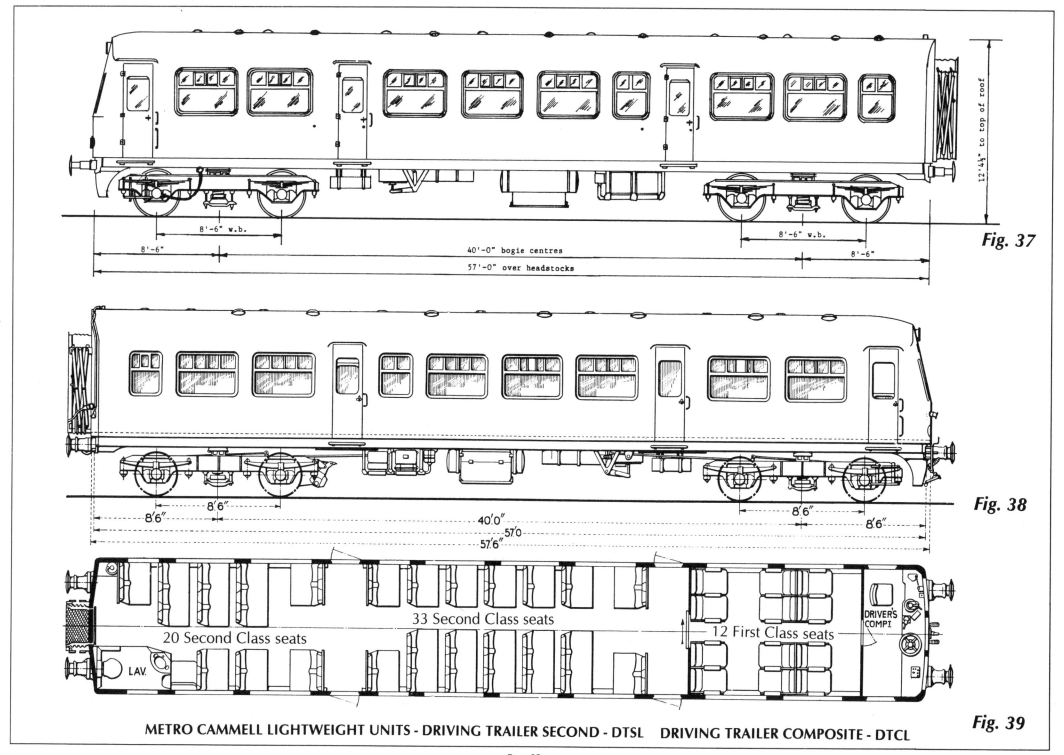

Fig. 37

Fig. 38

Fig. 39

METRO CAMMELL LIGHTWEIGHT UNITS - DRIVING TRAILER SECOND - DTSL   DRIVING TRAILER COMPOSITE - DTCL

CHAPTER THREE

BR Derby - Later Low-Density Units

Following the initial service experience with the original lightweight units, BR Derby developed a standard range of Low-Density cars. These fall into three separate categories:- Heavyweight Long-framed 2-car units; Lightweight 2,3,4-car units and Heavyweight Short-framed 3-car units.

All these units portrayed a distinct 'family' appearance with the stronger sloping front cabs (also used on the Gloucester Cross Country sets and all the High-Density cars) in place of the earlier 'Glasshouse' cabs which had proved to be less than satisfactory. This apart, the general layout was similar to the earlier series except that the Heavyweight sets had the side windows set slightly higher and the long-framed cars had a 4½-bay centre section.

a) Heavyweight Long-Framed 2-car Sets (TOPS Class 114)

Introduced in 1956, these units followed the last of the original lightweights in production and were the first units to feature the revised front end. They were the only Low-Density cars built on the long underframe.

The majority of these sets were built with two Leyland 150 bhp engines on each power car, but the first one, E50000 had two Rolls Royce 238 bhp engines with torque converter drive and the last in the series (E50049) was equipped with two 230 bhp Albion engines using standard mechanical transmission. Subsequently Albion engines were fitted throughout the class, which spent most of their lives at Lincoln Depot. Bodies were 63' 6" overall and the units had 'Blue Square' code control systems.

Driving Motor Brake Second - DMBS

Seats:	62 second
Nos.	E50000 (Lot No. 30341)
	E50001- 48 (Lot No. 30209)
	E50049 (Lot No. 30459)
Weight:	37.5 tons.
Drawings:	*Fig.40, fig.41* and *fig.42.*
	End view *fig.67.*

Driving Trailer Composite with Lavatory - DTCL

Seats:	12 first, 62 second.
Nos.	E56000 (Lot No. 30342)
	E56001- 49 (Lot No. 30210)
Weight:	29.5 tons.
Drawings:	*Fig.43, fig.44* and *fig.45.*
	End view *fig.67.*

b. Later Lightweight Units - (TOPS Class 108)

This large group of units includes 2, 3 and 4-car sets with two versions of the new front end and all were ultimately grouped under TOPS Class 108. These cars were developed directly from the original lightweight sets and retained the lower side windows.

Each power car was fitted with two Leyland 150 bhp horizontally mounted engines with standard mechanical drive. All were 57' 6" long, power cars weighed 28.0 to 29.9 tons and the trailers between 21.0 and 23.0 tons.

1. London Midland 2-car Power Twins

The first batch of 12 power twin sets for the LMR was introduced in 1959. They were fitted with the then standard 2-digit blind under the central cab window with a head/tail lamp either side.

Driving Motor Brake Second - DMBS

Seats:	52 second.
Nos.	M50924 - 35 (Lot No. 30460)
Drawings:	*Fig.46, fig.47* and *fig.48.*
	End view *fig.68.*

Driving Motor Composite with Lavatory - DMCL

Seats:	12 first, 53 second.
Nos.	M51561 - 72 (Lot No. 30461)
Drawings:	*Fig.49* (RHS) and *fig.59* (LHS body only)
	Seating plan *fig.51.*
	End view *fig.68.*

A further batch of 29 sets was produced in 1960 which incorporated the newly introduced 4-digit reporting number box in the roof dome, in place of the 2-digit box below the window. The destination blind was placed at the top of the centre cab window behind the glass. The two lamps were retained.

Driving Motor Brake Second - DMBS

Nos.	M51922 - 50 (Lot No.30601)
Drawings:	as M50924 - 35
	End view *fig.69.*

Driving Motor Composite with Lavatory - DMCL

Nos.	M52037 - 65 (Lot No.30660)
Drawings:	as M51561 - 72
	End view *fig.69*

2. North Eastern and London Midland Regions 2-car Sets

In 1958 BR Derby produced 21 of these sets for the NER and a further 5 for the LMR to the same pattern as the Power Twins described previously. They were equipped with 2-digit boxes and two lamps.

Driving Motor Brake Second - DMBS

Seats: 52 second
Nos.   E50599 - 619   (Lot No. 30406)
            M50625 - 29   (Lot No. 30407)
Drawings: as M50924 - 35
            End view *fig.68*.

Driving Trailer Composite with Lavatory - DTCL

Seats: 12 first, 53 second
Nos.   E56190 - 210   (Lot No. 30409)
            M56211 - 15   (Lot No. 30410)
Drawings: *Fig. 49* (LHS), *fig. 50* (RHS body only)
            Seating plan *fig. 51*
            End view *fig.68*

The LMR received 50 more in 1959.

Driving Motor Brake Second - DMBS

Nos.   M50938 - 87   (Lot No. 30465)

Driving Trailer Composite with Lavatory - DTCL

Nos.   M56221 - 56270   (Lot No. 30466)

1960 brought another 9 identical sets for the LMR.

Driving Motor Brake Second - DMBS

Nos.   M51416 - 24   (Lot No. 30498)

Driving Trailer Composite with Lavatory - DTCL

Nos.   M56271 - 79   (Lot No. 30499)

The final batch of 21 was delivered to the LMR in 1960 and these had the
4-digit roof mounted box.

Driving Motor Brake Second - DMBS

Nos.   M51901 - 21   (Lot No. 30601)
Drawings: as M50924 - 35

Driving Trailer Composite with Lavatory - DTCL

Nos.   M56484 - 504   (Lot No. 30602)
Drawings: as E56190 -210
            End view *fig. 69*.

3. North Eastern Region 3 - car Sets

Only 5 three car sets were built and these were delivered to the NER in
1958. They were similar to the contemporary 2-car sets.

Driving Motor Brake Second - DMBS

Seats: 52 second
Nos.   E50620 - 24   (Lot No. 30406)
Drawings: as M50924 - 35
            End view *fig.68*.

Trailer Second with Lavatory - TSL

Seats: 68 second
Nos.   E59386 - 90   (Lot No. 30493)
Drawings: *Fig.52, fig.53* and *fig.54*.

Driving Motor Composite with Lavatory - DMCL

Seats: 12 first, 53 seconds
Nos.   E50642 - 46   (Lot No. 30408)
Drawings: *Fig.50* (RHS), *fig.49* (LHS body only)
            Seating plan *fig.51*
            End view *fig.68*

Note: Some of these DMCL cars had only 50 second class seats. In these cases
the rear section layout is the same as the TSL in *fig.54.*

4. North Eastern Region 4-car Sets

BR Derby produced a batch of 6 of these sets concurrently with the
foregoing 3-car sets. The formation was similar to that of the original
lightweight sets.

Driving Motor Composite with Lavatory - DMCL

Seats: 12 first, 53 second
Nos.   E50630 - 41   (Lot No. 30408)
Drawings: *Fig.50* (RHS), *fig.49* (LHS body only)
            Seating plan *fig.51*
            End view *fig.68*

Note : Some of these DMCL cars had only 50 second class seats. In these
cases the rear section layout is the same as the TSL in *fig.54*
One DMCL is placed at each end of the set.

Trailer Brake Second with Lavatory - TBSL

Seats: 50 second
Nos.   E59245 - 50   (Lot No. 30412)
Drawings: *Fig.55, fig.56* and *fig.57.*

Trailer Second with Lavatory - TSL

Seats: 68 second
Nos.   E59380 - 85   (Lot No. 30411)
Drawings: *Fig.52, fig.53* and *fig.54.*

c) Heavyweight Short-Framed 3-car Sets (TOPS Class 107)

The final deliveries of the Derby Low-Density units were the 26 three-car sets
built in 1960 for the Scottish Region. In most respects they resembled the later
lightweight sets, but were of heavier construction. The side windows were
placed higher (like the long framed cars) and they had the 4-digit roof
mounted indicator box. These units had AEC 150 bhp engines, standard
mechanical transmission and were 'Blue Square' coded. In later years they
were downgraded to all-second and carried a variety of liveries including the
'Strathclyde Red'. Their working lives were spent entirely in Scotland.

Driving Motor Brake Second - DMBS

Seats: 52 second
Nos.   SC51985 - SC52010   (Lot No. 30611)
Weight: 34.5 tons.
Drawings: *Fig.58, fig.59* and *fig.60.*
End view: *Fig.70.*

Trailer Second with Lavatory - TSL

Seats:	71 second
Nos.	SC59782 - SC59807 (Lot No. 30613)
Weight:	28 tons 0 cwt.
Drawings:	*Fig.62, fig.62 and fig.63.*

Driving Motor Composite with Lavatory - DMCL

Seats:	12 first, 53 second
Nos.	SC52011 - 36 (Lot No. 30612)
Weight:	35 tons 0 cwt.
Drawings:	*Fig.64, fig.65 and fig.66.*
End view:	*Fig.70.*

General

These units were delivered in standard Multiple Unit green with two cream lines and plain ends. Later the yellow whiskers were added and, in turn, replaced by yellow warning panels. From around 1966 the livery changed to Rail Blue with the full yellow cab ends. In the mid 1970's a comprehensive refurbishment programme brought about a change yet again in livery to the 'all white' vehicle with a broad blue band below the windows until this was superseded by the two-tone blue and pale grey. Further livery changes occurred around 1984 when many units appeared in local PTE colour schemes.

BR Derby Class108 in refurbished livery with West Yorkshire PTE logo, yellow end and lining below the cantrail (to indicate the first class accommodation). The DMCL + DMBS set is seen at Ilkley with a service to Bradford. *Cheona Collection.*

BR Derby Class 108 with DMBS No. 51942 nearest the camera in later NSE livery. Note the four-position route box (out of use) on the roof dome which made these 108's like Class 107's. Bletchley in March, 1990. *C.Reid.*

A green liveried Derby 2-car set awaits its next duty whilst an AEC GWR railcar in BR Crimson and cream stands at the platform at Oxford. *J.Turner.*

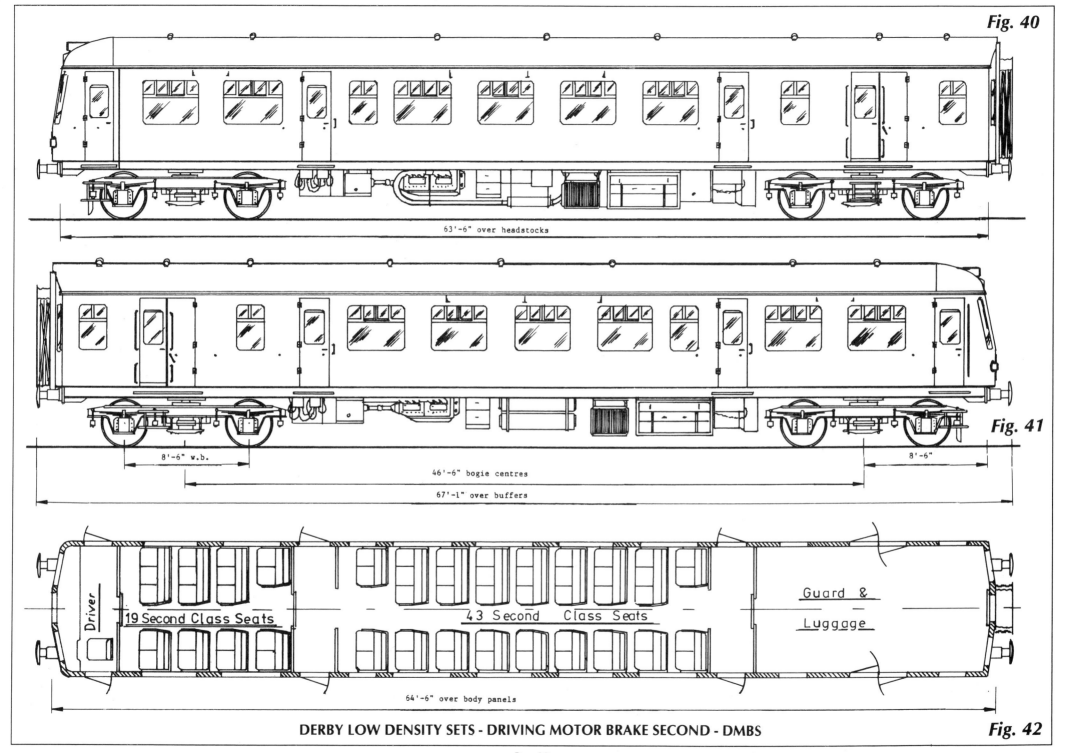

Fig. 40

63'-6" over headstocks

Fig. 41

8'-6" w.b.   46'-6" bogie centres   8'-6"

67'-1" over buffers

Driver | 19 Second Class Seats | 43 Second Class Seats | Guard & Luggage

64'-6" over body panels

DERBY LOW DENSITY SETS - DRIVING MOTOR BRAKE SECOND - DMBS   **Fig. 42**

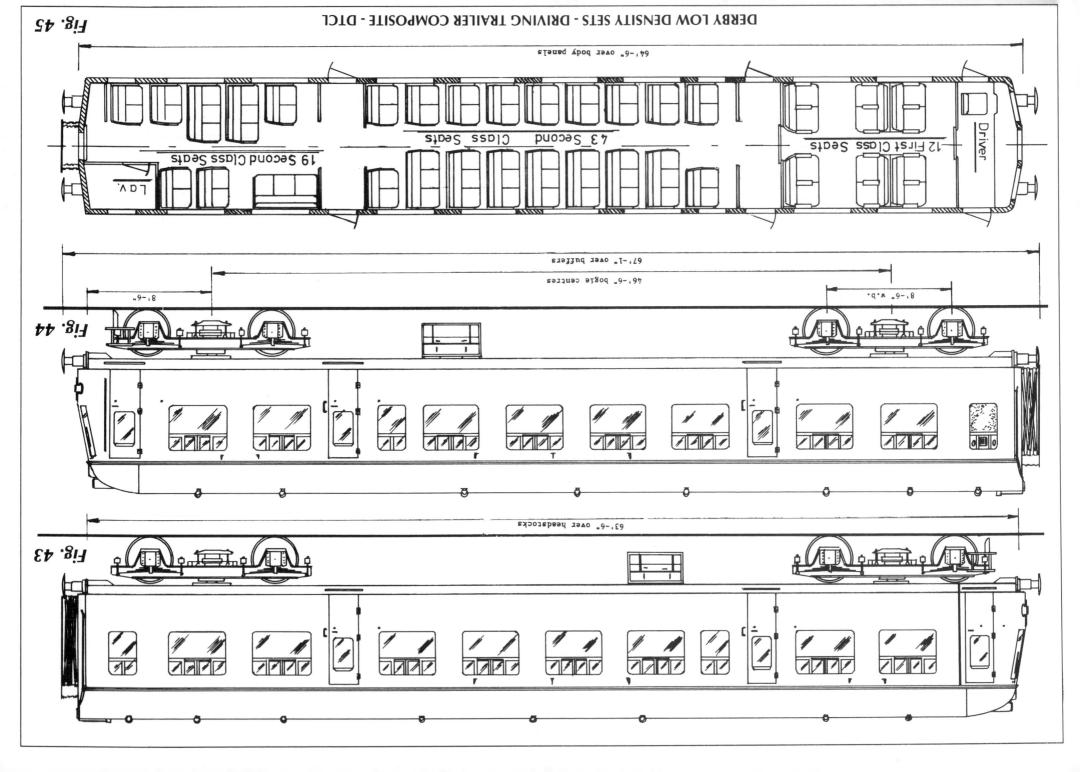

Fig. 45

64'-6" over body panels

Driver

12 First Class Seats

43 Second Class Seats

19 Second Class Seats

Lav.

Fig. 44

67'-1" over buffers

46'-6" bogie centres

8'-6"

8'-6" w.b.

Fig. 43

63'-6" over headstocks

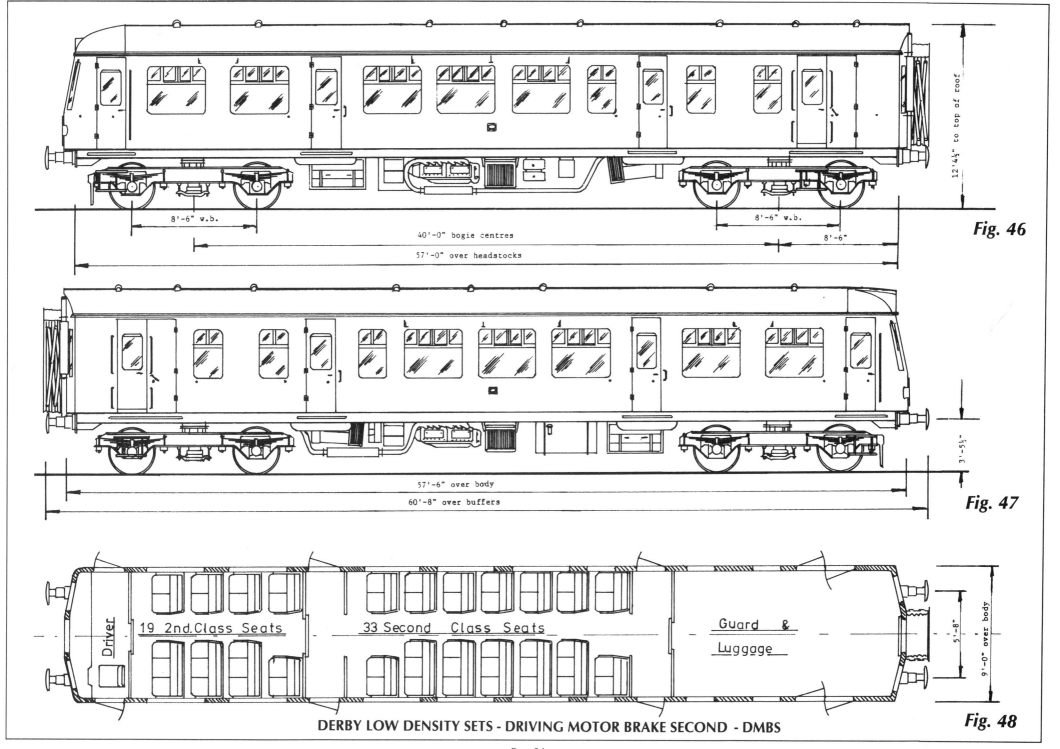

Fig. 46

8'-6" w.b.

8'-6" w.b.

8'-6"

40'-0" bogie centres

57'-0" over headstocks

12'4½" to top of roof

Fig. 47

57'-6" over body

60'-8" over buffers

3'-5½"

DERBY LOW DENSITY SETS - DRIVING MOTOR BRAKE SECOND - DMBS

Driver

19 2nd. Class Seats

33 Second Class Seats

Guard & Luggage

5'-8"

9'-0" over body

Fig. 48

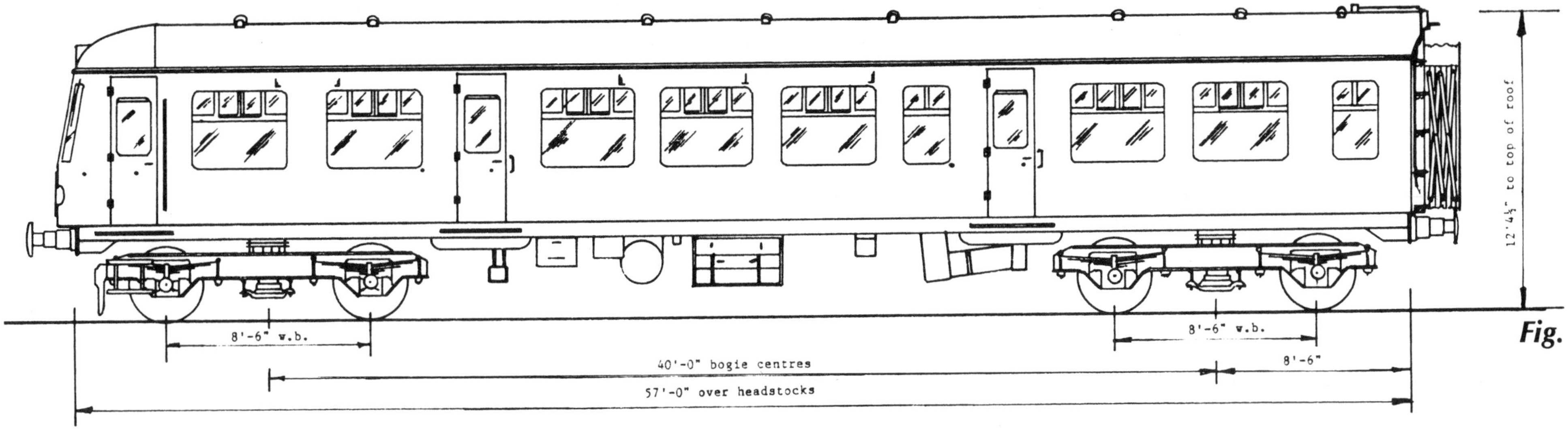

DERBY LOW DENSITY SETS - DRIVING MOTOR COMPOSITE - DMCL   DRIVING TRAILER COMPOSITE - DTCL

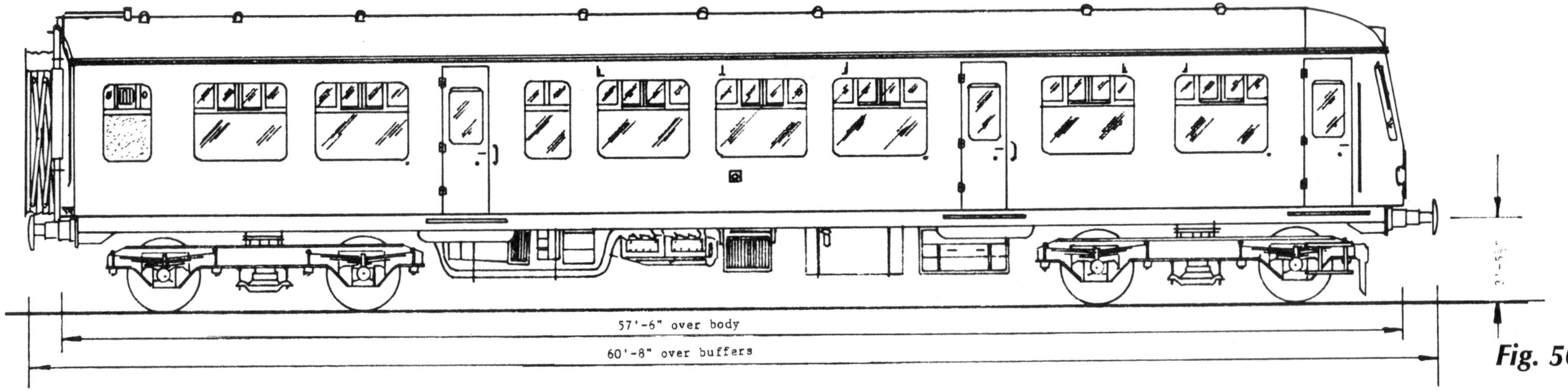

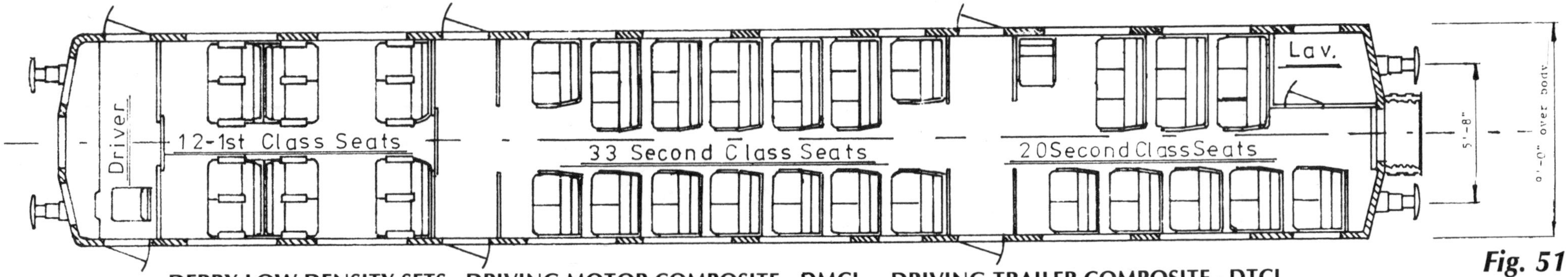

Fig. 51

20 Second Class Seats

33 Second Class Seats

12 - 1st Class Seats

Driver

Lav.

9'-0" over body

8'-8"

Fig. 50

60'-8" over buffers

57'-6" over body

Fig. 49

57'-0" over headstocks

40'-0" bogie centres

8'-6" w.b.

8'-6" w.b.

12'-4½" to top of roof

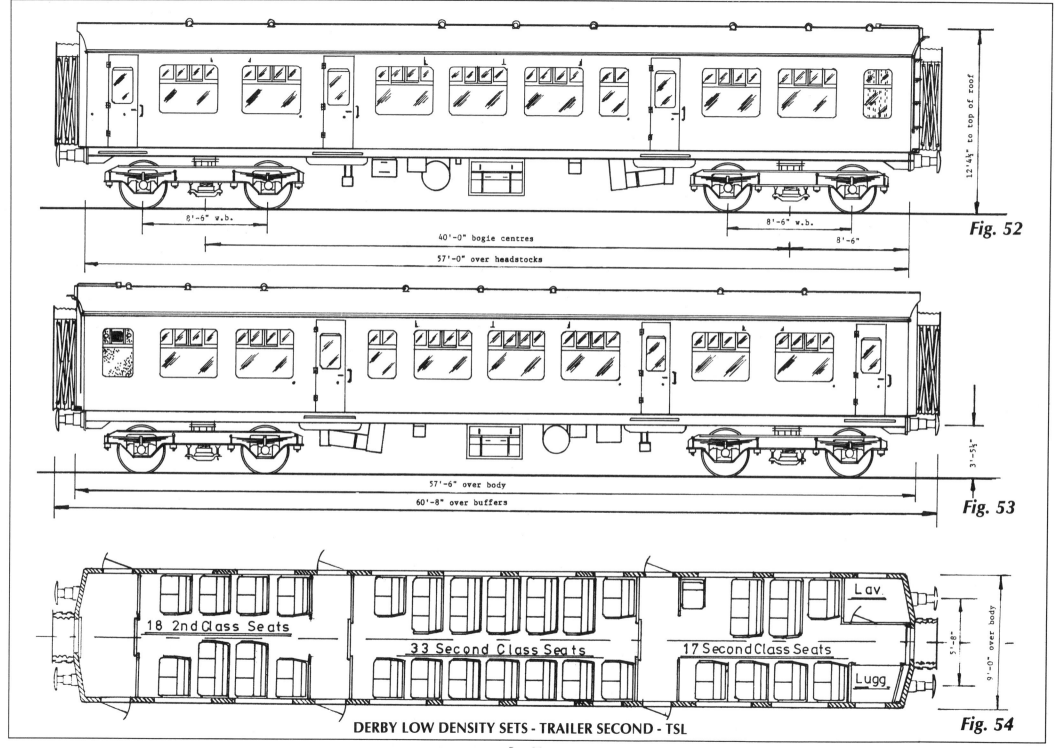

12'4½" to top of roof

8'-6" w.b.

8'-6" w.b.

8'-6"

40'-0" bogie centres

57'-0" over headstocks

Fig. 52

3'-5½"

57'-6" over body

60'-8" over buffers

Fig. 53

Lav.

18 2nd Class Seats

33 Second Class Seats

17 Second Class Seats

Lugg

5'-8"

9'-0" over body

DERBY LOW DENSITY SETS - TRAILER SECOND - TSL

Fig. 54

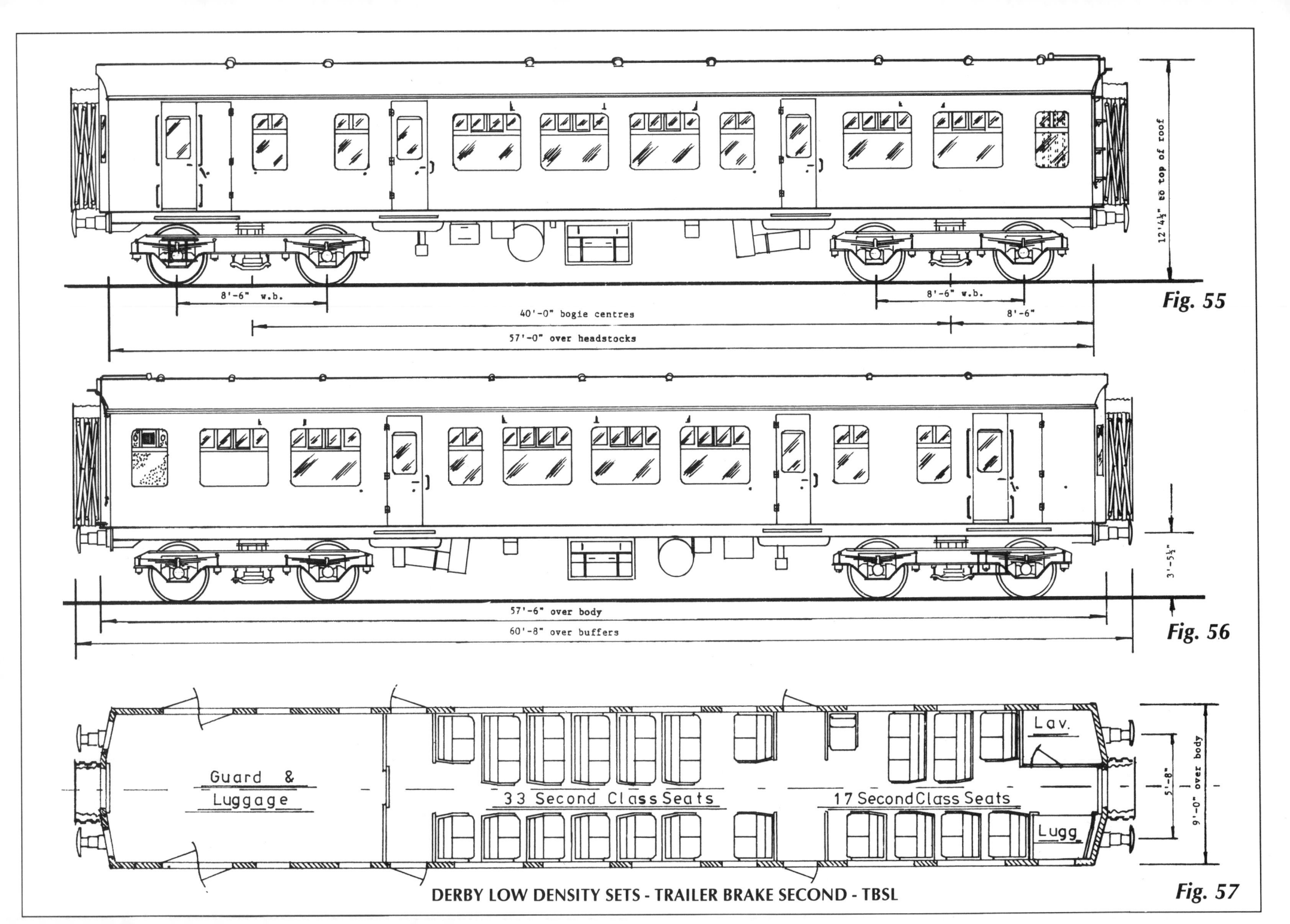

Fig. 55

12'4½" to top of roof

8'-6" w.b.   8'-6" w.b.

40'-0" bogie centres   8'-6"

57'-0" over headstocks

Fig. 56

3'-5½"

57'-6" over body

60'-8" over buffers

Fig. 57

Guard & Luggage   33 Second Class Seats   17 Second Class Seats   Lav.   Lugg

9'-0" over body

5'-8"

DERBY LOW DENSITY SETS - TRAILER BRAKE SECOND - TBSL

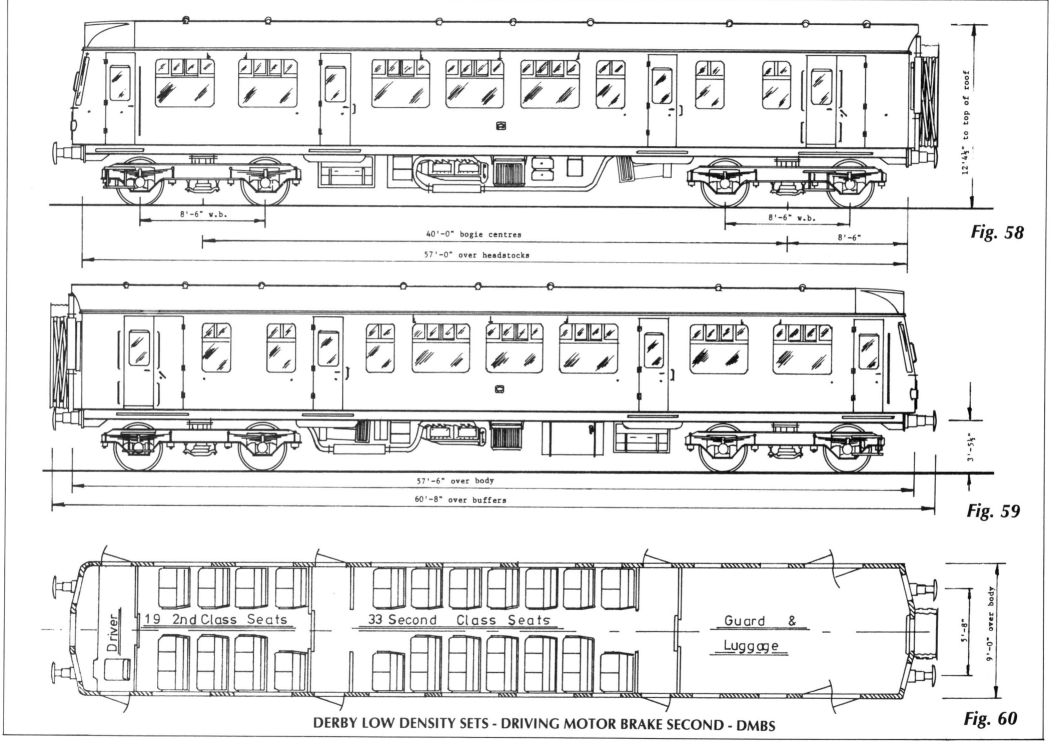

12'4½" to top of roof

8'-6" w.b.

8'-6" w.b.

40'-0" bogie centres

8'-6"

57'-0" over headstocks

Fig. 58

3'-5½"

57'-6" over body

60'-8" over buffers

Fig. 59

Driver

19 2nd Class Seats

33 Second Class Seats

Guard & Luggage

5'-8"

9'-0" over body

DERBY LOW DENSITY SETS - DRIVING MOTOR BRAKE SECOND - DMBS

Fig. 60

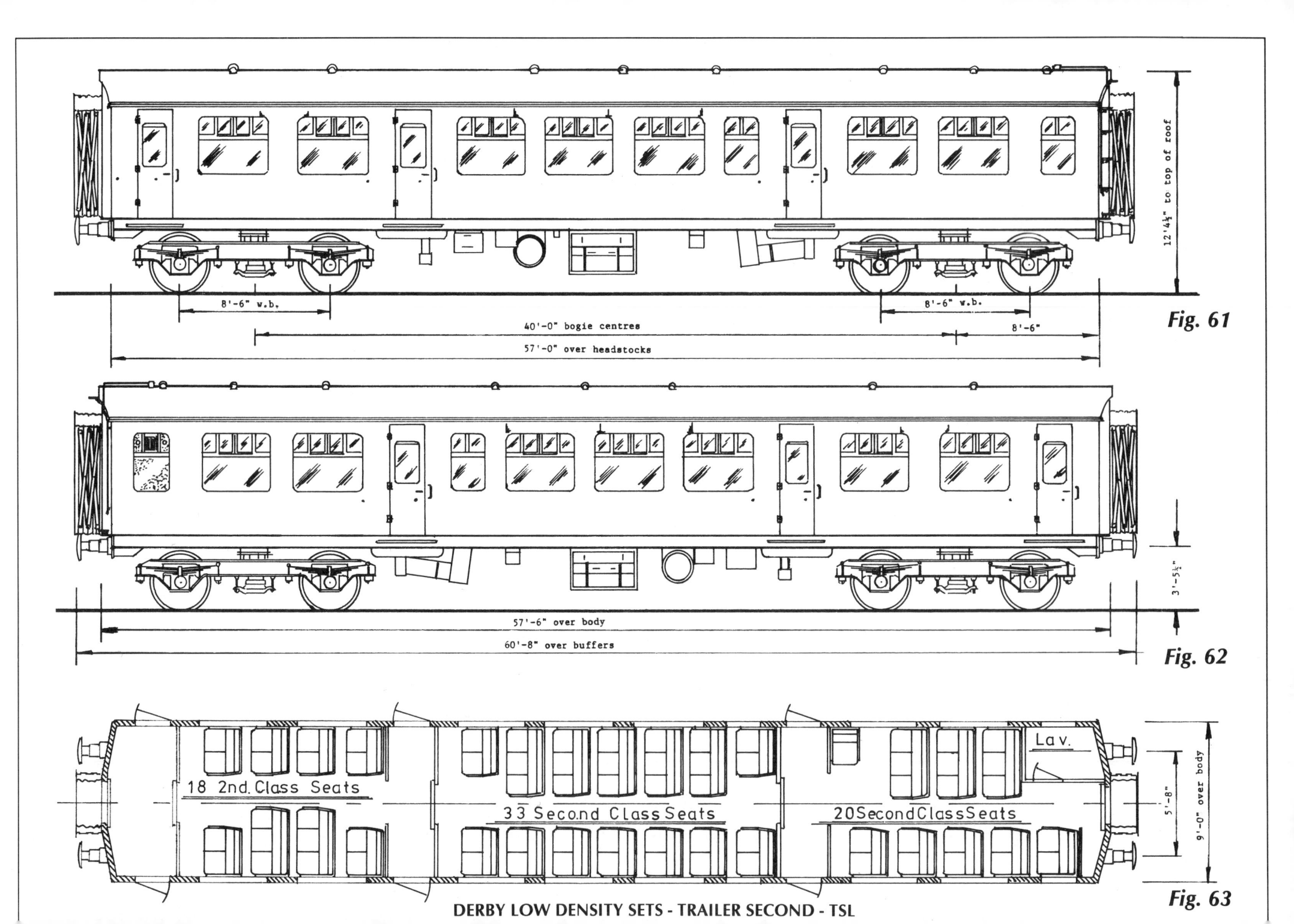

Fig. 61

12'4½" to top of roof

8'-6" w.b.

8'-6" w.b.

8'-6"

40'-0" bogie centres

57'-0" over headstocks

Fig. 62

3'-5½"

57'-6" over body

60'-8" over buffers

Fig. 63

18 2nd. Class Seats

33 Second Class Seats

20 Second Class Seats

Lav.

5'-8"

9'-0" over body

DERBY LOW DENSITY SETS - TRAILER SECOND - TSL

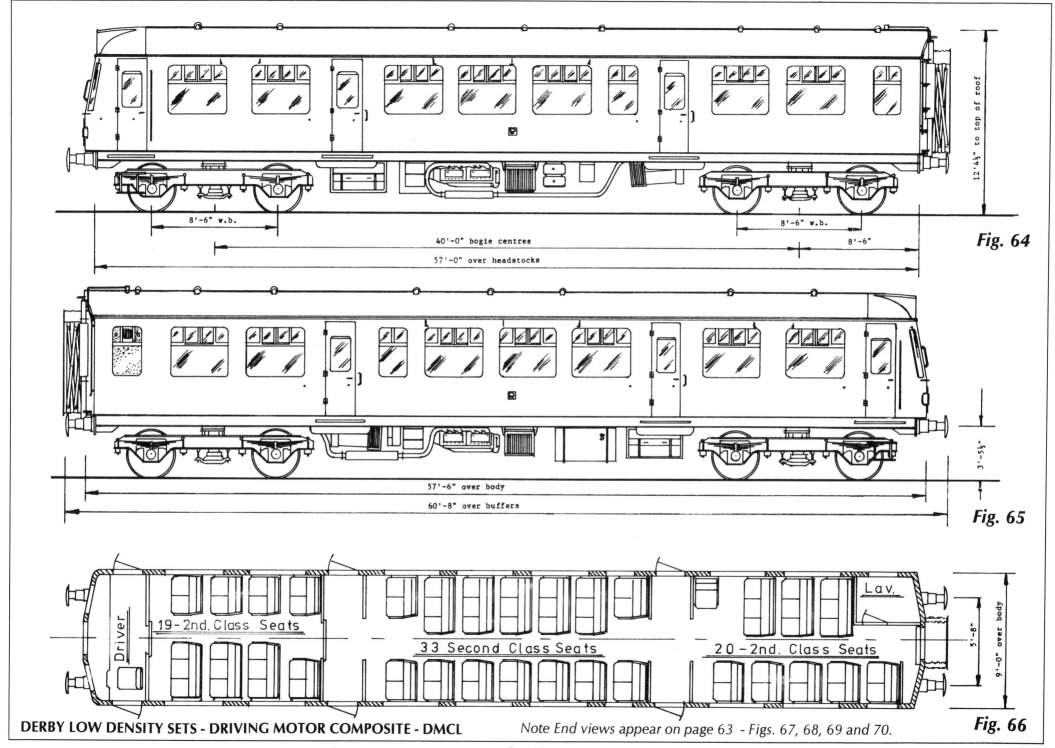

Fig. 64

12'4¾" to top of roof

8'-6" w.b.

8'-6" w.b.

8'-6"

40'-0" bogie centres

57'-0" over headstocks

Fig. 65

3'-5¼"

57'-6" over body

60'-8" over buffers

Fig. 66

Driver

19-2nd. Class Seats

33 Second Class Seats

20-2nd. Class Seats

Lav.

5'-8"

9'-0" over body

DERBY LOW DENSITY SETS - DRIVING MOTOR COMPOSITE - DMCL   *Note End views appear on page 63 - Figs. 67, 68, 69 and 70.*

CHAPTER FOUR

Metro-Cammell - Later Low Density units

The story of the Metro-Cammell units is quite complex, because of the large number of units and combinations involved. This was the largest of the private sector construction and the cars were probably the most attractive of all the low-density types.

As we have already seen, Metro-Cammell were involved from the start of the DMU programme and following on from their pioneering sets, discussed in *Chapter Two* , their later series of cars were very similar. On the introduction of the TOPS classifications the majority of these cars were placed in Class 101 (AEC powered) or Class 102 (Leyland) - although they were all subsequently merged into Class 101. These were followed by a further variation with Rolls-Royce engines - TOPS Class 111.

1). The Class 101/102 sets

These sets comprised two-car, power twins, three-car and four-car combinations. The basic bodyshell was common to all units as shown in the earlier chapter. As a result of experience gained with the earlier units a limited number of modifications were found to be necessary for the later production and between 1956 and 1960, a large number of cars were built. In addition to the formations outlined above, six buffet cars were produced for the North Eastern Region to be used randomly, marshalling with any of the other sets.

In order to clarify the original formations of these units we shall consider them by set type.

a). Two-car sets

A total of 123 of these sets were produced in five individual batches. The power cars were each fitted with two AEC 150 bhp engines with the standard mechanical transmission. The power cars weighed 32 tons and the trailers 25 tons.

1957 built units.

Driving Motor Brake Second - DMBS
Seats:	52 second (*44 second)
Nos.	E50198 - 209 (lot No. 30259)
	E50210 - 33 (Lot No. 30261)
	E50246 - 48* (Lot No. 30339)
	E50293 - 96 (Lot No. 30270)
Drawings:	*Fig.71,fig.72* and *fig.73* (guard's doors as main drg.)
	*Plan as *fig.80*.
	End views as *fig.81* and *fig.84*.

Driving Trailer Composite with Lavatory - DTCL
Seats:	12 first, 53 second (*12 first, 45 second)
Nos.	E56050 - 61 (Lot No. 30260)
	E56062 - 85 (Lot No. 30262)
	E56218 - 20* (Lot No. 30340)
	E56086 - 89 (Lot No. 30272)
Drawings:	*Fig.77,fig.78* and *fig.79*.
	Plan *fig.86*.
	End views as *fig.81* and *fig.90*.

1958 built units.

These units differed in having a 2-digit indicator and two lamps below the windscreens. The guard's doors were also altered on these and later deliveries.

Driving Motor Brake Second - DMBS
Seats:	52 second
Nos.	M51174 - 253 (lot No. 30467)
Drawings:	*Fig.71,fig.72* and *fig.73* (guard's door as inset)
	End views as *fig.82* and *fig.84*.

Driving Trailer Composite with Lavatory - DTCL
Seats:	12 first, 53 second
Nos.	M56332 - 411 (lot No. 30468)
Drawings:	*Fig.77,fig.78* and *fig.79*.
	End views as *fig.82* and *fig.90*.

b). Power-twin units

Fifty of these units were produced for the North Eastern Region in four batches. All had AEC engines except the last batch of ten which had Leyland engines, also of 150 bhp.

1957 built units

Driving Motor Brake Second - DMBS
Seats:	52 second
Nos.	E50152 - 57 (Lot No. 30252)
	E50164 - 67 (Lot No. 30254)
	E50250 - 59 (Lot No. 30266)
Drawings:	as E50198 etc.

Driving Motor Composite with Lavatory - DMCL
Seats:	12 first, 53 second
Nos.	E50158 - 63 (Lot No. 30253)
	E50168 - 71 (Lot No .30255)
	E50260 - 69 (Lot No. 30267)
Drawings:	*Fig.74,fig.75* and *fig.76*
	End views *fig.81* and *fig.85*.

1959 built units.

Like the 1958 two-car sets these incorporated the later end details and the altered guard's door arrangement.

Driving Motor Brake Second - DMBS
Seats:	52 second
Nos.	E51425 - 34 (Lot No. 30500)
Drawings:	as M51174 - 253

Driving Motor Composite with Lavatory - DMCL
Seats:	12 first, 53 second
Nos.	E51495 - 504 (Lot No. 30501)
Drawings:	*Fig.74, fig.75* and *fig.76.*
	End views as *fig.82* and *fig.85.*

c). Three-car Sets

A total of 54 three-car sets were built between 1957 and 1959. Of these, 21 were AEC powered for the North Eastern and London Midland Regions, the remainder being Leyland powered for the Scottish Region.

These sets are similar to the foregoing power twins with a centre trailer car. The first three sets had the four-lamp arrangement at the front end, but thereafter they were equipped with the 2-digit box and twin lamps. Ten sets were later modified by BR with a large four-digit display in the roof-end above the cab windows. The centre window was thereby reduced in height to accommodate the destination blind. *(see fig.83 and photograph on page 44).*

1957 built units.

Driving Motor Brake Second - DMBS
Seats:	52 second
Nos.	E50290 - 92 (Lot No. 30270)
Drawings:	as E50198 etc.

Trailer Second with Lavatory - TSL
Seats:	71 second
Nos.	E59302 - 304 (Lot No. 30273)
Drawings:	*Fig.87, fig.88,* plan view *fig.93.*
	End view *fig.90* and *fig.91.*

Driving Motor Composite with Lavatory - DMCL
Seats:	12 first, 53 second
Nos.	E50745 - 47 (Lot No. 30271)
Drawings;	as E50158 etc.

1958 built units

These units had the 2-digit box and two lamp arrangement, but did not have the revised guard's doors.

Driving Motor Brake Second - DMBS
Seats:	52 second
Nos.	M50303 - 20 (Lot No.30275)
Drawings;	*Fig.71, fig.72* and *fig.73.* (guard's doors as main drg.)
	End views as *fig.82* and *fig.84.*

Trailer Composite with Lavatory - TCL
Seats:	12 first, 53 second
Nos.	M59114 - 31 (Lot No. 30277)
Drawings:	*Fig.87, fig.88* and *fig.89.*
	End view as *fig.90* and *fig.91.*

Driving Motor Composite with Lavatory - DMCL
Seats:	12 first, 53 second
Nos.	M50321 - 38 (Lot No. 30276)
Drawings:	*Fig.77, fig.78* and *fig.79.*
	End view as *fig.82* and *fig.85.*

1959 built units.

These units were built for the Scottish Region and were equipped with Leyland engines and classified under TOPS as Class 102, but were later combined into Class 101. They had the later front end and revised guard's doors.

Driving Motor Brake Second - DMBS
Seats:	52 second
Nos.	SC51445 - 470 (Lot No. 30500)
	SC51795 - 801 (Lot No. 30587)
Drawings:	as M51174 - 253

Trailer Composite with Lavatory - TCL
Seats:	12 first, 53 second
Nos.	SC59543 - 68 (Lot No. 30502)
	SC59686 - 92 (Lot No. 30589)
Drawings:	as M59114 - 31

Driving Motor Composite with Lavatory - DMCL
Seats:	12 first, 53 second
Nos.	SC51515 - 40 (Lot No. 30501)
	SC51802 - 08 (Lot No. 30588)
Drawings :	as M50321 - 3

d). Four-car Sets

The four-car sets were of two different formations with the first 28 following the pattern of the Derby sets, whereas the final 10 were the same as the three-car sets described previously with the centre trailer. The first type were built in 1956/57 and equipped with AEC engines (Class 101), plus the four lamp front ends. The later batch were Leyland powered (Class 102) and were constructed with the later front end design.

1956/57 built units.

Driving Motor Composite with Lavatory - DMCL
(one of these cars was marshalled at each end of the set)

Seats:	12 first, 53 second (* 12 first, 45 second)
Nos.	E50138 - 51* (Lot No. 30249)
	E50172 - 97 (Lot No. 30256)
	E50234 - 45* (Lot No. 30263)
	E50748 - 51‡ (Lot No. 30271)
Drawings:	*Fig.77, fig.78* and *fig.79*. (* cars plan as *fig.86*)
	End views *fig.81* and *fig.85*.

Trailer Second with Lavatory - TSL

Seats:	71 second (* 61 second)
Nos.	E59042 - 48* (Lot No. 30250)
	E59060 - 72 (Lot No. 30257)
	E59086 - 91 (Lot No. 30264)
	E59305 - 06‡ (Lot No. 30273)
Drawings;	*Fig.87* and *fig.88*. Plan as *fig.93* (**fig.92*).
	End views as *fig.90* and *fig.91*.

Trailer Brake Second with Lavatory - TBSL

Seats:	53 second (* 45 second)
Nos.	E59049 - 55* (Lot No. 30251)
	E59073 - 85 (Lot No. 30258)
	E59092 - 97* (Lot No. 30265)
	E29112 - 13‡ (Lot No. 30274)
Drawings:	*Fig.94* and *fig.95*. Plan as *fig.95a*. (* cars *fig.97*)
	End views *fig.91* and *fig.96*.

‡ these cars were transferred to Scottish Region early in their lives and acquired SC prefixes.

1959 built units.

Driving Motor Brake Second - DMBS

Seats:	52 second
Nos.	E51435 - 44 (Lot No. 30500)
Drawings:	as M51174 - 253

Trailer Composite with Lavatory - TCL
(two of these cars were marshalled in each set)

Seats:	12 first, 53 second
Nos.	E59523 - 42 (Lot No. 30502)
Drawings:	as M59114 - 31

Driving Motor Composite with Lavatory - DMCL

Seats:	12 first, 53 second
Nos.	E51505 - 14 (Lot No. 30501)
Drawings:	as M50321 - 38

2). The Class 111 Sets.

In addition to the AEC and Leyland powered units, Metro-Cammell also produced a number of sets with Rolls-Royce diesel engines. Like their more numerous cousins, they appeared in various formations:

a). Two-car sets   b). Power twin sets and   c). Three-car sets.

Being 'Blue Square' coded cars, these were fully compatible with the standard DMU's.

a). Two-car sets.

Four of these sets were built in 1957 for the London Midland Region and, externally were very similar to the contemporary Class 101/102. Each power car was equipped with two Rolls Royce 180 bhp horizontal engines and standard transmission. DMBS No. M50136 had both its engines supercharged to 230 bhp.

Driving Motor Brake Second - DMBS

Seats:	52 second
Nos.	M50134 - 37 (Lot No. 30248)
Drawings:	as E50198 etc.

Driving Trailer Composite with Lavatory - DTCL

Seats:	12 first, 53 second
Nos.	M56090 - 93 (Lot No. 30337)
Drawings:	as E56050 etc

b). Power twin sets.

1960 saw six of these twin sets built which were the last complete sets of the distinctive Metro-Cammell design DMU to be produced. Similarly powered as the other Class 111 sets, they incorporated the later cab ends and revised guard's doors.

Driving Motor Brake Second - DMBS

Seats:	52 second
Nos.	E51545 - 50 (Lot No. 30508)
Drawings:	as M51174 - 263

Driving Motor Composite with Lavatory - DMCL

Seats:	12 first, 53 second
Nos.	E51555 - 60 (Lot No. 30509)
Drawings:	as M50321 - 38

c). Three-car sets.

These units preceded the power twins just described with 10 being produced in 1957 and a further 4 in 1959. The first batch had the four-lamp front ends and the original guard's door arrangement whilst the last four had 2-digit boxes and the revised doors.

Driving Motor Brake Second - DMBS

Seats:	52 second
Nos.	E50280 - 89 (Lot No. 30338)
	E51541 - 44 (Lot No. 30508)
Drawings:	*Fig.71* (guard's doors - 1st batch as main drg.)
	Fig.72 . fig.73 (second batch as inset)
	End views *fig.81*(first batch and *fig.82* (second batch)
	and *fig.84*.

Trailer Second with Lavatory - TSL

Seats:	71 second
Nos.	E59100 - 09 (Lot No. 30269)
	E59569 - 72 (Lot No. 30510)
Drawings:	*Fig.87* and *fig.88*. Plan as *fig.93*
	End views *fig.90* and *fig.91*.

Driving Motor Composite with Lavatory - DMCL

Seats:	12 first, 53 second
Nos.	E50270 - 79 (Lot No. 30268)
	E51551 - 54 (Lot No. 30509)
Drawings:	*Fig.74, fig.75* and *fig.76*.
	End views *fig.81* (first batch) and *fig.82* (second batch) plus *fig.85*.

3). Trailer Buffet Cars

The very last DMU cars built by Metro-Cammell (until the Sprinter Series in the late 1980's) were six Trailer Buffet cars for the North Eastern Region, which appeared in 1960. They were intended as 'loose' vehicles for inclusion in certain scheduled trains according to the requirements of the daily rosters. In layout they were a Trailer Second with a miniature buffet installed in the front two-bay saloon section. The two side windows behind the buffet section were replaced by blank panels set in simple rubber mountings into the standard apertures. The seating capacity was reduced by 19. In later years the cars were treated as simple TSL's with the buffets out of use.

Trailer Second Buffet with Lavatory - TSLRB

Seats:	53 second
Nos.	E59573 - 78 (Lot No. 30615)
Drawings:	*Fig.98,fig.99* and *fig.100*.
	End views *fig.90* and *fig.91*.

General

Metro-Cammell sets were delivered in the same style of livery as their earlier lightweight cousins. Being amongst the longest serving units they carried most of the various liveries through their long service lives.

They seem to have been very well constructed and in the mid 1990's the survivors still manage to look good in Regional Railways stripes, Network South East or Strathclyde 'Red' liveries.

In the mid-1970's a refurbishment programme was initiated on these units which included removal of the top marker lights, blanking off the two headcode panels, fitting larger silencers on the inner ends of the power cars and an expansion box below the underframes. The small gutters over the doors were removed and replaced by full-length rain gutters in the conventional position at the top of the sides. Later still high intensity lamps were fitted to the cab ends of the driving cars. Some of these modifications were also applied to classes 104, 105, 108 etc.

Metro Cammell 1959-built, Class 101, 2-car set in green and cream livery with whiskers. This was one of ten sets modified by BR when they fitted the 4-digit headcode box in the roofend and the destination box in the centre window. Seen here at Cononley on a Skipton to Bradford service, 29th May, 1960.   *R.S.Carpenter.*

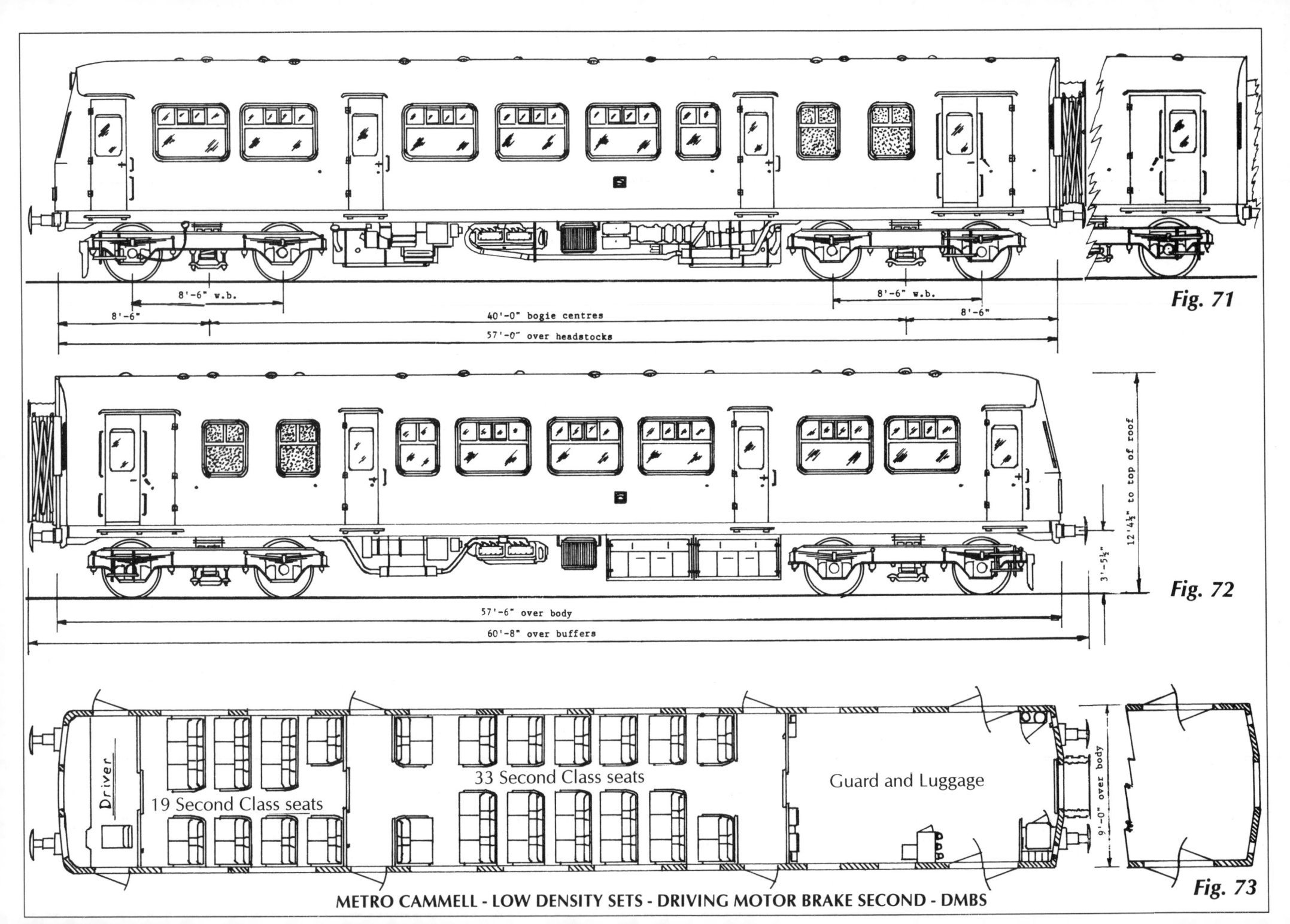

Fig. 71

8'-6" w.b.

8'-6"

40'-0" bogie centres

57'-0" over headstocks

8'-6" w.b.

8'-6"

Fig. 72

12'-4½" to top of roof

3'-5½"

57'-6" over body

60'-8" over buffers

Driver

19 Second Class seats

33 Second Class seats

Guard and Luggage

9'-0" over body

Fig. 73

METRO CAMMELL - LOW DENSITY SETS - DRIVING MOTOR BRAKE SECOND - DMBS

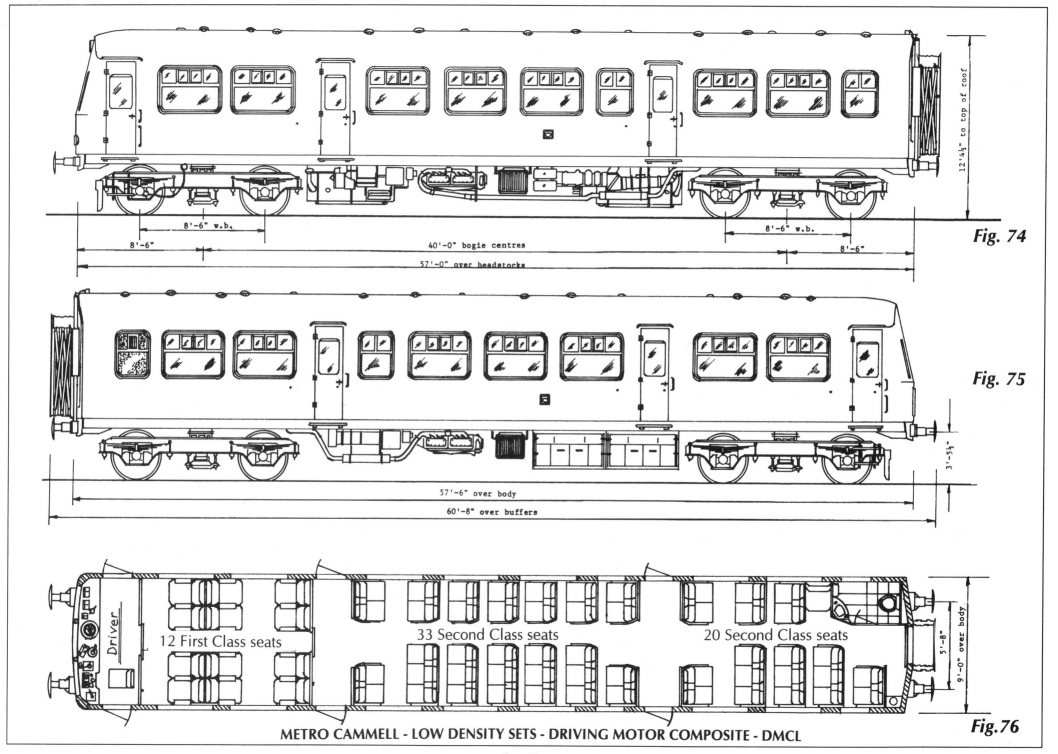

Fig. 74

12'4½" to top of roof

8'-6" w.b.

8'-6" w.b.

8'-6"

40'-0" bogie centres

8'-6"

57'-0" over headstocks

Fig. 75

3'-5½"

57'-6" over body

60'-8" over buffers

Driver

12 First Class seats

33 Second Class seats

20 Second Class seats

5'-8"

9'-0" over body

Fig.76

METRO CAMMELL - LOW DENSITY SETS - DRIVING MOTOR COMPOSITE - DMCL

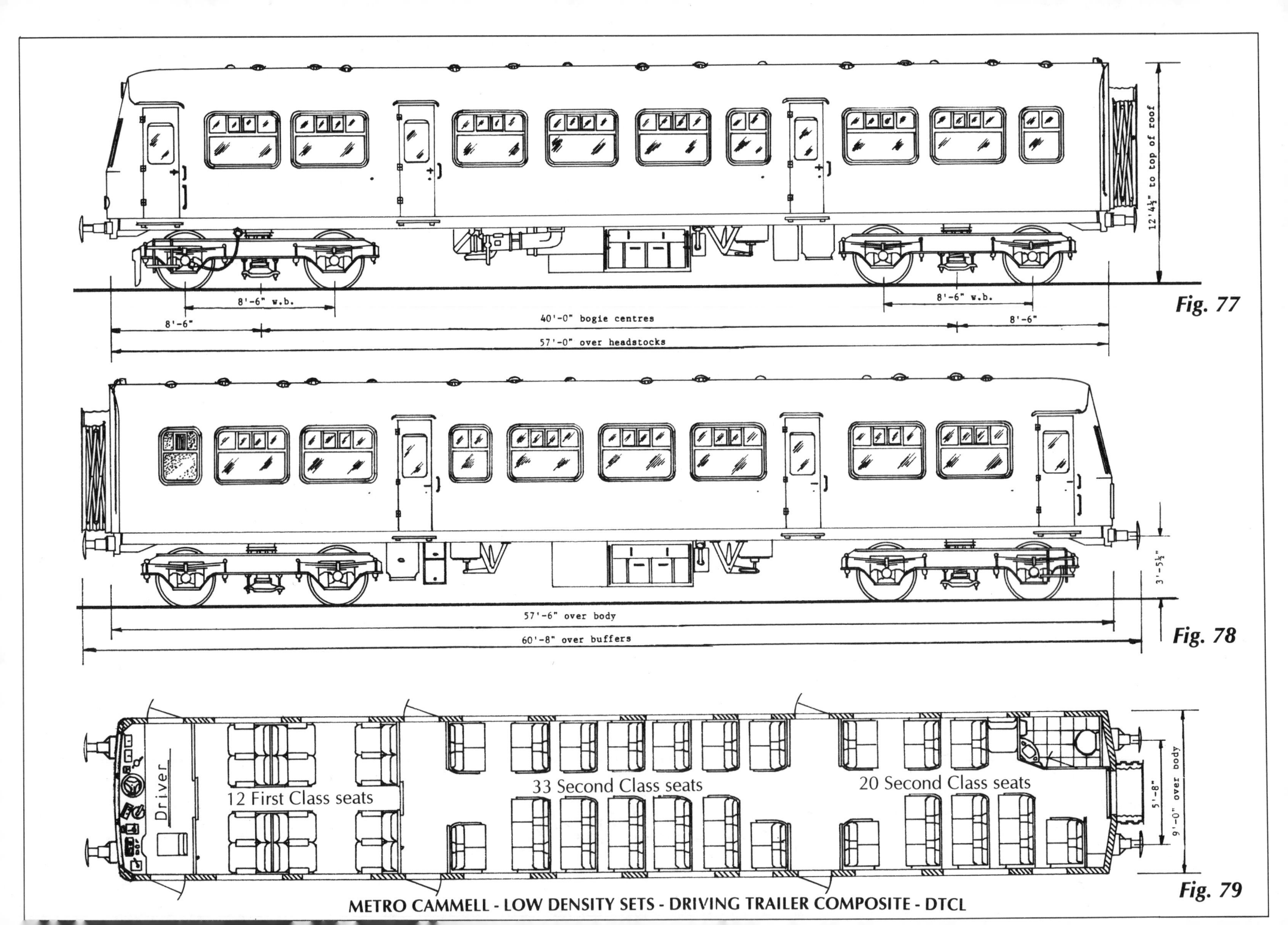

Fig. 77

12'-4½" to top of roof

8'-6" w.b.

8'-6" w.b.

8'-6"

40'-0" bogie centres

8'-6"

57'-0" over headstocks

Fig. 78

3'-5½"

57'-6" over body

60'-8" over buffers

Fig. 79

Driver

12 First Class seats

33 Second Class seats

20 Second Class seats

5'-8" over body

9'-0" over body

METRO CAMMELL - LOW DENSITY SETS - DRIVING TRAILER COMPOSITE - DTCL

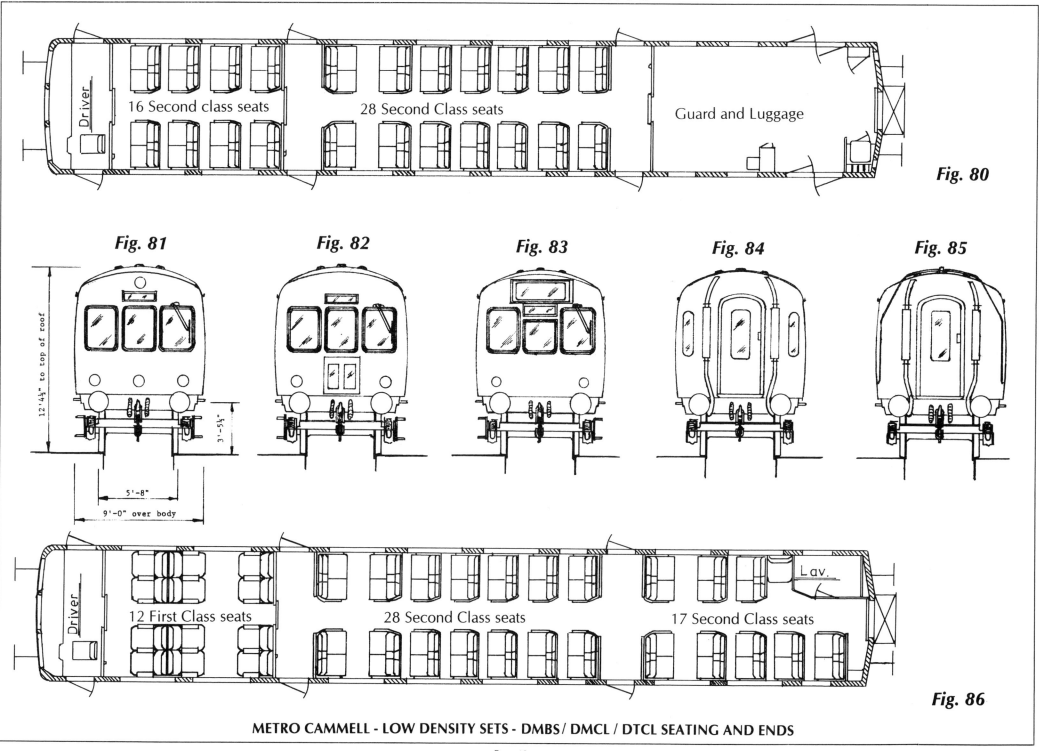

Fig. 80

Fig. 81   Fig. 82   Fig. 83   Fig. 84   Fig. 85

16 Second class seats   28 Second Class seats   Guard and Luggage

12'4½" to top of roof

3'-5½"

5'-8"

9'-0" over body

12 First Class seats   28 Second Class seats   17 Second Class seats

Lav.

Fig. 86

METRO CAMMELL - LOW DENSITY SETS - DMBS / DMCL / DTCL SEATING AND ENDS

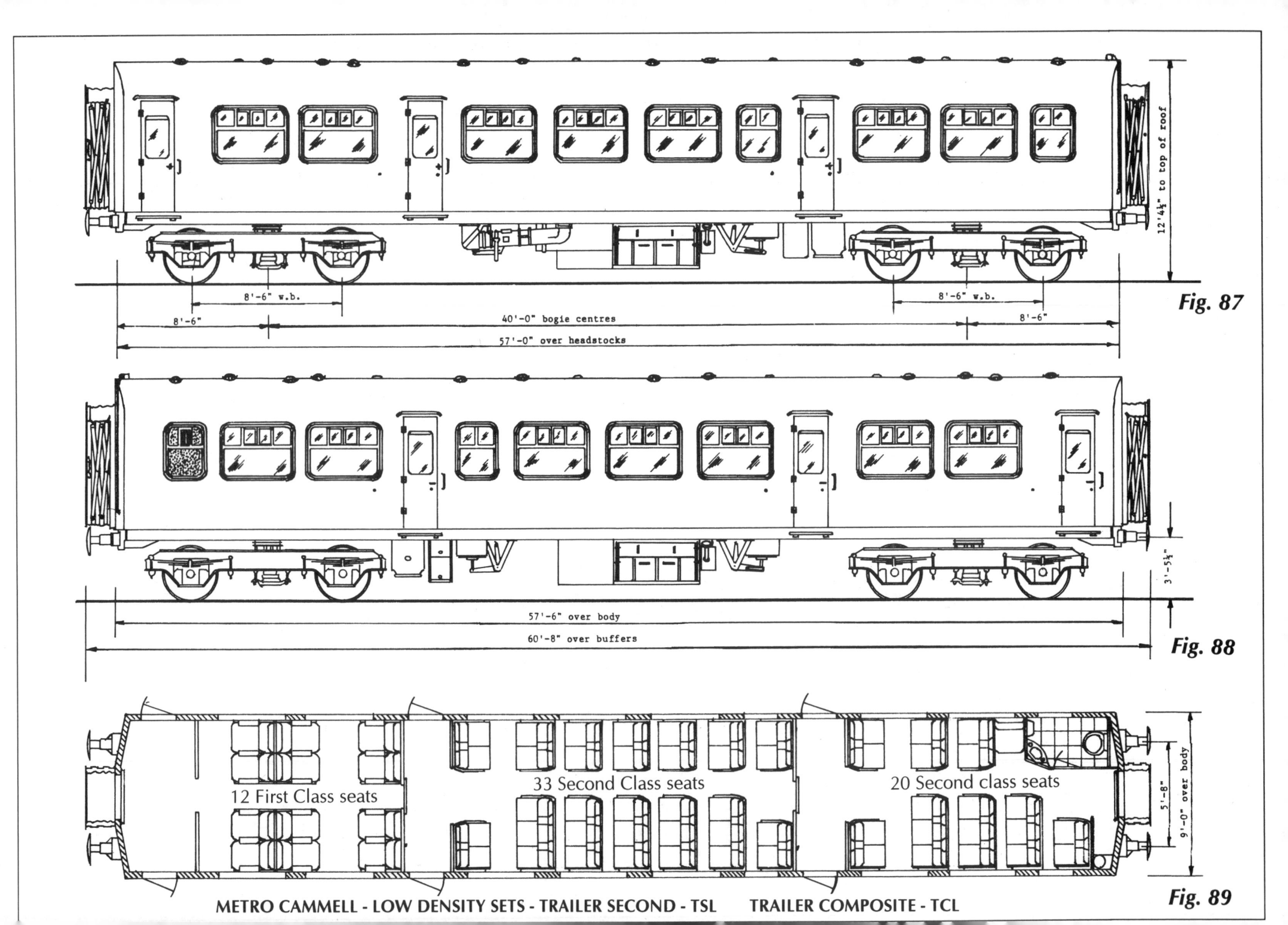

Fig. 87

12'4¼" to top of roof

8'-6" w.b.

8'-6"   40'-0" bogie centres   8'-6" w.b.   8'-6"

57'-0" over headstocks

Fig. 88

3'-5¼"

57'-6" over body

60'-8" over buffers

Fig. 89

5'-8"

9'-0" over body

12 First Class seats   33 Second Class seats   20 Second class seats

METRO CAMMELL - LOW DENSITY SETS - TRAILER SECOND - TSL   TRAILER COMPOSITE - TCL

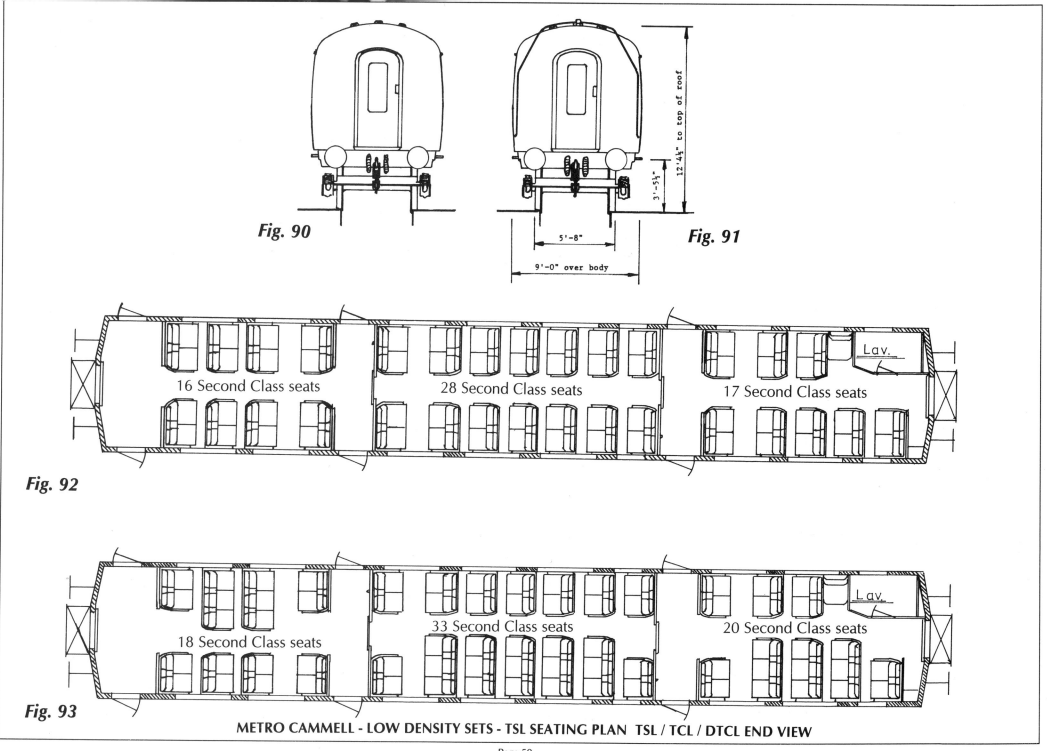

Fig. 90

Fig. 91

12'4½" to top of roof

3'-5½"

5'-8"

9'-0" over body

Fig. 92

16 Second Class seats

28 Second Class seats

17 Second Class seats

Lav.

Fig. 93

18 Second Class seats

33 Second Class seats

20 Second Class seats

Lav.

METRO CAMMELL - LOW DENSITY SETS - TSL SEATING PLAN TSL / TCL / DTCL END VIEW

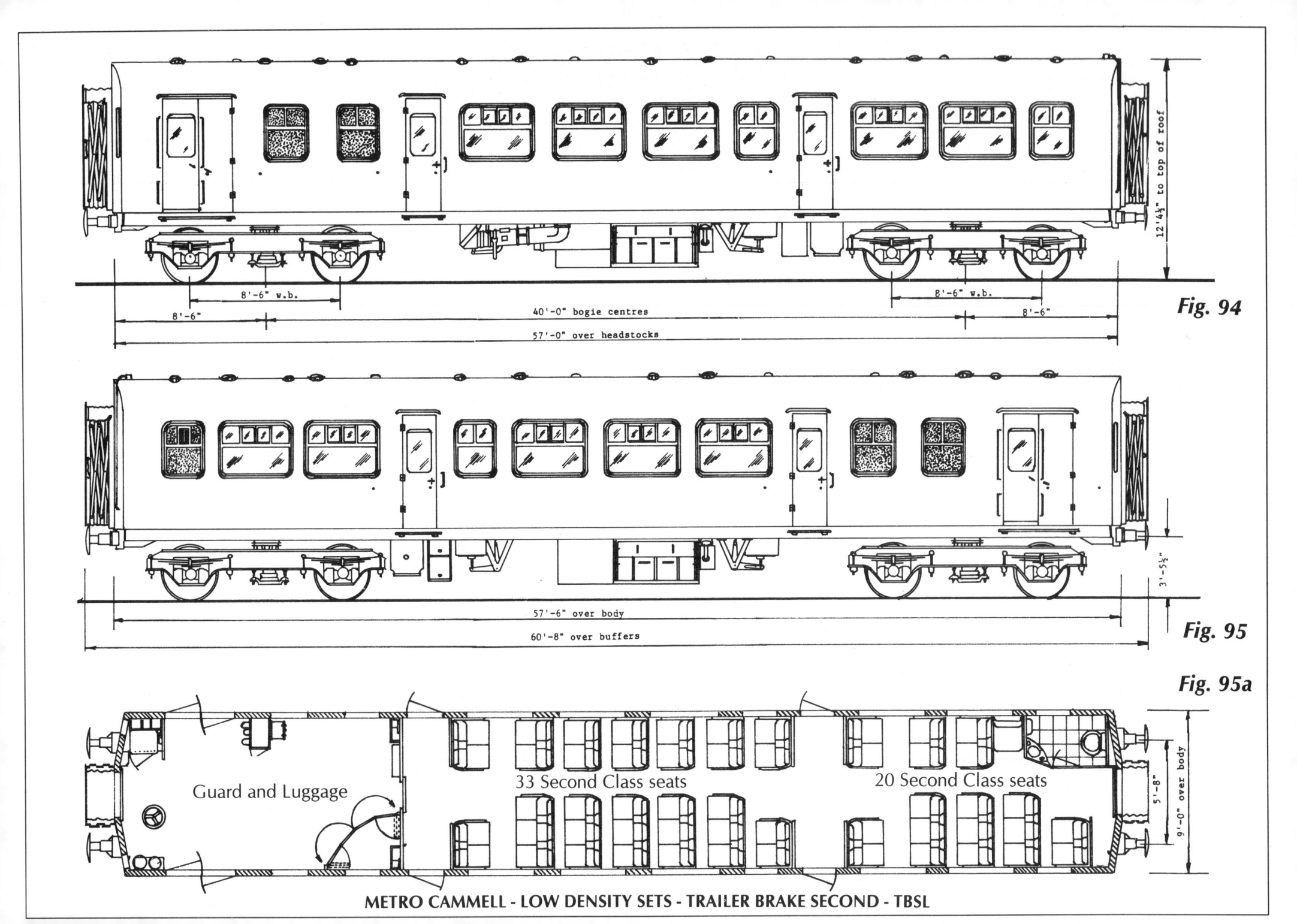

Fig. 94

12'4½" to top of roof

8'-6" w.b.

8'-6"

8'-6" w.b.

8'-6"

40'-0" bogie centres

57'-0" over headstocks

Fig. 95

3'-5¼"

57'-6" over body

60'-8" over buffers

Fig. 95a

5'-8"

9'-0" over body

Guard and Luggage

33 Second Class seats

20 Second Class seats

METRO CAMMELL - LOW DENSITY SETS - TRAILER BRAKE SECOND - TBSL

Guard and Luggage

28 Second Class seats

17 Second Class seats

Lav.

Fig. 97

METRO CAMMELL - LOW DENSITY SETS - TRAILER BRAKE SECOND - TBSL ALTERNATIVE

12'4½" to top of roof

3'-5½"

5'-8"

Fig. 96

Right : A Metro Cammell set at Luton Bute Street on a football special from Wolverhampton. Note the end and roof details.
Cheona Collection.

Below : Metro Cammell Class 101, 3-car set in refurbished livery leaving Middlesbrough with the 15.47 Darlington to Saltburn service on 22nd July, 1980. *G.Gamble.*

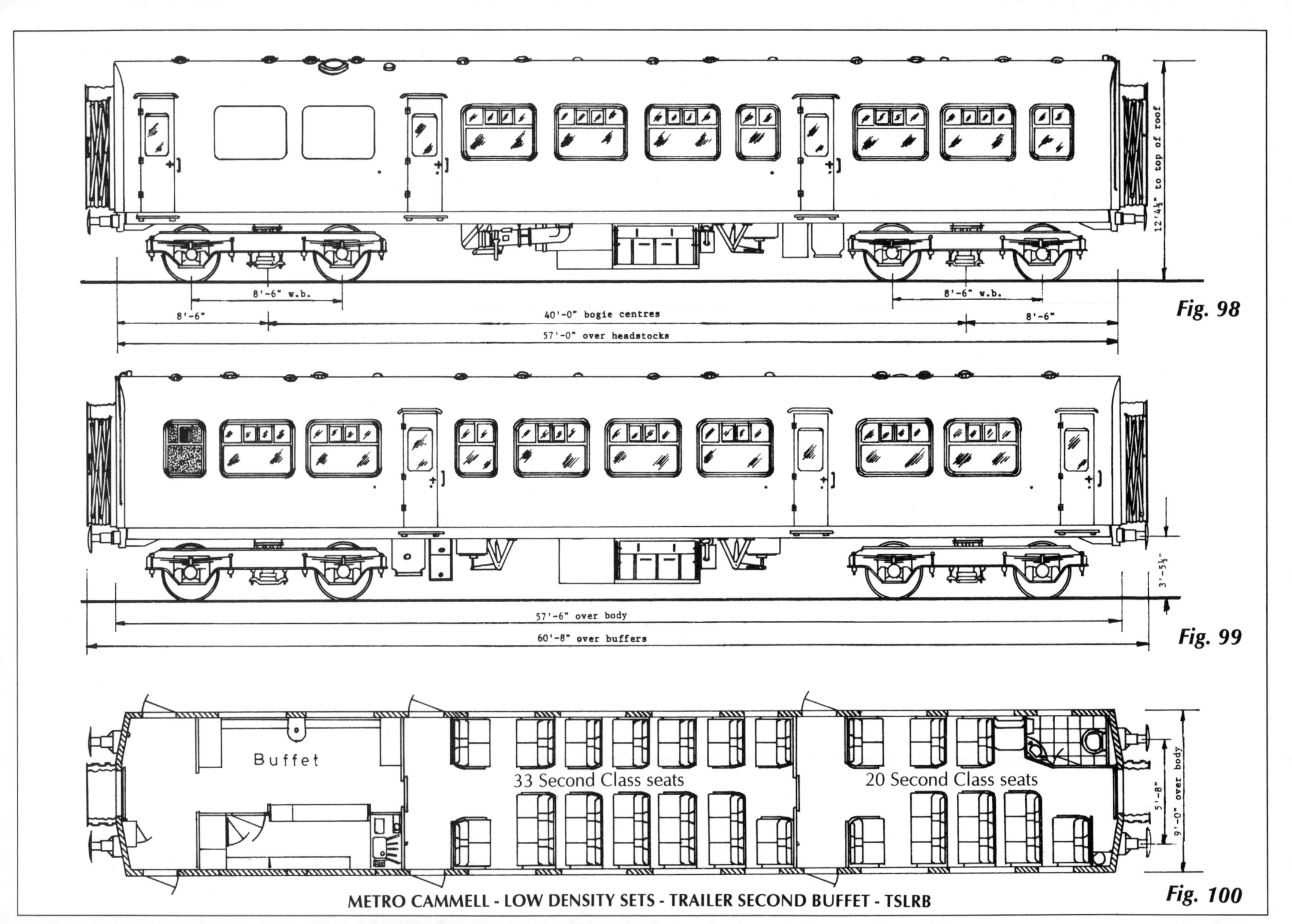

Fig. 98

12'4½" to top of roof

8'-6" w.b.

8'-6"

40'-0" bogie centres

8'-6" w.b.

8'-6"

57'-0" over headstocks

Fig. 99

3'-5¼"

57'-6" over body

60'-8" over buffers

Fig. 100

Buffet

33 Second Class seats

20 Second Class seats

5'-8"

9'-0" over body

METRO CAMMELL - LOW DENSITY SETS - TRAILER SECOND BUFFET - TSLRB

CHAPTER FIVE

Gloucester RC & W. Units

The Gloucester Railway Carriage and Wagon Company Limited had been involved in the construction of diesel railcars from the early days of the Great Western Railway railcars and therefore it was logical that they would be involved in the DMU programme. They produced Cross Country sets (Class 119), High Density single units (Class 122), and Motor Parcels cars. Here we are concerned with their Class 100 two-car Low Density sets.

Surprisingly, only forty of these were produced in two batches. Their general layout followed the pattern established by the early Derby and Metro-Cammell sets although they were quite distinctive in their external appearance. The front section of each car had a small window followed by a full one, although the front saloon contained the usual two seating bays. The centre section had four full sized windows conforming to the standard size and layout. Finally, the rear section of the DTCL had a most unusual window arrangement. The seating in this rear section differed from most of the other designs in accommodating 21 second class passengers.

All the Low-Density units supplied by outside builders had their own front end characteristics and the Gloucester units were certainly distinctive. They had a pronounced dome at each end and this, combined with the rather severe line of the cab windows gave the units a distinct 'frown'.

Introduced in 1957 these forty sets were AEC (150 bhp) powered and were divided between the London Midland Region with 11 sets and the Scottish Region who had the other 29. The bodies were 57' 6" long.

Driving Motor Brake Second - DMBS

Seats:	52 second
Nos.	Sc50339 - 47 (Lot No. 30278)
	M50348 - 58 (Lot No. 30278)
	SC51108 - 27 (Lot No. 30444)
Weight:	30tons 5cwt.
Drawings:	*Fig.101, fig.102* and *fig.103.*
	End views. *Fig.107* (first batch) or *fig.108* (second batch) and *fig.110.*

Driving Trailer Composite with Lavatory - DTCL

Seats:	12 first, 54 second.
Nos.	Sc56094 - 102 (Lot No.30279)
	M56103 - 113 (Lot No. 30279)
	SC56300 - 19 (Lot No. 30445)
Weight:	25 tons.
Drawings:	*Fig.104, fig.105* and *fig.106.*
	End views *fig.107* (first batch) or *fig.108* (second batch) and *fig.109.*

The first batch had a single lamp mounted in the roof whereas the others had a marker lamp on either side of the two-digit indicator box which both batches carried under the centre cab window. From the early 1980's those cars with two marker lamps fitted, had red lenses fitted into the lamp frames as tail lamps, when running in the rear position. This practice was also used on other classes. Until then oil lamps had been used on conventional lamp brackets. When new they all carried the standard lined green livery, but do not ever appeared to have carried whiskers although they did receive yellow warning panels below the windows eventually. The survivors of the class received the 'all-blue' livery with the 'all-yellow' ends.

Gloucester RC & W Co. Class 100, DMBS car No. 51112 in Rail Blue livery with yellow end seen here at Haymarket, 1973.   *Cheona Collection.*

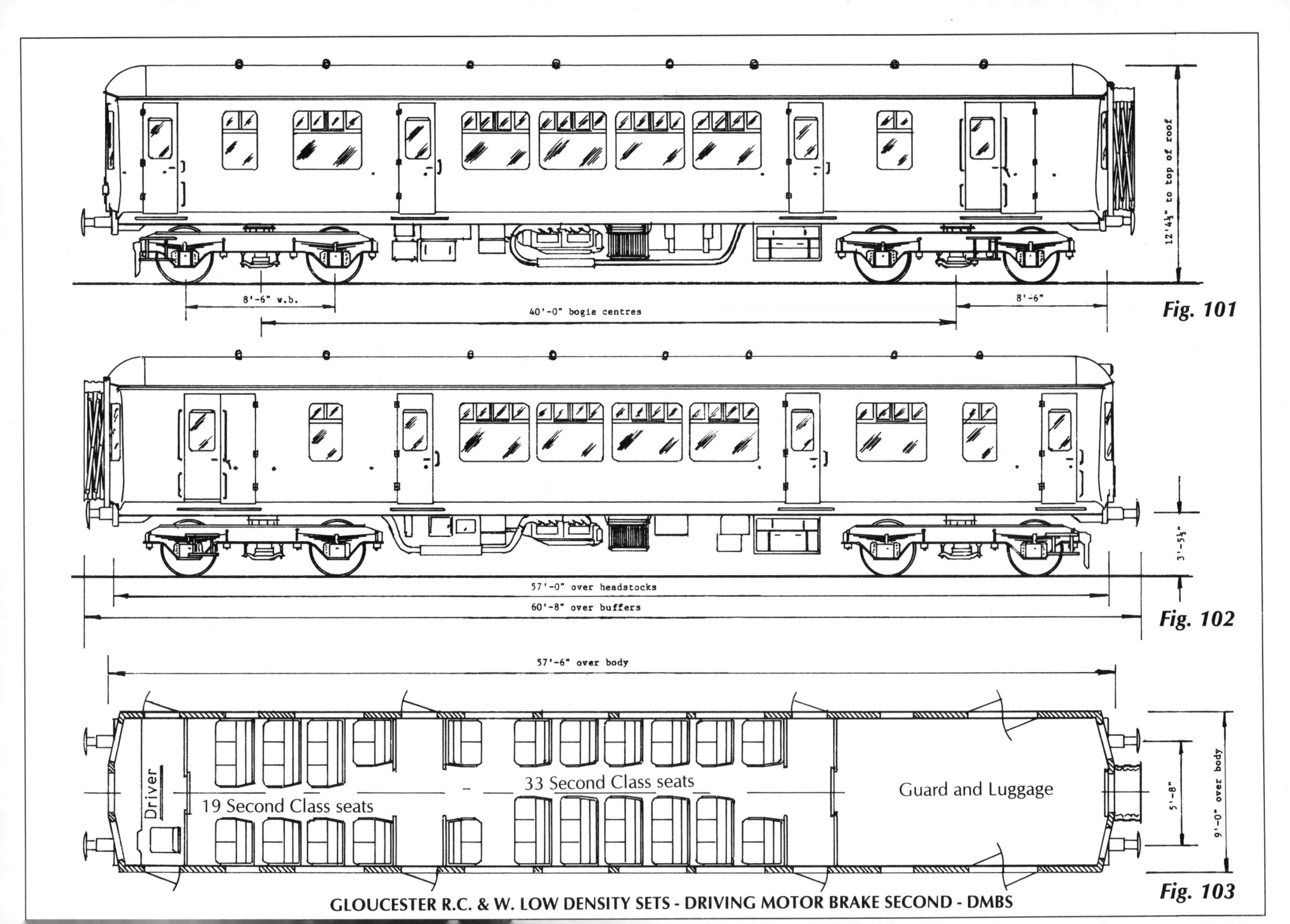

Fig. 101

12'-4½" to top of roof

8'-6" w.b.

40'-0" bogie centres

8'-6"

Fig. 102

57'-0" over headstocks

60'-8" over buffers

3'-5½"

Fig. 103

57'-6" over body

Driver

19 Second Class seats

33 Second Class seats

Guard and Luggage

5'-8"

9'-0" over body

GLOUCESTER R.C. & W. LOW DENSITY SETS - DRIVING MOTOR BRAKE SECOND - DMBS

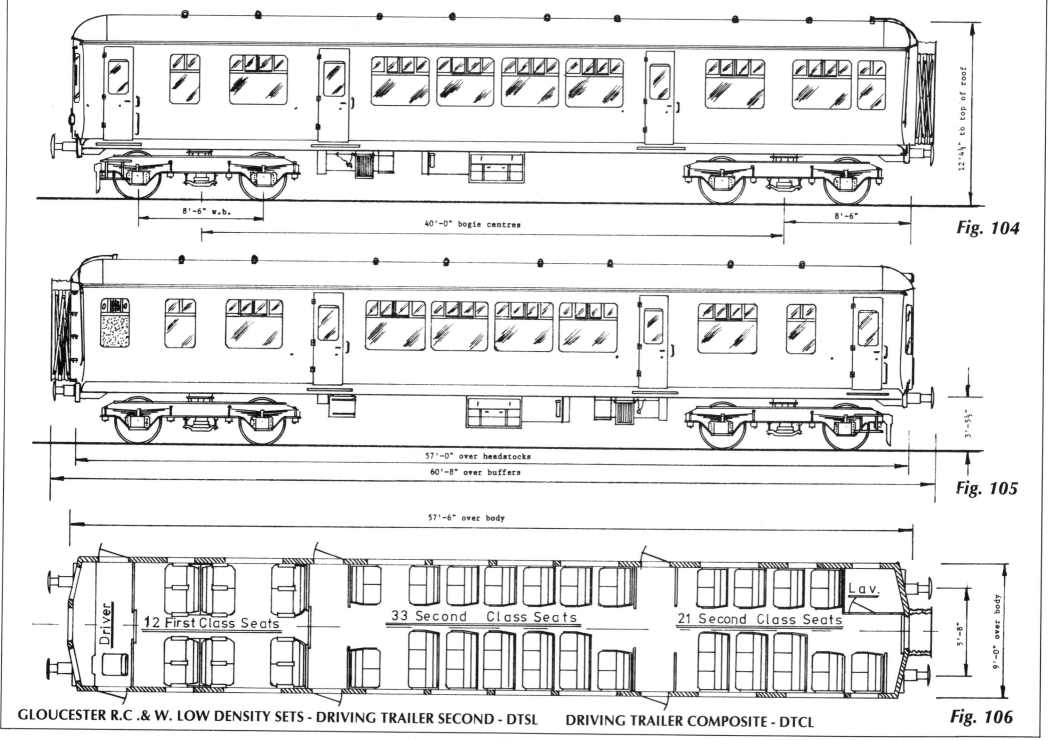

12'-4½" to top of roof

8'-6" w.b.

40'-0" bogie centres

8'-6"

Fig. 104

57'-0" over headstocks

60'-8" over buffers

3'-5½"

Fig. 105

57'-6" over body

Driver

12 First Class Seats

33 Second Class Seats

21 Second Class Seats

Lav.

5'-8"

9'-0" over body

GLOUCESTER R.C .& W. LOW DENSITY SETS - DRIVING TRAILER SECOND - DTSL   DRIVING TRAILER COMPOSITE - DTCL

Fig. 106

CHAPTER SIX

Park Royal Units

Following the success of the initial Derby and Metro-Cammell lightweight sets a number of other private sector builders were invited to submit proposals for further units. One of these was Park Royal Vehicles Ltd of Park Royal, London, then an associate of AEC and a major 'bus builder. They supplied 20 two-car sets to the London Midland Region in 1957, but these were in fact constructed at their Stockport works which was formerly Crossley Motors Ltd. This company had a long history of building chassis and bodies for 'buses and trolleybuses which were widely used by Municipal Transport undertakings. However, we know these units as the Park Royal sets and that is how they will be remembered.

Like the Gloucester units dealt with in the previous chapter, they had their own individuality although based on the original Derby design. Built to the standard 57' 6" length, they had a larger than usual front saloon, accommodating 16 first or 24 second class seats. This saloon had three large windows as did the shorter than normal centre section. The high waist line and heavy looking chassis gave these sets a very sturdy and solid appearance.

Naturally, being a member of the ACV group, they fitted AEC engines - two 150 bhp units being supplied in each power car.

The front of the cars incorporated the two-blind display below the centre cab window and the destination indicator was mounted at the top of this same window, within the frame and behind the glass. When built they carried the dark green livery with the two cream bands. Later a yellow warning panel was added below the cab windows and later still the standard Rail Blue with yellow ends was universally carried. Being relatively non-standard these cars had a comparatively short life, most of which was spent at Chester Depot. The last four two-car sets (50411 - 4, 56166 - 69) were transferred to the Western Region and were finally withdrawn on that region.

Driving Motor Brake Second - DMBS

Seats: 52 second
Nos.   M50395 - 414   (Lot No. 30286)
Weight: 33 tons 6 cwt.
Drawings: *Fig.114, fig.115* and *fig.116.*
            End views *fig.111* and *fig.112.*

Driving Trailer Composite with Lavatory - DTCL

Seats: 16 first, 48 second
Nos.   M56150 - 69   (Lot No. 30287)
Weight: 26 tons 6 cwt.
Drawings: *Fig.117, fig.118* and *fig.119.*
            End views *fig.111* and *fig.113.*

A Park Royal twin unit with DMBS No. M50395 in green and cream livery, nearest the camera.   *The late M.Gregory collection.*

A Park Royal twin unit with DTCL No. M56152 (nearest the camera) in green and cream livery (with whiskers).   *The late M.Gregory collection.*

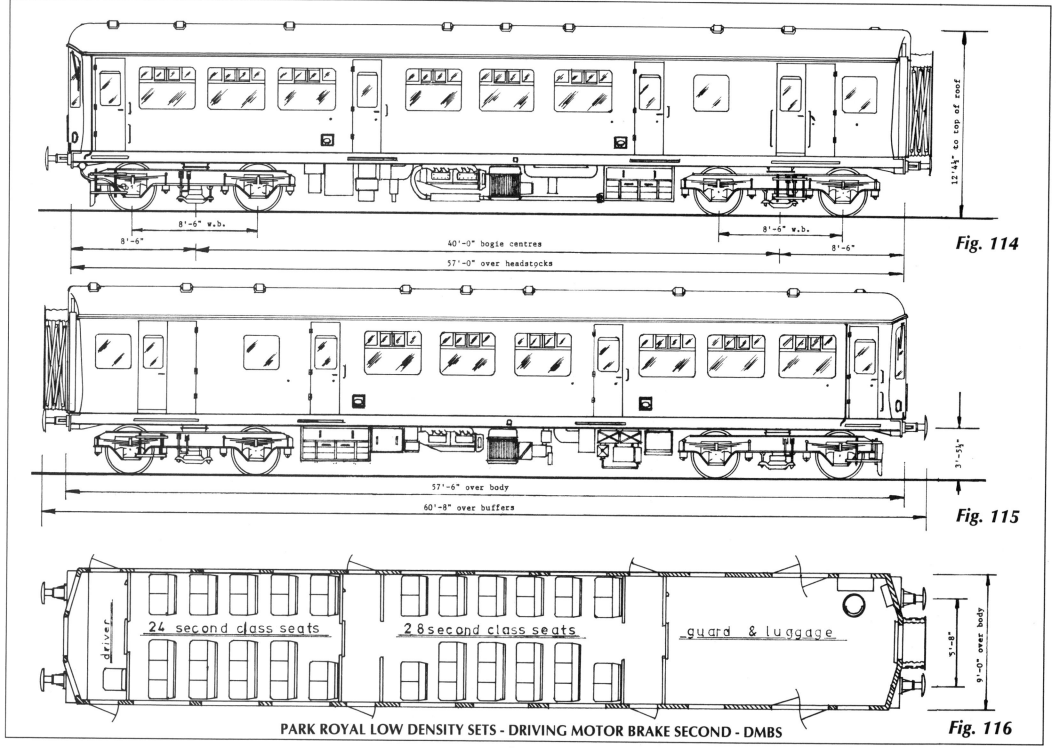

Fig. 114

12'4¼" to top of roof

8'-6" w.b.

8'-6"

40'-0" bogie centres

57'-0" over headstocks

8'-6" w.b.

8'-6"

Fig. 115

3'-5½"

57'-6" over body

60'-8" over buffers

driver

24 second class seats

28 second class seats

guard & luggage

5'-8"

9'-0" over body

Fig. 116

PARK ROYAL LOW DENSITY SETS - DRIVING MOTOR BRAKE SECOND - DMBS

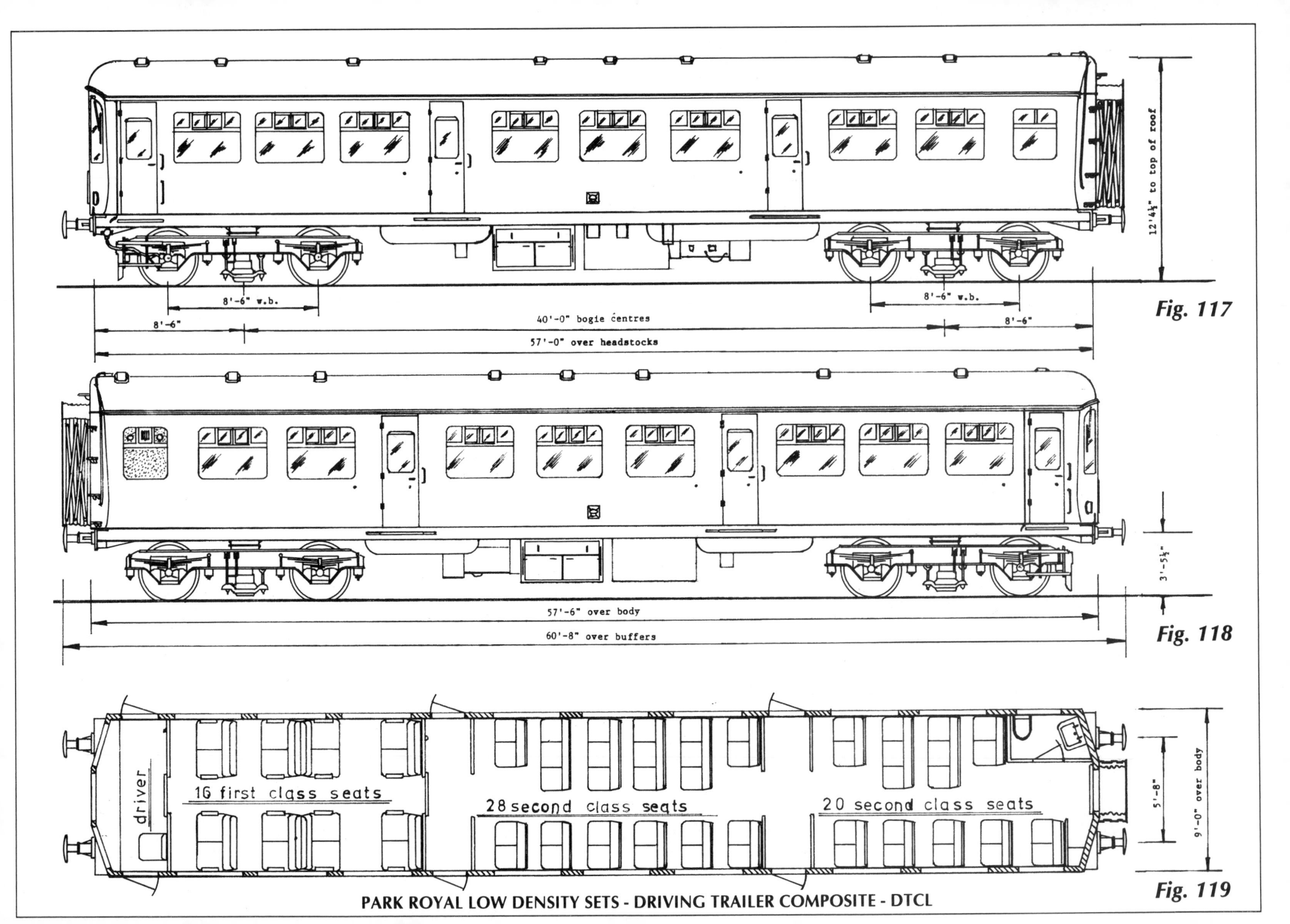

Fig. 117

12'4¾" to top of roof

8'-6" w.b. 8'-6" w.b.

8'-6" 8'-6"

40'-0" bogie centres

57'-0" over headstocks

Fig. 118

3'-5½"

57'-6" over body

60'-8" over buffers

Fig. 119

driver

16 first class seats   28 second class seats   20 second class seats

5'-8"

9'-0" over body

PARK ROYAL LOW DENSITY SETS - DRIVING TRAILER COMPOSITE - DTCL

CHAPTER SEVEN

The Wickham Units

D. Wickham & Co. Ltd have a long history of producing rail inspection vehicles and it was perhaps more than a little surprising at the time for them to be given an order for five two-car sets in 1955. These entered service with the Eastern Region in 1957.

Being of lightweight construction, the body and chassis formed an integral unit which contributed to the low weight of the finished units. Although conforming to the Derby saloon layout they differed in most other respects.

The front section had three closely spaced windows and accommodated 16 first or 23 second class passengers. The centre section had four (equally closely spaced) windows and 28 second class seats. The rear section of the DMBS had 8 second class seats followed by the guard's and luggage van. In the DTCL this section had three closely spaced windows on the left hand side and two large and two small on the other side. The second of these being the lavatory compartment.

Power cars each carried two Leyland 150 bhp engines using the standard mechanical transmission.

The very distinctive cab ends had the cantrail gutters swept down below the destination blinds fitted over the centre cab window. A two-digit blind and three lamps were fitted below this window and as built these cars carried the green livery with two cream lines (whiskers were added very soon after entering service). The usual process was followed whereby yellow warning panels appeared later. The later survivors just made it into the Rail Blue era.

Driving Motor Brake Second - DMBS
Seats:	59 second
Nos.	E50415 - 19 (Lot No. 30288)
Weight:	31 tons 0 cwt.
Drawings:	*Fig.120, fig.121* and *fig.122*.
	End views as *fig.126* and *fig.127*.

Driving Trailer Composite with Lavatory - DTCL
Seats:	16 first, 50 second
Nos.	E56170 - 74 (Lot No. 30289)
Weight:	20 tons 10 cwt.
Drawings:	*Fig.123, fig.124* and *fig.125*.
	End views as *fig.126* and *fig. 128*.

Nos. E50415/9, E56170/4 were sold back to the builders in 1960 to meet an export order from Trinidad and Tobago Railways.

The interior of the Wickham car with the characteristic scalloped partitions. Note how the seats, lights and luggage racks resemble those used in 'buses. *Railway Gazette.*

A Wickham 2-car low density set with DTCL No. E56173 nearest the camera - one of the cars which went to Trinidad in 1960. Note how the cantrail gutter is swept below the destination box on the end and that the livery is green and cream.

M.Smith / Kelland collection.

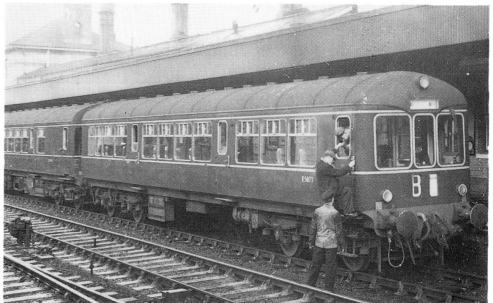

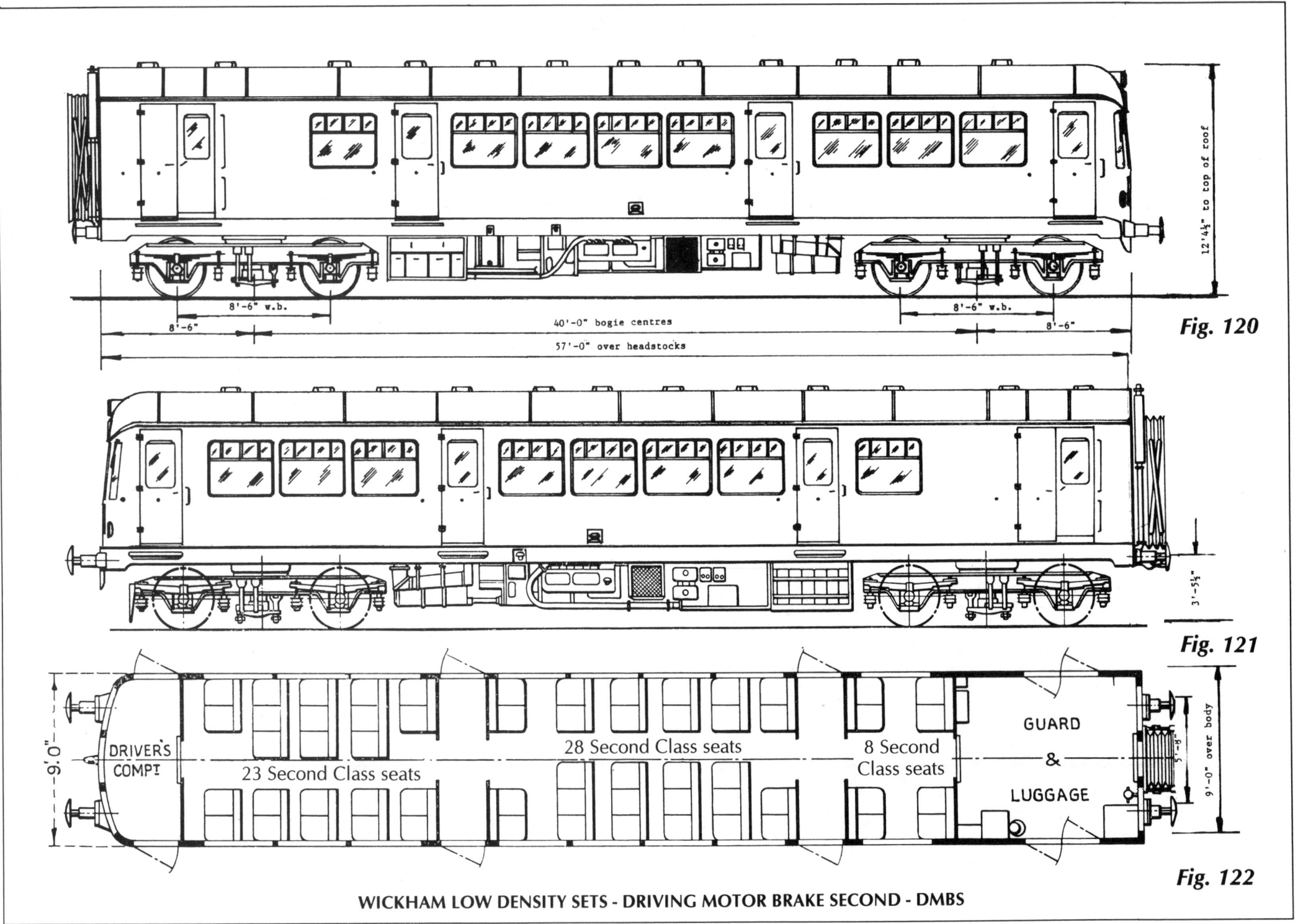

Fig. 120

12'4½" to top of roof

8'-6" w.b.

8'-6"

8'-6" w.b.

8'-6"

40'-0" bogie centres

57'-0" over headstocks

Fig. 121

3'-5½"

Fig. 122

9'-0"

DRIVER'S COMP!

23 Second Class seats

28 Second Class seats

8 Second Class seats

GUARD & LUGGAGE

5'-8"

9'-0" over body

WICKHAM LOW DENSITY SETS - DRIVING MOTOR BRAKE SECOND - DMBS

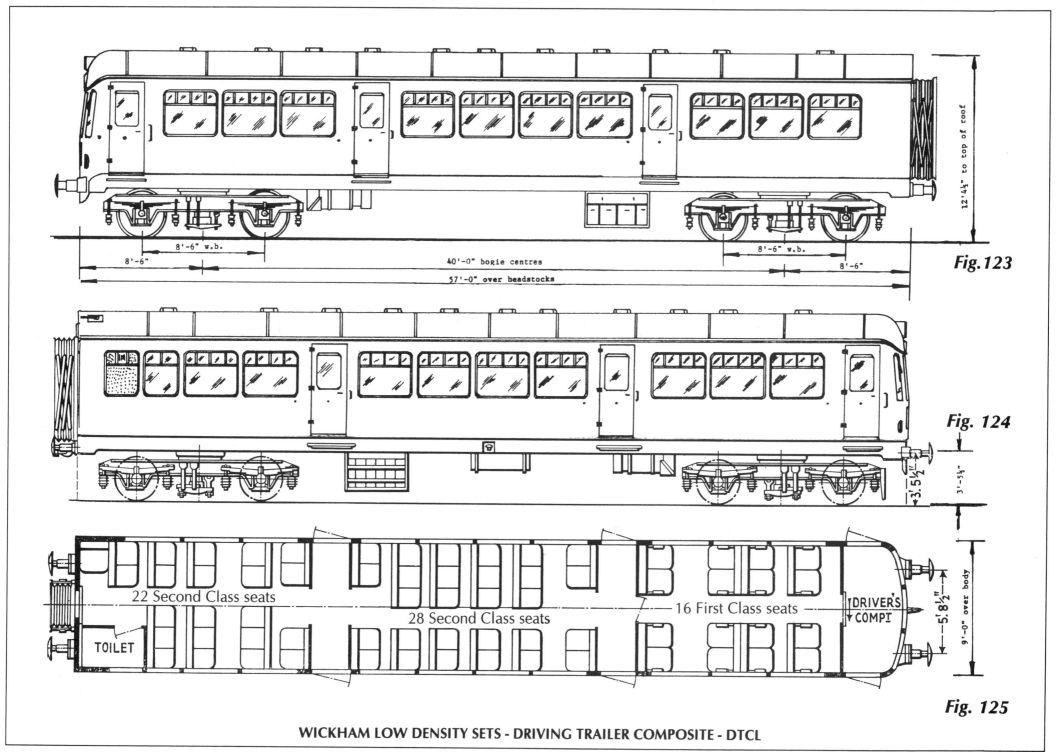

Fig. 123

Fig. 124

22 Second Class seats

28 Second Class seats

16 First Class seats

TOILET

DRIVER'S COMPT

Fig. 125

WICKHAM LOW DENSITY SETS - DRIVING TRAILER COMPOSITE - DTCL

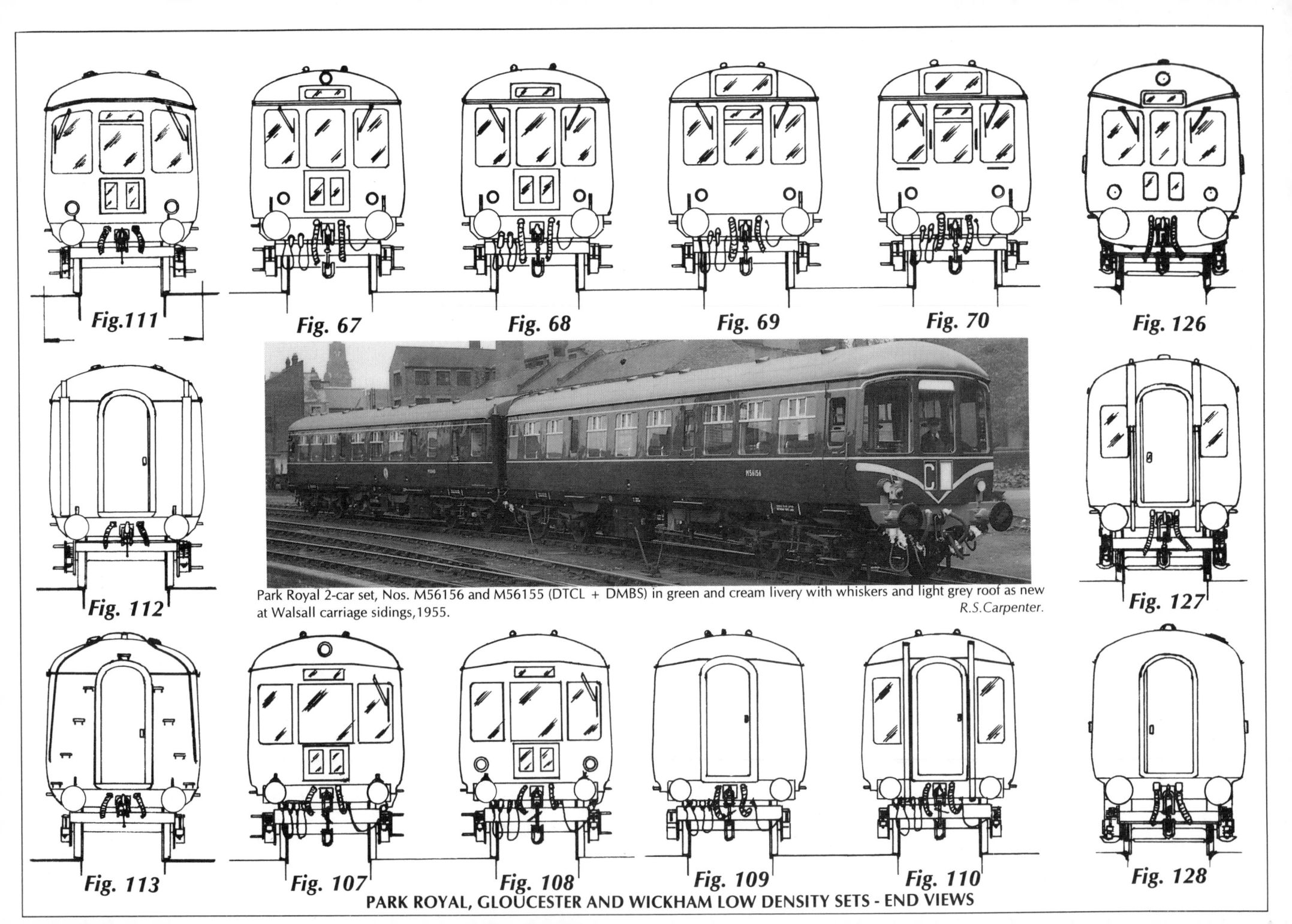

Fig.111

Fig. 67

Fig. 68

Fig. 69

Fig. 70

Fig. 126

Fig. 112

Park Royal 2-car set, Nos. M56156 and M56155 (DTCL + DMBS) in green and cream livery with whiskers and light grey roof as new at Walsall carriage sidings,1955.

R.S.Carpenter.

Fig. 127

Fig. 113

Fig. 107

Fig. 108

Fig. 109

Fig. 110

Fig. 128

PARK ROYAL, GLOUCESTER AND WICKHAM LOW DENSITY SETS - END VIEWS

CHAPTER EIGHT

The Cravens Units

Cravens Ltd of Sheffield had been heavily involved in the Standard Mk 1 coach construction programme and so it was probably not surprising that they should be invited to supply some of the DMU fleet. It was also not surprising that their version of the DMU design featured the Mk 1 bodyside profile and door.

At first glance the observer could be forgiven for thinking these cars were all built to the same design. However, there were a significant number of variations which we will pick out as we go through this whole series of units.

They can be divided into four main groups:

a)	Two-car sets (DMBS + DTCL)	
b)	Three-car sets (DMBS + TCL + DMCL)	
c)	Power Twin sets (DMBS + DMCL)	
d)	Rolls Royce powered sets (DMBS + DMCL)	

The situation is further complicated by the fact that there were two different types of DMBS used in the two-car sets, namely A1 and A3. The Rolls Royce cars were different again.

All the Cravens cars were built to the short frame size of 57' 6" and had the distinctive two-window front end. Whilst the front saloon followed the Derby pattern with two window bays, the centre section had only three equally-spaced large windows. The rear section was similar to the normal design but, again had its own individual character.

When new the Cravens cars carried the standard green livery with two cream bands. Some of them carried the 'Speed Whiskers', but all eventually received the yellow warning panels. From the late 1960's they were repainted into standard Rail Blue with all-yellow ends and a few later received the blue/grey livery.

a) Two-car sets

Delivered in four batches these sets and one odd DMBS (E50249 built in 1959 as a replacement for E50173 lost in an accident at Hexham in 1957) are dealt with as follows:

1956 sets (TOPS Class 106 - later Class 105)

There were 14 of these sets built in 1956 for the North Eastern Region. Type A1 DMBS cars were each powered by two 150bhp Leyland engines with standard transmission. They carried the early four-lamp headcode arrangement with the destination blind centrally above the windscreens and splitting the rain guttering. The A1 type had a single window in the brake van and the double doors are fitted near the end of the car.

Driving Motor Brake Second - Type A1 - DMBS
Seats:	52 seconds
Nos.	E50359 - 72 (Lot No. 30280)
Weight:	29 tons 0 cwt.
Drawings:	*Fig.129, fig.130* and *fig.131.*
End views:	*Fig.144* and *fig.147.*

Driving Trailer Composite with Lavatory - DTCL
Seats:	12 frist, 51 second
Nos.	E56114 - 27 (Lot No. 30281)
Weight:	23 tons 0 cwt.
Drawings:	*Fig.132, fig.133* and *fig.134.*
End views:	*Fig.144* and *fig.148.*

1957 sets (Tops Class 105)

A further 22 sets followed in 1957, 17 for the North Eastern Region and 5 for the London Midland Region. All were originally fitted with AEC engines, but these were later replaced by Leyland units. The DMBS cars were Type A1 and identical to those in the 1956 series.

Driving Motor Brake Second - Type A1 - DMBS
Seats:	52 second
Nos.	E50373 - 89 (Lot No. 30282)
	M50390 - 94 (Lot No. 30284)
Weight:	29 tons 0 cwt.
Drawings:	As E50359

Driving Trailer Composite with Lavatory - DTCL
Seats:	12 first, 51 second
Nos.	E56128 - 44 (Lot No. 30283)
	M56145 - 49 (Lot No. 30285)
Weight:	25 tons 0 cwt.
Drawings:	as E56114 - 27

1958 sets (TOPS Class 105)

These 48 sets for the North Eastern Region had type A3 DMBS in place of the A1 used in the previous units and featured 2-digit indicator boxes with a marker lamp either side. Each power car had two AEC 150bhp engines.

The type A3 differed from the type A1 in having the double doors nearer to the centre of the guard's/luggage van and also having a small window either side of the doors.

Driving Motor Brake Second - Type A3 - DMBS
Seats:	52 second
Nos:	E51254 - 301 (Lot No. 30469)
Weight :	30 tons 0cwt.
Drawings:	*Fig. 135, fig. 136* and *fig. 137.*
	End views *fig.145* and *fig.147.*

Driving Trailer Composite with Lavatory - DTCL

Seats :	12 first, 51 second
Nos:	E56412 - 59 (Lot No. 30470)
Weight :	24 tons 0cwt.
Drawings :	as E56114 - 27

1959 sets (TOPS Class 105)

A final batch of 24 sets was built in 1959, two sets for the Eastern Region and 22 for the Scottish Region. These had AEC engines, but reverted to the Type A1 DMBS. The two-digit box and two-lamp arrangement introduced with the 1958 build was retained. The odd DMBS was also built in this year to the same design, but with a separate Lot No. for the North Eastern Region.

Driving Motor Brake Second - Type A1 - DMBS

Seats:	52 second
Nos.	E51471 - 92 (Lot No. 30503)
	SC51473 - 94 (Lot No. 30503)
	E50249 (Lot No. 30505)
Drawings:	Fig.129, fig.130 and fig.131.
	End views as Fig.145 and fig.147.

Driving Trailer Composite with Lavatory - DTCL

Seats:	12 first, 51 second
Nos.	E56460 - 1 (Lot No. 30504)
	SC56462 - 83 (Lot No. 30504)
Weight:	24 tons 0cwt.
Drawings:	as E56114 - 27

b) Three-car sets

A single batch of three-car sets was produced in 1957 for the London Midland Region. They comprised a DMBS, a TCL and a DMCL. In later years the centre trailer cars were withdrawn resulting in the sets becoming Power-Twins identical to those described later.

Like the Power Twins these sets had AEC engines and the DMBS cars were to Type A3. They had the two-digit indicator and two lamps. Some of the TCL cars were later down graded to Trailer Second units with seating for 70.

Driving Motor Brake Second - Type A3 - DMBS

Seats:	52 second
Nos.	M50752 - 70 (Lot No. 30352)
Weight:	30 tons 0cwt.
Drawings:	as E51254 - 301

Trailer Composite with Lavatory - TCL

Seats:	12 first, 51 second
Nos.	M59307 - 25 (Lot No. 30354)
Weight:	23 tons 0cwt.
Drawings:	Fig.138, fig.139 and fig.140.
	End views as fig. 148 and fig.149.

Driving Motor Composite with Lavatory - Type A2 - DMCL

Seats:	12 first, 51 second
Nos.	M50785 - 803 (Lot No. 30353)
Weight:	30 tons 0 cwt.
Drawings:	Fig.141, fig.142 and fig.143.
	End views as fig.145 and fig.148.

c) Power-Twin sets

The London Midland region received 14 Power-Twin sets in 1957 at the same time as the triplets described above. They were built to the same Lot numbers and the cars were interchangeable with them. After the withdrawal of the centre trailer cars from the triplets, all 33 sets became identical.

Driving Motor Brake Second - Type A3 - DMBS

Seats:	52 second
Nos.	M50771 - 84 (Lot No. 30352)
Weight:	30 tons 0 cwt.
Drawings:	as E52154 - 301

Driving Motor Composite with Lavatory - Type A2 - DMCL

Seats:	12 first, 51 second
Nos.	M50804 - 17 (Lot No.30353)
Weight:	30 tons 0 cwt.
Drawings:	as M50785 - 803

d) Rolls Royce powered sets

A series of 50 two-car sets was introduced which proved to be less than successful and were withdrawn after a relatively short service life. The first 25 of these had mechanical transmission whilst the others had hydraulic transmission. They differed from all the other DMU's in having a single Rolls Royce 8-cylinder 238 bhp horizontal engine for each car giving a total of 476 bhp for each two car set.

These sets were delivered new to Accrington and Newton Heath for the North -East Lancashire services in 1959-60. By 1967 all the survivors of the M51681-51730 batch had been transferred to Cricklewood depot and were withdrawn from there. Seventeen of the second batch (M51731-80) had previously been transferred to Cricklewood by 1965, for the Kentish Town -

Barking service. The remainder of this batch (less withdrawals due to fire or mishap) saw out their days at Accrington. Many of these cars retained their dark green livery right up to withdrawal, although others had been repainted in blue with small warning panels or full yellow ends. An article by the late Peter Mallaband on the Cravens DMU's appeared in 'Motive Power Monthly' in February 1987 and mentioned TOPS classifications 112 & 113, although an earlier TOPS list showed both these classifications as blank. In the article the following are quoted :

M51681 - 51706	112/1	M51706 - 51730	112/2
M51731 - 51755	113/1	M51756 - 51779	113/2

Note : (M51780 was withdrawn in 1962)

Exactly why British Rail chose to adopt this arrangement at the height of the DMU programme is something of a mystery, but it did give the opportunity of studying mechanical and hydraulic drive systems under similar conditions. The bodies were similar to the other Cravens units with the front ends of M51681-51730 as *fig.145*, but the front ends of M51731-80 incorporated a four-digit indicator box in the roof dome whilst retaining the two-lamp arrangement as *fig.146*.

Mechanical Transmission (TOPS Class 112)

Driving Motor Brake Second - Type A3 DMBS

Seats:	52 second
Nos.	M51681 - 705 (Lot No. 30533)
Drawings:	No separate drawing has been prepared for these short lived cars, but the body details can be taken from *fig.135*, *fig.136* and *fig.137*, with the end views as *fig.145* and *fig.147*.

Driving Motor Composite with Lavatory - Type A2 - DMCL

Seats:	12 first, 51 second
Nos.	M51706 - 30 (Lot No. 30534)
Weight:	29 tons 10 cwt.
Drawings:	As above, but refer to *Fig.141*, *fig142* and *fig.143* with end views as *fig.145* and *fig.148*.

Hydraulic Transmission (TOPS Class 113)

Driving Motor Brake Second - Type A3 - DMBS

Seats:	52 second
Nos.	M51731 - 55 (Lot No. 30535)
Weight:	29 tons 0 cwt.
Drawings:	as above, except end views as *fig.146* and *fig.147*.

Driving Motor Composite with Lavatory - Type A2 - DMCL

Seats:	12 first, 51 second
Nos:	M51756 - 80 (Lot No. 30535)
Weight:	29 tons 0 cwt.
Drawing:	as above, except end views as *fig.146* and *fig.147*.

General

In one other respect the Cravens cars were unique. When built they had an internal exhaust system. In DMBS cars the exhaust trunking was located against the partition to the vestibule and in the DMCL it passed up the wall of the lavatory compartment. In both cases it then passed through the roof of the car. Most retained this feature to the end, but some had more normal external exhaust system fitted.

Note

Some Class 105 units (also some early Derby lightweights and some Wickham two car sets) destined for service on ex - M & GN lines with long single track sections (in Lincolnshire and Norfolk), had a recess in the side next to the driver's door window. This was to house a tablet catcher which in the event was never fitted as the lines in question closed in 1959 and the recesses were plated over.

See Bibliography ref. 2, page 4, 6 and 29.

A Cravens Class 105, 2-car set leaves March station on 12th April, 1983, with the 10.35 Peterborough to Cambridge service. It carries the Rail Blue with yellow ends livery.

G.Gamble.

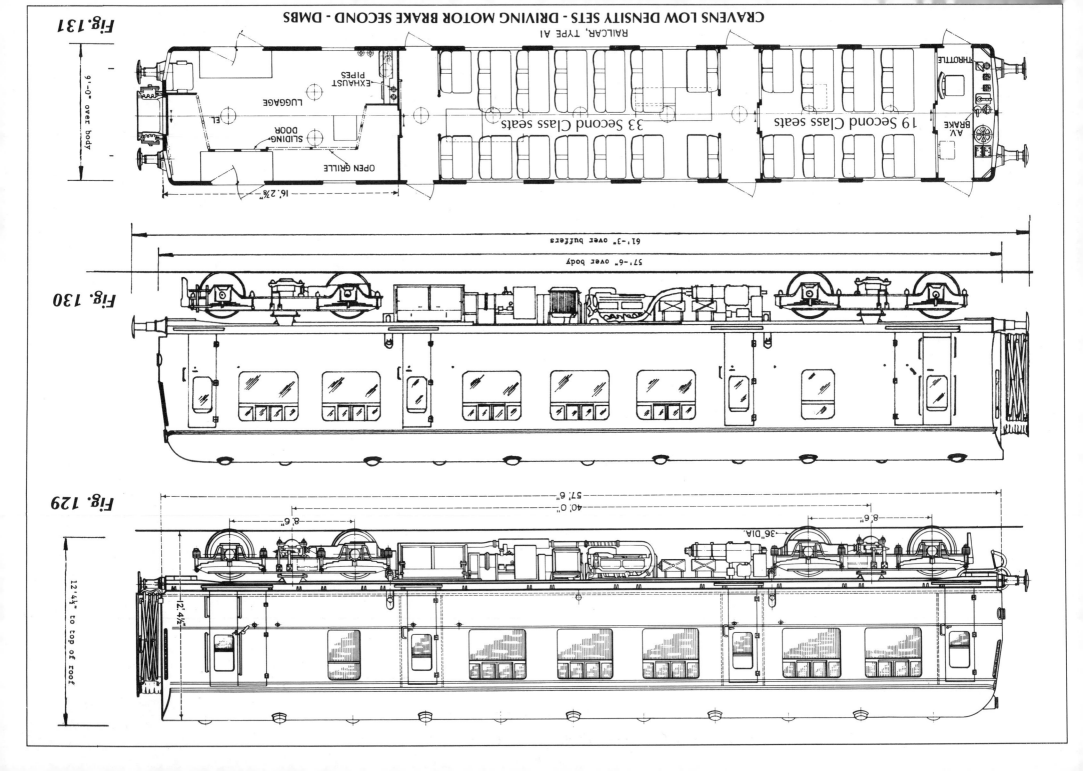

CRAVENS LOW DENSITY SETS - DRIVING MOTOR BRAKE SECOND - DMBS

RAILCAR, TYPE A1

Fig. 131

Fig. 130

Fig. 129

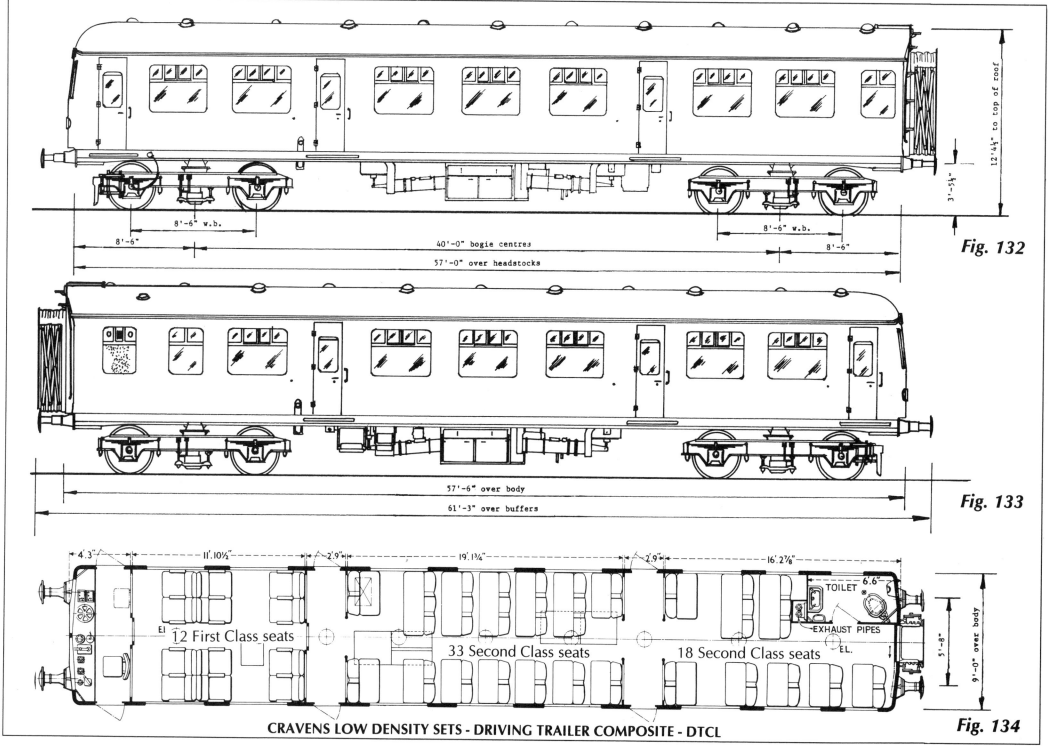

Fig. 132

12'4¼" to top of roof

3'-5¼"

8'-6" w.b.

8'-6"

40'-0" bogie centres

8'-6" w.b.

8'-6"

57'-0" over headstocks

Fig. 133

57'-6" over body

61'-3" over buffers

4'.3"

11'.10½"

2'.9"

19'.1¾"

2'.9"

16'.2⅞"

TOILET

6.6"

EXHAUST PIPES

E.L.

E.L.

12 First Class seats

33 Second Class seats

18 Second Class seats

5'-8"

9'-0" over body

CRAVENS LOW DENSITY SETS - DRIVING TRAILER COMPOSITE - DTCL

Fig. 134

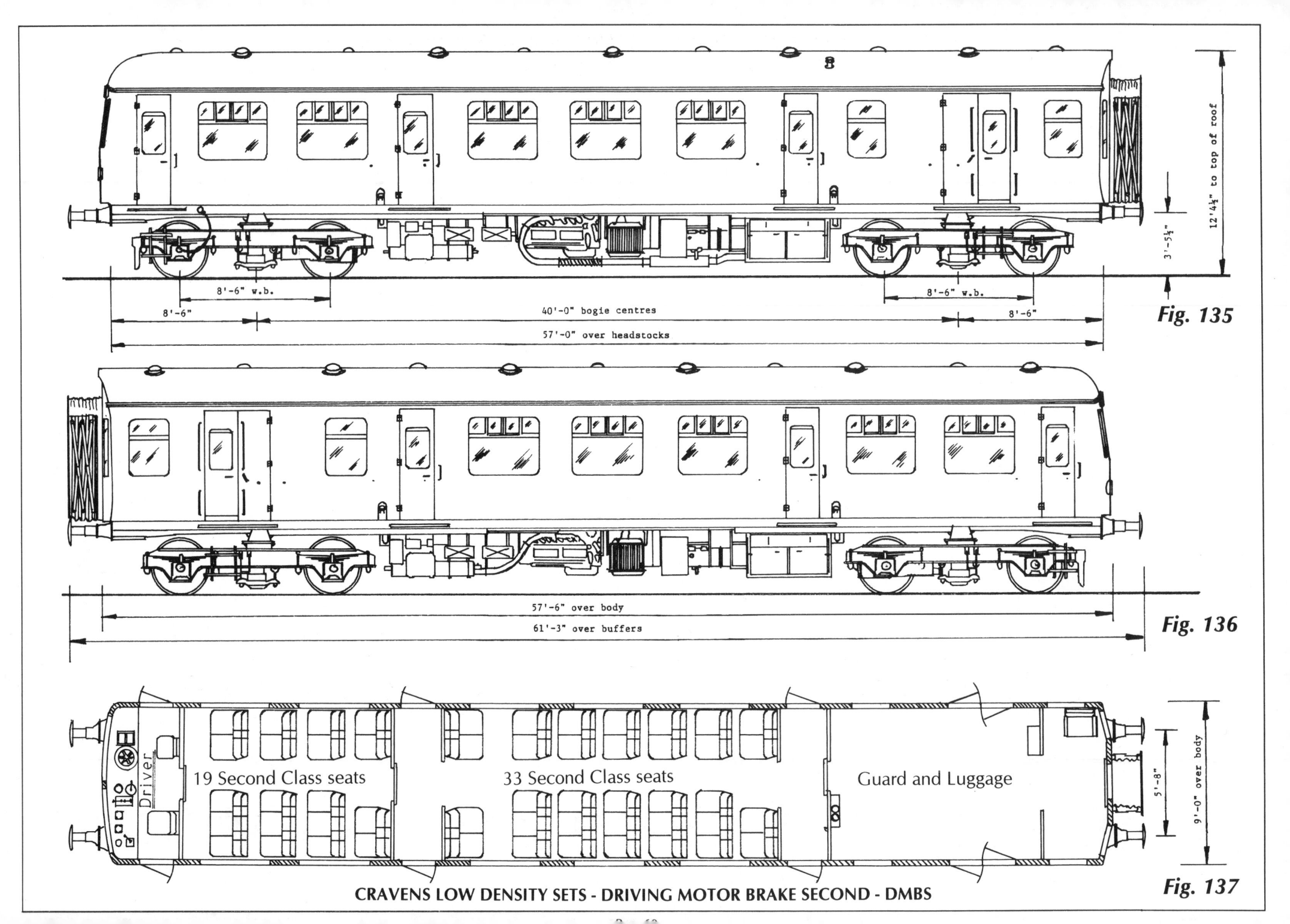

12'4¼" to top of roof

3'-5¼"

8'-6" w.b.

8'-6"

40'-0" bogie centres

8'-6" w.b.

8'-6"

57'-0" over headstocks

Fig. 135

57'-6" over body

61'-3" over buffers

Fig. 136

Driver

19 Second Class seats

33 Second Class seats

Guard and Luggage

5'-8"

9'-0" over body

CRAVENS LOW DENSITY SETS - DRIVING MOTOR BRAKE SECOND - DMBS

Fig. 137

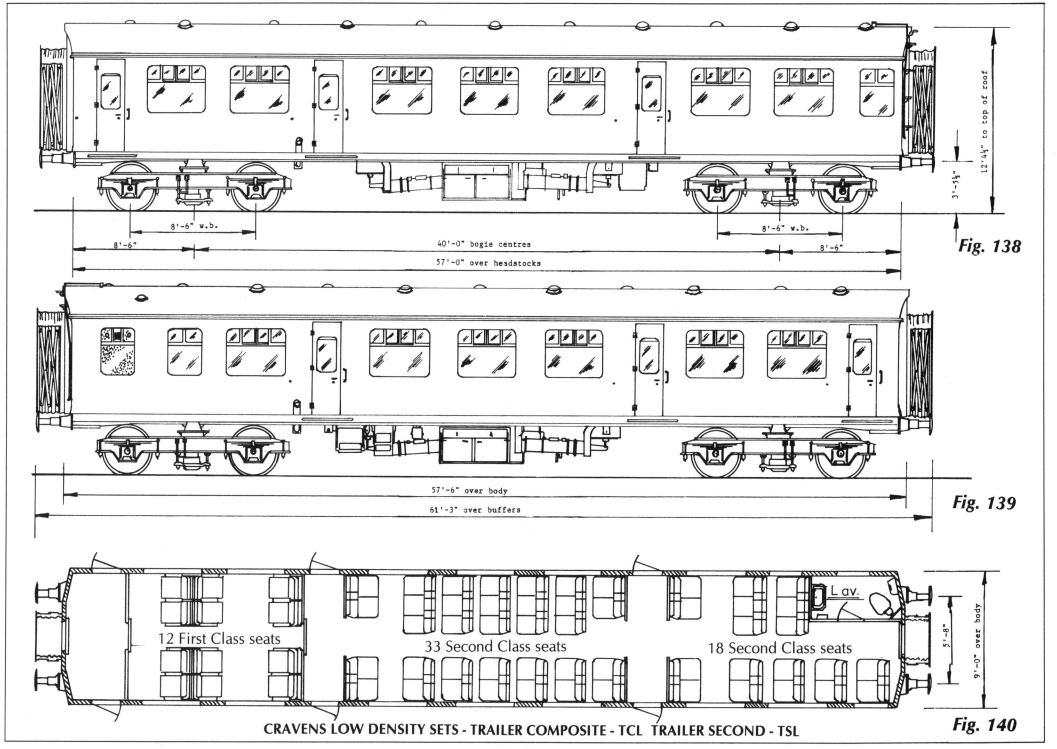

Fig. 138

8'-6" w.b.   8'-6" w.b.

8'-6"   40'-0" bogie centres   8'-6"

57'-0" over headstocks

12'4½" to top of roof

3'-5¼"

Fig. 139

57'-6" over body

61'-3" over buffers

12 First Class seats   33 Second Class seats   Lav.   18 Second Class seats

5'-8"

9'-0" over body

CRAVENS LOW DENSITY SETS - TRAILER COMPOSITE - TCL TRAILER SECOND - TSL

Fig. 140

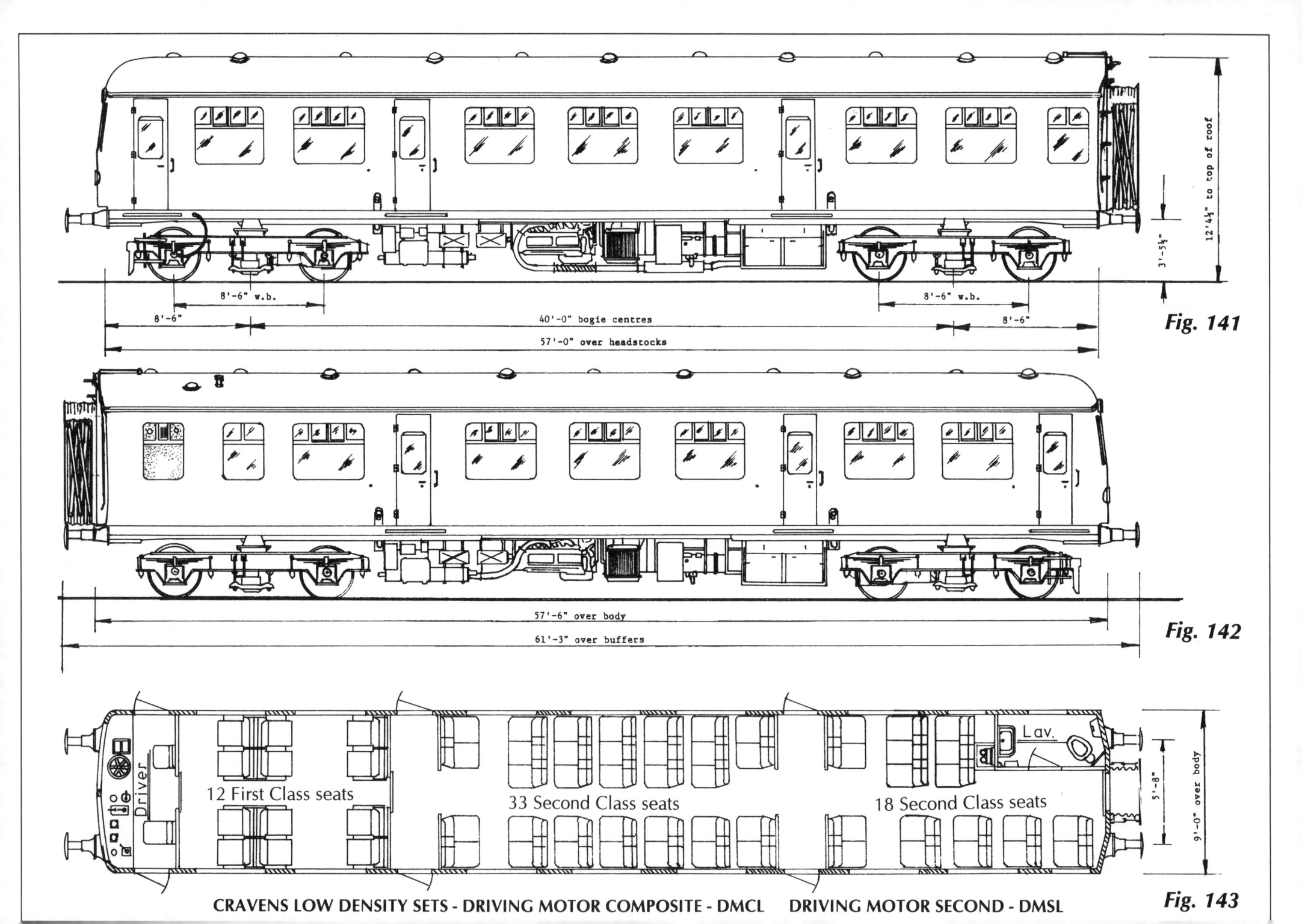

Fig. 141

12'4¼" to top of roof

3'-5½"

8'-6" w.b.

8'-6" w.b.

8'-6"

40'-0" bogie centres

8'-6"

57'-0" over headstocks

Fig. 142

57'-6" over body

61'-3" over buffers

Driver

12 First Class seats

33 Second Class seats

18 Second Class seats

Lav.

5'-8"

9'-0" over body

Fig. 143

CRAVENS LOW DENSITY SETS - DRIVING MOTOR COMPOSITE - DMCL   DRIVING MOTOR SECOND - DMSL

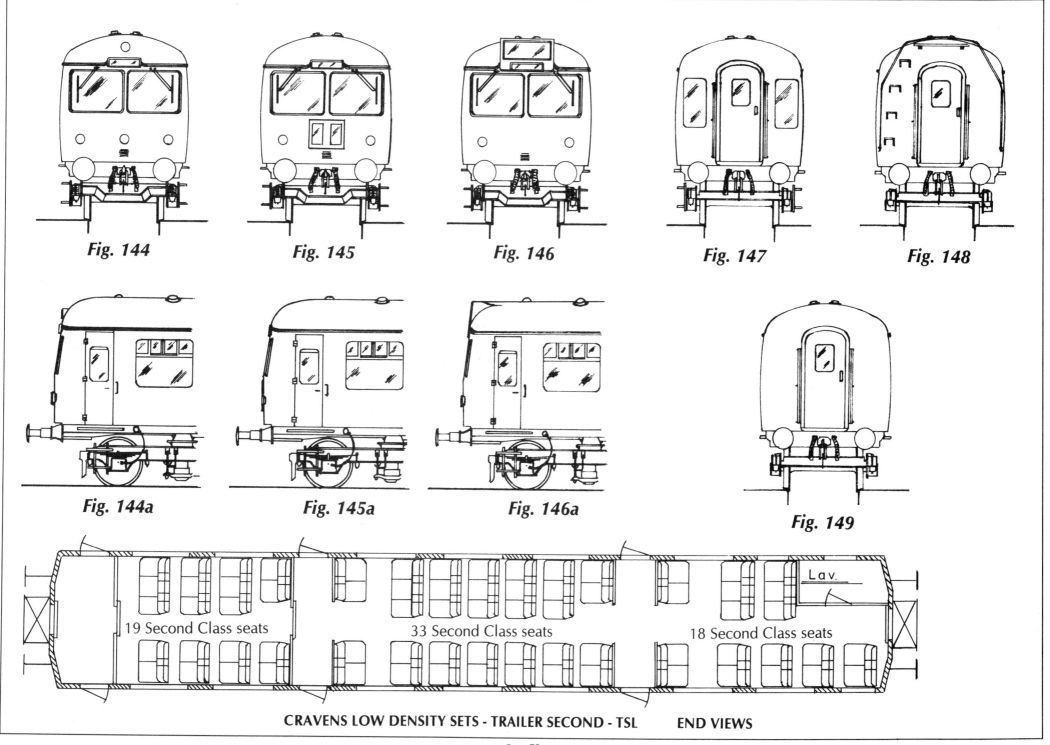

Fig. 144

Fig. 145

Fig. 146

Fig. 147

Fig. 148

Fig. 144a

Fig. 145a

Fig. 146a

Fig. 149

19 Second Class seats

33 Second Class seats

Lav.

18 Second Class seats

CRAVENS LOW DENSITY SETS - TRAILER SECOND - TSL   END VIEWS

CHAPTER NINE

The Birmingham RCW Sets.

These sets fall into two separate series - the first and largest of these became TOPS Class 104 - which itself divides into three types of set. The later series became TOPS Class 110.

Class 104 series

These were the first of the BRCW units and were very distinctive with their three-window cab front being starkly upright with very tall windows giving the appearance of a thin roof. The general layout of the coach bodies followed the Derby design very closely and yet they managed to appear totally different to them.

All the driving cars were built with a two-digit box under the centre cab window with a head/tail lamp either side. Some cars actually had a third lamp situated on the roof dome immediately above the roof-mounted destination indicator blind.

The Class 104 series was delivered in the following set formations:

  a) Two-car sets
  b) Three-car sets
  c) Four-car sets

Each power car had two Leyland 150 bhp engines with a normal mechanical transmission and the sets were 'blue square' coupling code. They were delivered in the standard green livery with cream lining, but did not have the whiskers. Most later acquired yellow warning panels. They carried most of the later liveries also.

a) Two-car sets

Two batches were built in 1957 & 1958 for the London Midland and the North Eastern Regions respectively. They were virtually identical although the first batch had the roof lamp.

Driving Motor Brake Second - DMBS
Seats:	52 second
Nos.	M50532 - 41 (Lot No. 30296)
	E50594 - 98 (Lot No. 30404)
Weight:	31 tons 0 cwt.
Drawings:	*Fig.150, fig.151* and *fig.152.*
	End views *fig.162* (1st Batch) or *fig.163* (2nd batch) and *fig.164.*

Driving Trailer Composite with Lavatory - DTCL
Seats:	12 first, 54 second
Nos.	M56175 - 84 (Lot No. 30297)
	E56185 - 89 (Lot No. 30405)
Weight:	24 tons 0 cwt.
Drawings:	*Fig.153* (LHS),*fig.154* (RHS body only)
Seating plan:	*Fig.155,* End view as *fig.162* (1st batch) or *fig.163* (2nd batch) and *fig.167.*

b) Three-car sets

There were also two batches of these contemporary three-car sets supplied to the London Midland Region in 1957 the first of which had the roof-mounted third lamp.

Driving Motor Brake Second - DMBS
Seats:	52 second
Nos.	M50420 - 23 (Lot No. 30290)
	M50428 - 79 (Lot No. 30293)
Weight:	31 tons 0 cwt.
Drawings:	as M50532 - 41 etc.

Trailer Composite with Lavatory - TCL
Seats:	12 first, 54 second
Nos.	M59312 - 35 (Lot No. 30292)
	M59136 - 87 (Lot No. 30295)
Weight:	24 tons 0 cwt.
Drawing:	*Fig.156, fig.157* and *fig.158.*
	End views *fig.166* and *fig.167.*

Driving Motor Composite with Lavatory - DMCL
Seats:	12 first, 54 second
Nos.	M50424 - 27 (Lot No. 30291)
	M50480 - 531 (Lot No. 30294)
Weight:	24 tons 0 cwt.
Drawings:	*Fig.153* (LHS body only), *fig.154* and *fig.155.*
	End view *fig.162* (1st batch) or *fig. 163* (2nd batch) and *fig.165.*

c) Four-car sets

The final form of the Class 104 series is represented by the 26 four-car sets in two batches for the North Eastern Region. These followed the pattern of the Derby four-car sets and many of these later lost the trailer second and ran as three-car sets.

Driving Motor Composite - DMCL *(one marshalled at each end of set)*

Seats: 12 first, 54 second
Nos. E50542 - 83 (Lot No. 30298)
E50584 - 93 (Lot No. 30301)
Weight: 31 tons 0 cwt.
Drawings: as M50424 - 27 etc.

Trailer Second with Lavatory - TSL

Seats: 69 second
Nos. E59188 - 208 (Lot No. 30299)
E59230 - 34 (Lot No. 30302)
Weight: 24 tons 0 cwt.
Drawings: *Fig.156, fig.157* plan.
End views *fig.166* and *fig.167*.

Trailer Brake Second with Lavatory - TBSL

Seats: 51 second
Nos. E59209 - 29 (Lot No. 30300)
E59240 - 44 (Lot No. 30303)
Weight: 24 tons 0 cwt.
Drawings: *Fig.159, fig.160* and *fig.161*.
End views as *fig.166* and *fig.167*.

A Birmingham RC & W Co. Class 104 unit composed of cars No. 53437 and 53479.

Milepost 92½.

Class 110 units

In 1961, 30 of these three-car sets were built for the London Midland Region and North Eastern Region Calder Valley Line services. Two 180bhp Rolls Royce engines were fitted in each power car with standard mechanical transmission. They differed from the earlier BRCW units in a number of ways. The side windows were mounted in bright metal raised frames giving a more modern appearance. The ends were considerably improved, incorporating a four-digit display in the roof dome displacing the destination blind to the top of the centre cab window which was shortened accordingly. The bottom of all three cab windows were lowered to align with the side windows and the outer two were given sloping tops. The change was quite dramatic and these cars were much more attractive than their predecessors. These sets were also unique amongst the Low Density units in having a Driving Motor Brake Composite car in their formation.

As built they sported the green livery with the cream lines. The waist lining was swept down at the front end to incorporate the whiskers to give a streamlined effect. Most of the 'blue era' liveries were carried.

Driving Motor Brake Composite - DMBC

Seats: 12 first, 33 second
Nos. E51809 - 28 (Lot No. 30592)
M52066 - 75 (Lot No. 30691)
Weight: 32 tons 0 cwt.
Drawings: *Fig.173, fig.174* and *fig.175*.
End views as *fig.168* and *fig.169*.

Trailer Second with Lavatory - TSL

Seats: 72 second
Nos. E59693 - 712 (Lot No. 30594)
M59808 - 17 (Lot No. 30693)
Weight: 24 tons 0 cwt.
Drawings: *Fig.176, fig.177* and *fig.178*.
End views as *fig.171* to *fig.176* and *fig.172*.

Driving Motor Composite with Lavatory - DMCL

Seats: 12 first, 54 second
Nos. E51829 - 48 (Lot No. 30593)
M52076 - 85 (Lot No. 30692)
Weight: 31 tons 10 cwt.
Drawings: *Fig.179, fig.180* and *fig.181*.
End views as *fig.168* and *fig.170*.

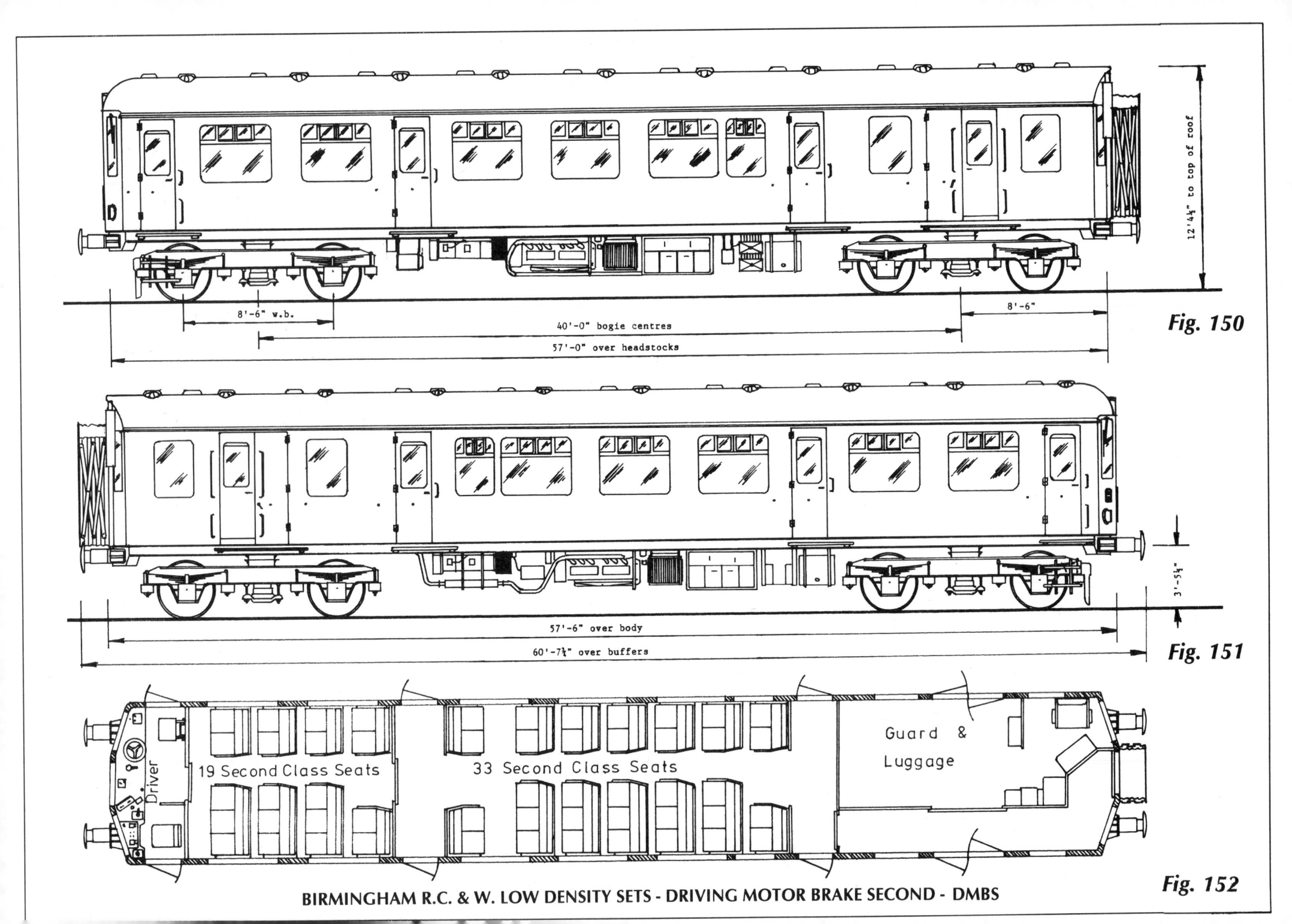

Fig. 150

12'4¼" to top of roof

8'-6" w.b.

40'-0" bogie centres

57'-0" over headstocks

8'-6"

Fig. 151

57'-6" over body

60'-7¼" over buffers

3'-5¼"

Fig. 152

Driver

19 Second Class Seats

33 Second Class Seats

Guard & Luggage

BIRMINGHAM R.C. & W. LOW DENSITY SETS - DRIVING MOTOR BRAKE SECOND - DMBS

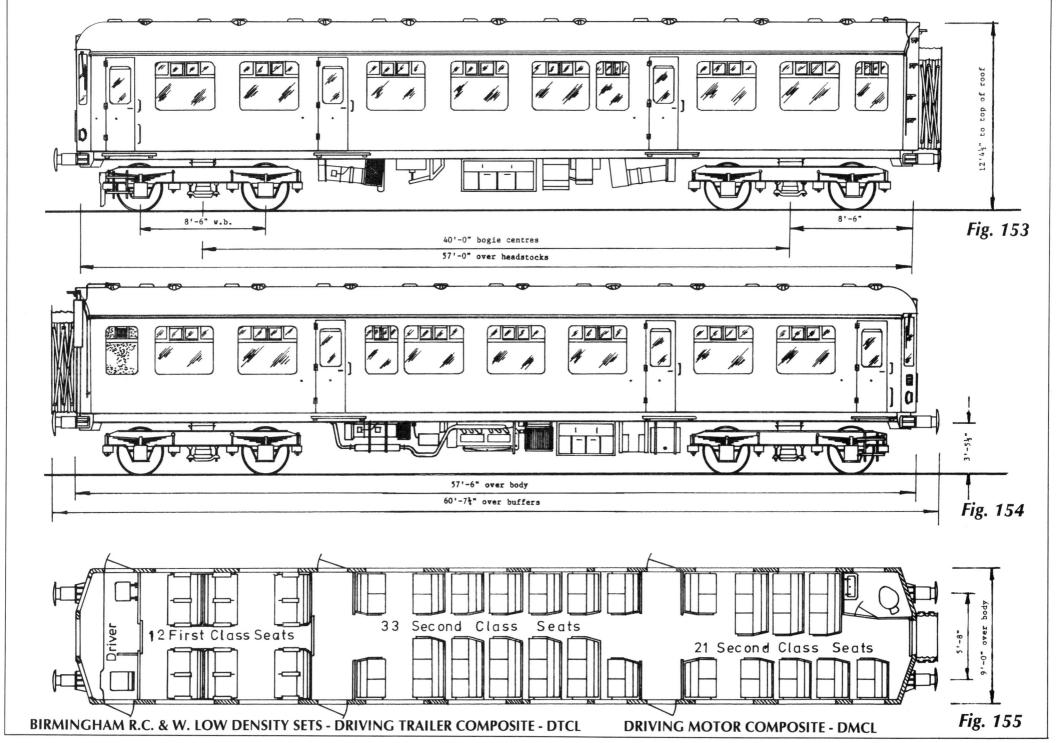

12'4½" to top of roof

Fig. 153

8'-6" w.b.

8'-6"

40'-0" bogie centres

57'-0" over headstocks

3'-5¼"

57'-6" over body

60'-7¾" over buffers

Fig. 154

Driver

12 First Class Seats

33 Second Class Seats

21 Second Class Seats

5'-8"

9'-0" over body

BIRMINGHAM R.C. & W. LOW DENSITY SETS - DRIVING TRAILER COMPOSITE - DTCL   **DRIVING MOTOR COMPOSITE - DMCL**   **Fig. 155**

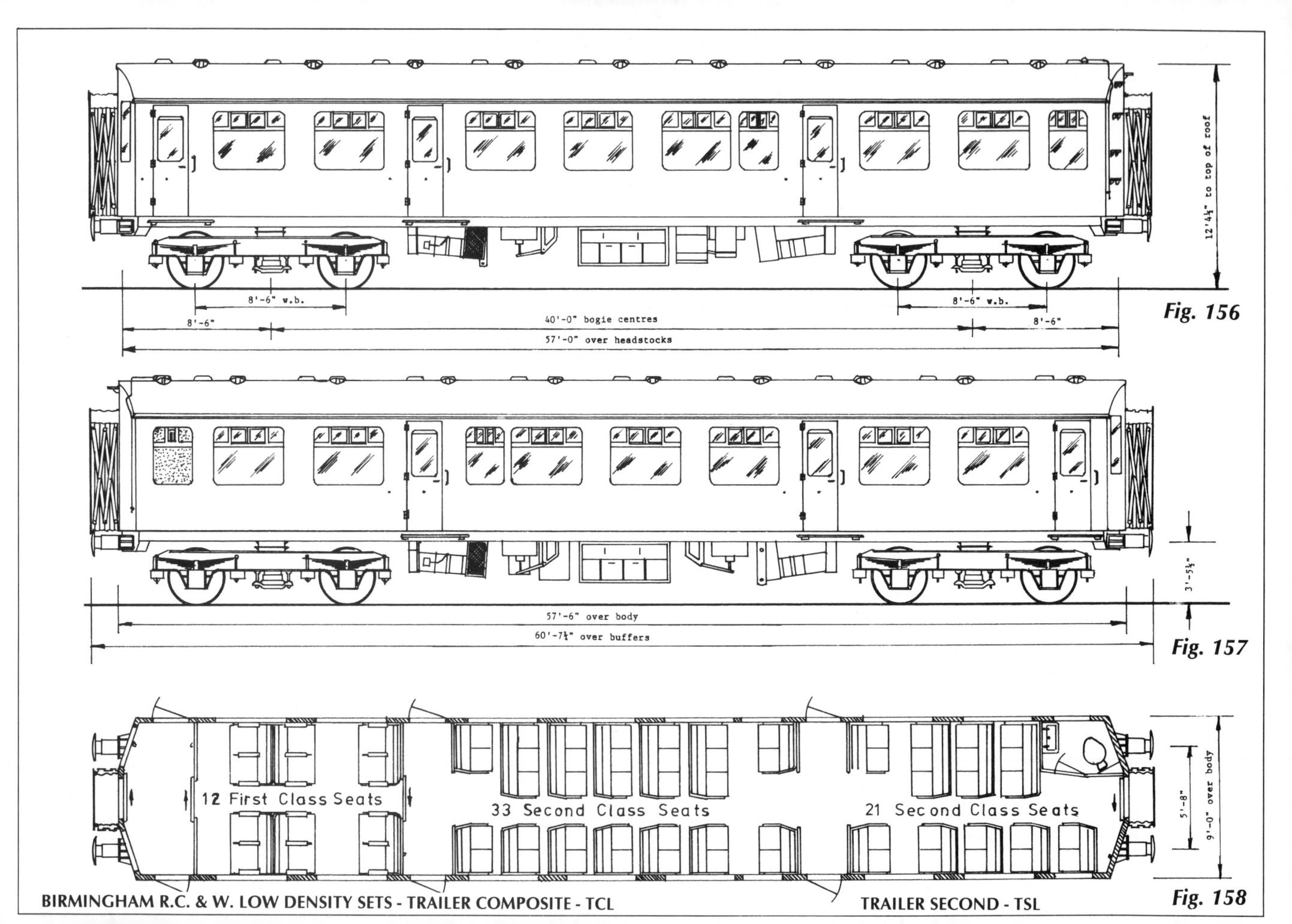

Fig. 156

12'-4½" to top of roof

8'-6" w.b.

8'-6" w.b.

8'-6"

40'-0" bogie centres

8'-6"

57'-0" over headstocks

Fig. 157

3'-5¼"

57'-6" over body

60'-7¼" over buffers

Fig. 158

12 First Class Seats

33 Second Class Seats

21 Second Class Seats

5'-8"

9'-0" over body

BIRMINGHAM R.C. & W. LOW DENSITY SETS - TRAILER COMPOSITE - TCL

TRAILER SECOND - TSL

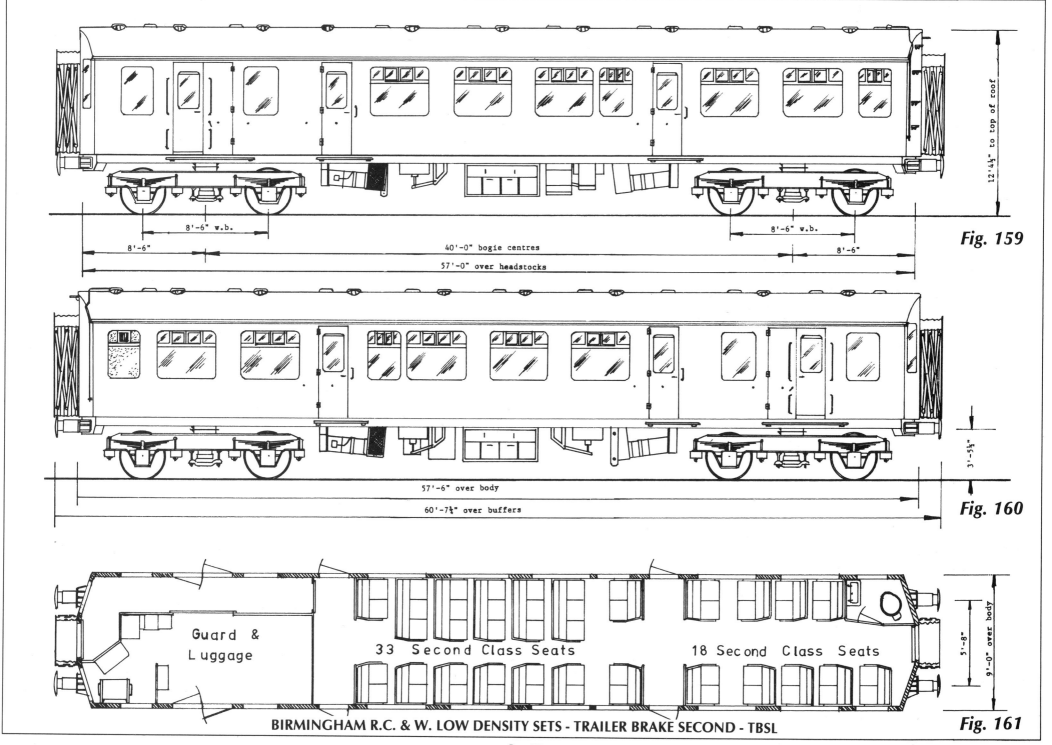

Fig. 159

12'4½" to top of roof

8'-6" w.b.

8'-6" w.b.

8'-6"

40'-0" bogie centres

8'-6"

57'-0" over headstocks

Fig. 160

3'-5¼"

57'-6" over body

60'-7½" over buffers

Fig. 161

5'-8"

9'-0" over body

Guard & Luggage

33 Second Class Seats

18 Second Class Seats

BIRMINGHAM R.C. & W. LOW DENSITY SETS - TRAILER BRAKE SECOND - TBSL

BIRMINGHAM R.C. & W. LOW DENSITY SETS - END ELEVATIONS

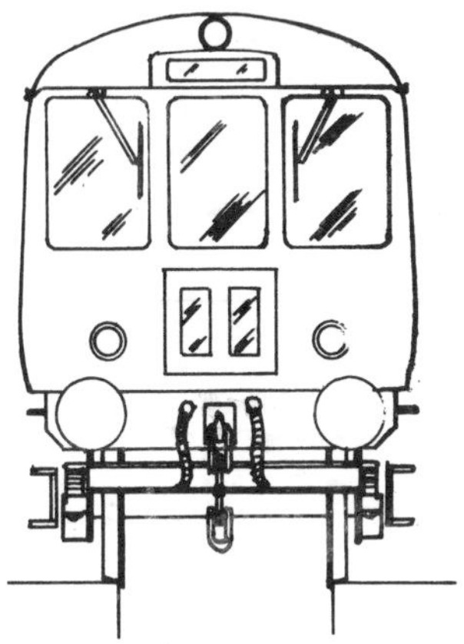

Fig. 162    *Fig. 163* 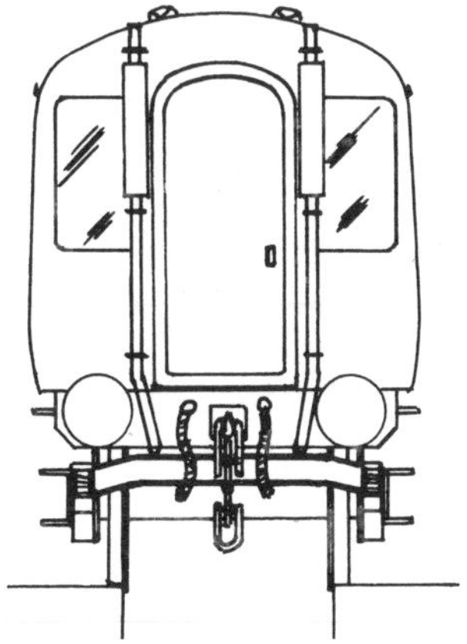   *Fig. 164* 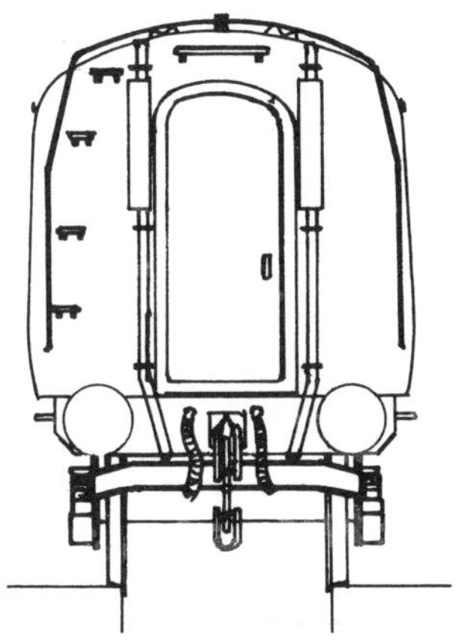   *Fig. 165* 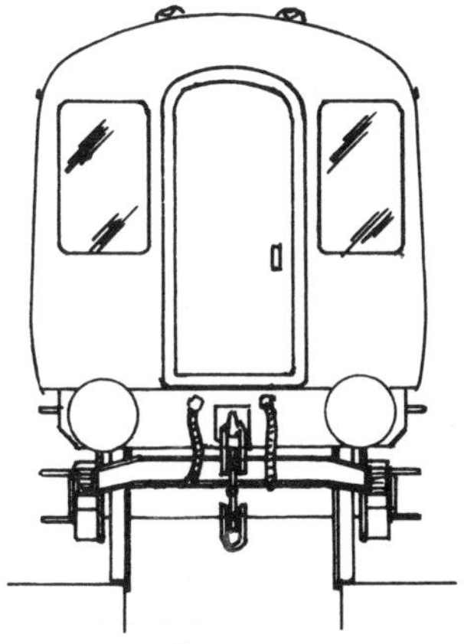   *Fig. 166* 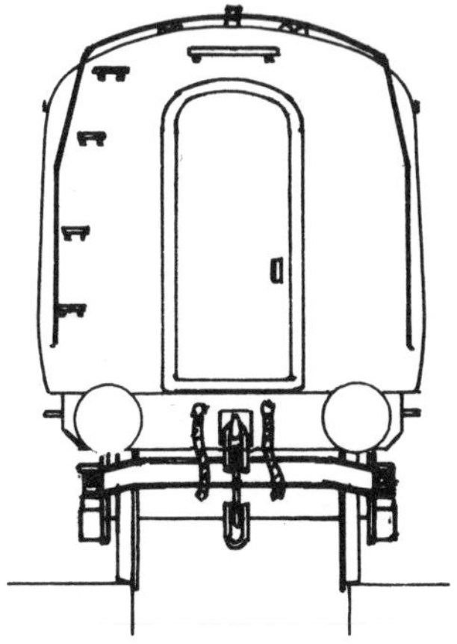   *Fig. 167*

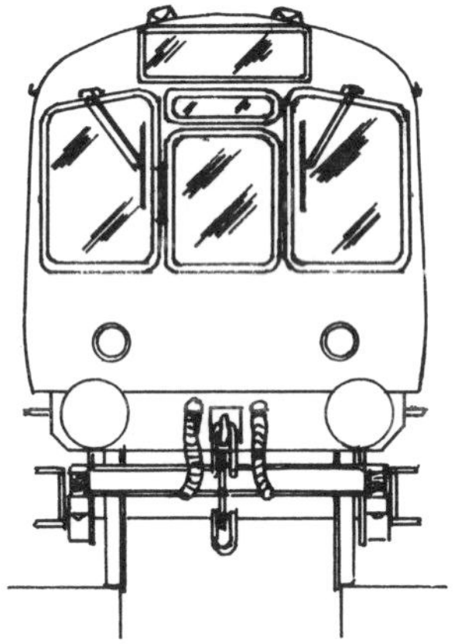

Fig. 168 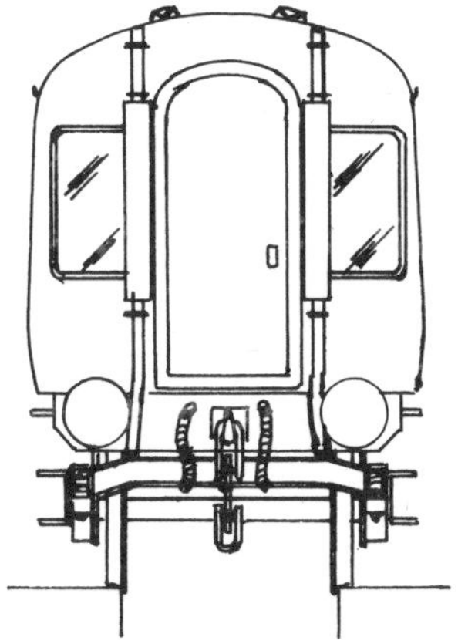   *Fig. 169* 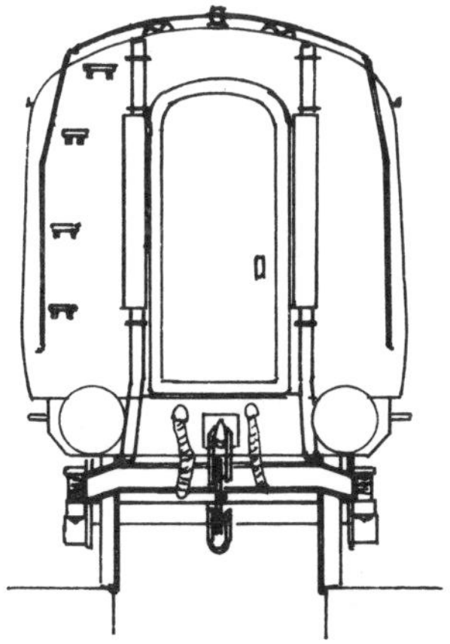   *Fig. 170* 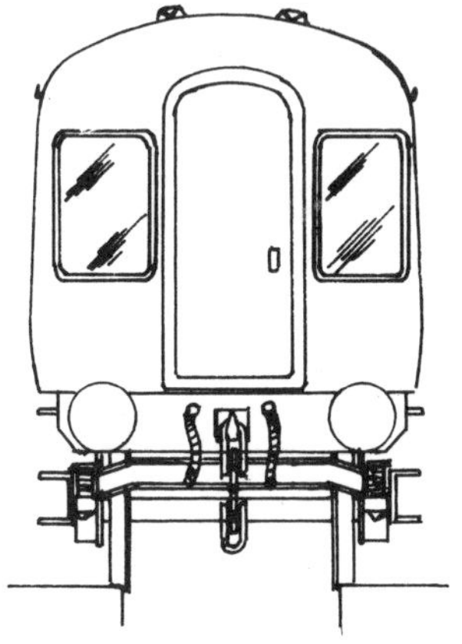   *Fig. 171* 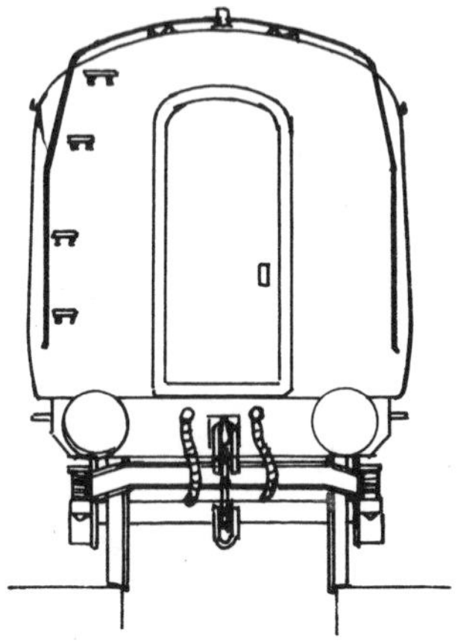   *Fig. 172*

BR C & W Class 110 'Calder Valley' DMBC in Rail Blue with yellow end, leads a rake of Metro Cammell cars bound for York.   *Cheona Collection.*

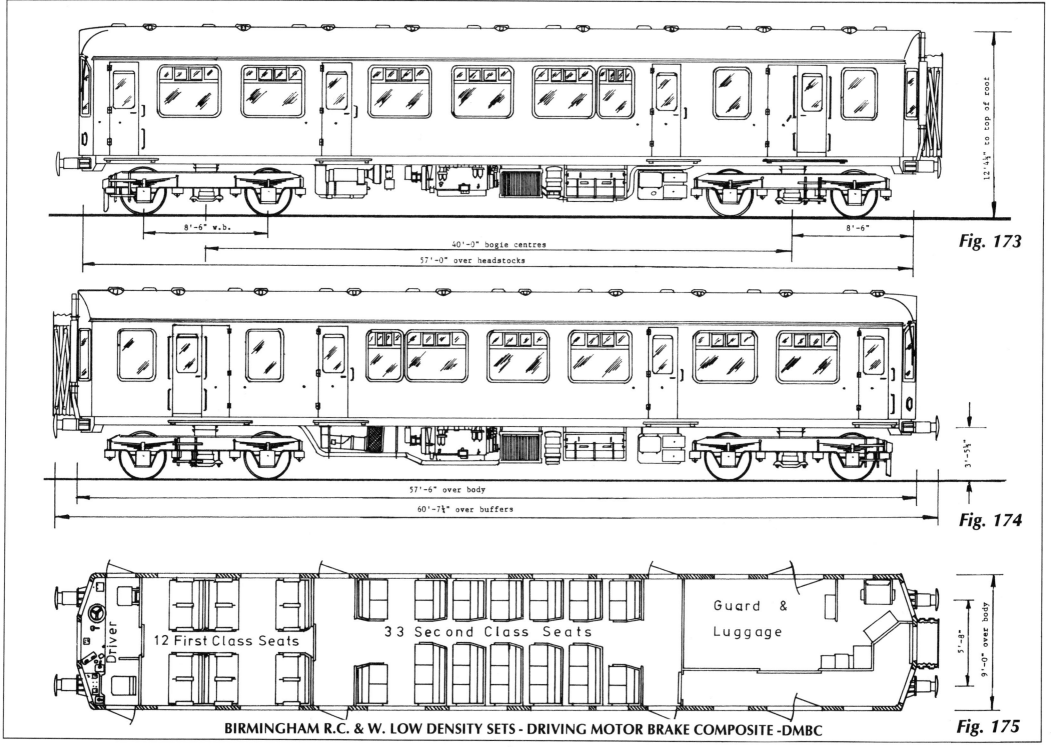

8'-6" w.b.   8'-6"

40'-0" bogie centres

57'-0" over headstocks

12'4¾" to top of roof

Fig. 173

57'-6" over body

60'-7¼" over buffers

3'-5½"

Fig. 174

Driver

12 First Class Seats   33 Second Class Seats   Guard & Luggage

5'-8"

9'-0" over body

Fig. 175

BIRMINGHAM R.C. & W. LOW DENSITY SETS - DRIVING MOTOR BRAKE COMPOSITE -DMBC

Fig. 178

Fig. 177

Fig. 176

BIRMINGHAM R.C. & W. LOW DENSITY SETS - TRAILER SECOND - TSL

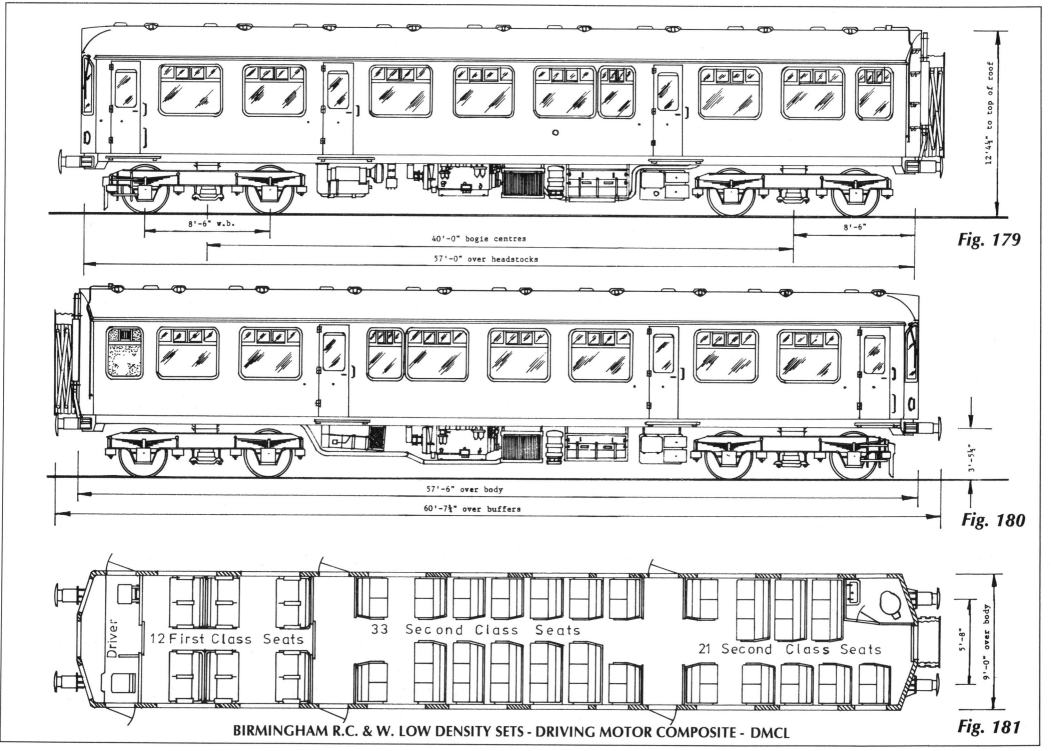

Fig. 179

12'-4½" to top of roof

8'-6" w.b.

40'-0" bogie centres

57'-0" over headstocks

8'-6"

Fig. 180

3'-5¼"

57'-6" over body

60'-7¾" over buffers

Fig. 181

Driver

12 First Class Seats

33 Second Class Seats

21 Second Class Seats

5'-8"

9'-0" over body

BIRMINGHAM R.C. & W. LOW DENSITY SETS - DRIVING MOTOR COMPOSITE - DMCL

CHAPTER TEN

The High-Density or Suburban series of units was far more standardised than the Low-Density type. In very broad terms it was a logical development of the loco-hauled non-gangway coach which it replaced on the suburban services.

At the time of the Modernisation Plan the Birmingham, Bristol, Paddington, Plymouth and South Wales suburban services of the Western Region had changed little since the days of the GWR. Non-corridor trains hauled by ex-GWR Prairie tanks or their BR Standard cousins. The BR Standard non-corridor coach was built on either a 57' 0"or 63' 5"underframe with nine or ten compartments respectively. First and second class compartments had the same dimensions and brake coaches had five or six compartments of standard dimensions. London Midland Region services from their London termini were provided with similar vehicles whereas the Eastern Region commuter services used non-corridor sets which included some lavatory facilities with some coaches having internal side corridors without gangway connections.

The Modernisation Plan resulted in the electrification of the Euston mainline and outer suburban services and some of the Eastern Region London area routes. Otherwise diesel locomotives replaced steam as motive power for the remaining services still utilising the same coaching stock. To bring these services up to date the High-Density DMU was produced.

Designed at Derby - where the majority were also built-these units met the demands of suburban and commuter traffic. All were built on the long underframe, the layout being based on the former non-corridor coach. Essentially a ten compartment format with a slam door to each but, in order to improve peak hour capacity and passenger flow, a semi-open plan similar to the Eastleigh designed EMU was adopted. Where no internal partition occurred the adjacent quarterlights were combined to form a single window.

Driving cars had the seating bays displaced rearwards by half a bay to accommodate the cab. This followed the standard Derby design as used on their later Low-Density cars. Guard's and luggage space was located at the opposite end of the vehicle. The single cars had a second cab fitted into the luggage area.

These units can be considered in the following three sub-groups:

    a) Western Region 3-car and single units.
    b) Eastern Region 3-car hydraulic units.
    c) London Midland Region 4-car sets.

Because of the high degree of standardisation of these cars and in order to keep the number of individual drawings to a manageable level, most have been produced as 'composites'. In the notes which follow the individual differences are highlighted.

In contrast to the Low-Density sets the High-Density units represent the most standardised of all the DMU types and the differences between the various classes are not obvious without close observation. The changing fashions in front-end treatment were reflected in the High-Density series, the early cars having the four lamp arrangement whilst the later units had the two-digit indicator box with two lamps. Finally the roof mounted four-digit reporting number box appeared sometimes with the two lamps.

Initial deliveries were in plain unlined Multiple Unit Green with the whiskers added later. Subsequent deliveries had the two cream lines and whiskers from new. Yellow warning panels were later introduced and after 1966 they all gradually appeared in Rail Blue with full yellow ends and with yellow cantrail bands over the first class accommodation. These cars carried most of the later livery variations dependant upon their actual location. It should be borne in mind that the regional descriptions above refer to their original allocation. Regional boundary changes meant that the cars moved from one region to another and later migrations and re-marshalling meant that these cars saw widespread use during their long service life. Classes 116,117,118,121,122 cars had low-backed seating whereas high-backed seats were fitted to classes 115 and 127.

a) Western Region 3-car and Single Units

The first design of the High-Density unit was for the Birmingham area of the Western Region and these were built at Derby. They later became TOPS Class 116 and comprised DMBS,TS and DMS although some had a TC in place of the TS. Later Class 116 deliveries standardised on the TC even though in later years they were down graded to TS. The Paddington services received deliveries of these sets shortly afterwards. They later saw service on the Welsh Valleys routes and also in the Glasgow area. Those working in the Birmingham area later received non-asbestos trailers from class 127 and displaced Marylebone class 115 sets in place of their 'asbestos' trailers. A further later modification was the fitting of gangway connections within the sets as was first instigated on the Western Region sets.

The Western Region received further HD sets from the Pressed Steel (TOPS Class 117) and the Birmingham Carriage & Wagon Co. Ltd (Class 118). These were all built to the Derby design with the centre car being a TCL with four first class bays at one end, five second class at the other with two lavatories in the centre. These two classes differed from the Derby 116 class in having the four-digit reporting box in the roof dome. The improvement in passenger accommodation compared with the previous loco-hauled stock was considerable and it was further enhanced by the subsequent fitting of gangways between the cars within the sets. This modification gave access to the lavatory facilities to every passenger and was provided on all High Density sets then allocated to the Western Region, but not on those units transferred to other regions at that time.

The Western Region identified a need for a dual purpose type of car which would be used on lightly used lines, but could also augment the standard three-car sets in peak hours. This resulted in the Single units, the first of which were the Gloucester-built (TOPS Class 122) cars. Derived from the Derby 116 type they had a second cab at the luggage van end with the exhaust pipes rising along the line of the pillars between the three cab windows. These had the same cab-end design as the Class 116 and a series of unpowered driving seconds was also produced to strengthen the singles to form two-car units where traffic demanded.

This format proved successful and a further series was produced by Pressed Steel Co. (TOPS Class 121) at the same time as their three-car sets. The only noticeable difference between these and the Gloucester cars was the fitting of four-digit boxes in the roof domes. This resulted in a very fancy sweep to the tops of the exhaust stacks.

When new classes 117 and 121 cars were fitted with buffers having flats at both top and bottom but these were later replaced by the standard round buffers. A further variation was the oval buffer which appeared later on all High Density types, though not universally.

Later modifications included the fitting of high intensity lamps. Some Class 116 cars had their original roof vents replaced by fewer of the new design, the vacant positions being crudely concealed by patches.

Three of the Gloucester Single cars were later modified by the Scottish Region as Driving Motor Luggage Vans (Class 131) by removing all internal partitions and seats and fitting a second pair of double doors on each side. These doors were fitted in different positions on each car and the drawing is based on observation of the specific car illustrated. All other doors were locked and the handles removed. A similar, though less drastic modification (Class 130) was carried out on some Class 116 power cars which involved locking some of the side doors and removing seats. These ran with modified GUV vans (Nos. 86174 and 86572) as 3- or 4- car express parcels units. Most of them later reverted back to normal passenger cars.

Derby built 3 - car Sets (TOPS Class 116)

There were a total of 42 sets in the first series introduced in 1957, the first 10 having second class trailers and the remainder equipped with composites. All had two Leyland 150 bhp engines in each power car, standard mechanical transmission and four-lamp front ends.

Driving Motor Brake Second - DMBS

Seats:	65 second (gangway or non-gangway)
Nos.	W50050 - 91 (Lot No. 30211)
	Gangways later fitted to 50080 - 91
Weight:	35 tons 10 cwt.
Drawings:	*Fig.182* (LHS) and *fig.183* (RHS - except roof dome)
	Plan *fig.184* (non-gangway same except connection).
	End views *fig. 222, fig. 230 or fig. 231.*

Trailer Second - TS

Seats:	106 second (non-gangway)
	98 second (gangway)
Nos.	W59032 - 41 (Lot No. 30385)
	Gangways later fitted to all.
Weight:	28 tons 10 cwt
Drawings:	*Fig.185* and *fig.186.*
	Plan *fig.190* (non-gangway)
	Fig.189 (gangway)
	End view *fig.228 or fig.229.*

Trailer Composite - TC.

Seats:	28 first, 74 second (non-gangway)
	22 first, 68 second (gangway)
Nos.	W59000 - 31 (Lot No. 30212)
	Gangways later fitted to 59030 & 31.
Weight:	28 tons 10 cwt.
Drawings:	*Fig.185* and *fig.186.* Plan *fig.188* (non-gangway)
	Fig.187 (gangway)
	End views *fig.228 or fig.229.*

Driving Motor Second - DMS

Seats:	95 second (non-gangway)
	89 second (gangway)
Nos.	W50092 - 133 (Lot No. 30213)
	Gangways later fitted to 50122 - 124/6/8 - 33.
Weight:	35 tons 10 cwt.
Drawing:	*Fig.191* and *fig.192.* Plan *fig.195* (non-gangway)
	Fig.193 (gangway)
	End view *fig.222* and *fig.230 or fig.231.*

In the same year a further 53 sets were produced to the same design, but with the two-digit box and two lamp arrangement, and these were followed by 13 additional sets, but with only 11 trailer cars.

Driving Motor Brake Second - DMBS

Seats and Weight - *as above.*

Nos.
W50818 - 70   (Lot No. 30363)
W51128 - 40   (Lot No. 30446)
Gangways later fitted to 50834/6/9/42 - 5/7/8/51 -54 8/63-9/51128/32/34-40.

Drawings: As above except end view *fig.223* and *fig.230* or *fig.231.*

Trailer Composite - TC

Seats and Weight - *as above*

Nos.
W59326 - 76   (Lot No. 30365)
W59438 - 48   (Lot No. 30448)
Gangways later fitted to 59335/40/4/6/7/50/2/3/55 -7 9/62-6/8-75/59444-8.

Drawings.   As above.

Driving Motor Second - DMS

Seats and Weight *as above.*

Nos.
W50871 - 923   (Lot No. 30364)
W51141 - 53   (Lot No. 30447)
Gangways later fitted to 50887/9/92/5 -8/900/1/4/7- 11/16 -22/51141/5/7-53.

Drawings.   As above except end view *fig.223* and *fig.230* or *fig.231.*

The original grouping of this class was as follows:

W50050 - 78	Lot No. 30211	W59000 - 28	Lot No. 30212
W50092 - 120	Lot No. 30213		
W50079 - 88	Lot No. 30211	W59032 - 41	Lot No. 30385
W50121 - 30	Lot No. 30213		
W50089	Lot No. 30211	W50818 - 70	Lot No. 30363
W50131	Lot No. 30213	W50871 - 923	Lot No. 30364
W59029 - 31	Lot No. 30212	W59326 - 76	Lot No. 30365
W50090 - 91	Lot No. 30211	W50132 - 3	Lot No. 30213
W51128 - 40	Lot No. 30446	W51141 - 53	Lot No. 30447
W59438 - 48	Lot No. 30448		

Pressed Steel built 3 - car sets (TOPS Class 117)

In 1959, the Western Region introduced 42 sets (only 39 trailers) with improved facilities, into the London area. They followed the Derby design and incorporated a number of features which Derby had included in the sets they built for the LMR. The main improvement was the inclusion of a lavatory in the centre car which was later made accessible to the whole set when gangways were fitted to all these sets.

These units had the four-digit box in the roof and could be distinguished by the 'flat topped' appearance of these boxes compared with other classes. Not all the driving cars had the two lamps fitted. DMS 51396 was fitted with a complete cab end from a scrap 116 class car at Doncaster Works in the early 1990's following an accident and thereafter looked very much like a 116 car.

Driving Motor Brake Second - DMBS

Seats: 65 second (gangway or non-gangway)
Nos.   W51332 - 73   (Lot No. 30546)
Weight: 36 tons 0 cwt.
Drawings: *Fig.182* (except roof dome) *fig.183.*   Plan *fig.184* (except connection for non-gangway version) End view *fig.225* and *fig.230* or *fig.231.*

Trailer Composite with Lavatory - TCL

Seats: 24 first, 50 second (non-gangway)
22 first, 48 second (gangway)
Nos.   W59484 - 522   (Lot No. 30547)
Weight: 30 tons 0 cwt.
Drawings: *Fig.196* and *fig. 97* - Plan *fig.198* (gangway) or *fig.199.*
End view *fig.228* and *fig.232* or *fig.229* and *fig.233.*

Driving Motor Second - DMS

Seats: 91 second (non-gangway)
89 second (gangway)
Nos.   W51374 - 415   (Lot No. 30548)
Weight: 36 tons 0 cwt.
Drawings: *Fig.191* (except roof dome) *fig.192.*
Plan *fig.194* (non-gangway) *fig.193* gangway.
End view *fig.225* and *fig.230* or *fig.231.*

Birmingham R. C & W Co. Ltd built sets (TOPS Class 118)

The final deliveries of High-Density units to the Western Region were the 15 sets from BRCW in 1960. Virtually identical to the Pressed Steel sets they could be identified by the pronounced 'arch' to the indicator box. Window mounting rubbers were a more subtle difference. These sets spent most of their service life in the Plymouth and Bristol areas. All were later fitted with gangways.

Driving Motor brake Second - DMBS
Seats and Weight as Class 117
Nos.   W51302 - 16   (Lot No. 30543)
Drawing: Fig.182 and fig. 83 (except roof domes plan as Class 117)
          End view *fig.225* and *fig.232* or *fig.233*.

Trailer Composite with Lavatory - TCL
Seats and Weight as Class 117
Nos.   W59469 - 83   (Lot No. 30544)
Drawing: As Class 117

Driving Motor Second - DMS
Seats and Weight as Class 117
Nos.   W51317 - 31   (Lot No. 30545)
Drawing: *Fig. 191* and *fig. 192* (except roof domes). Plan as Class 117.
          End view as DMBS

Gloucester R C & W Co. Ltd built Single units (TOPS Class 122)

When Derby were completing the last of the Class 116, 3-car sets the WR had a requirement for some single units with matching Driving Trailers. It seems likely that at that stage in the DMU programme Derby were unable to supply and so the contract was placed with Gloucester. The power cars were effectively a Class 116 DMBS with a second cab fitted. Two AEC engines were fitted instead of the Leyland in the 116's. Later Leyland units were fitted to some cars during overhaul. To complement the 20 single cars a total of 9 Driving Trailer Seconds with a layout similar to the Class 116 DMS's were provided. All 29 cars had the two-digit indicator and two-lamp style of front end. As we shall see when we deal with the Cross-Country units, Gloucester successfully grafted this same Derby front end on to the basic Swindon design to produce the very attractive Class 119 units.

Driving Motor Brake Second - DMBS
Seats: 65 second
Nos.   W55000 - 19   (Lot No. 30419)
Weight: 35 tons 0 cwt.
Drawings: *Fig.201* and *fig.202* (except roof domes) Plan *fig.203*
          End views *fig.223* and *fig.224*.

Driving Motor Luggage Van (TOPS Class 131 ex-Class122)
Seats: Nil
Nos.   SC55013 - 5   (Lot No. 30419)
Drawings: *Fig.204, fig.205* and *fig.206*. This shows the conversion carried out on SC55013. Others may have had the additional double doors nearer the centre of the car. End views are the same as the original format.

Driving Trailer Second - DTS
Seats: 95 second (later reduced to 91)
Nos.   W56291 - 9   (Lot No.30420)
Drawings: *Fig.207* and *fig.208* (except roof domes) Plan *fig.209* End views as *fig.223* and *fig.228*.

Pressed Steel built Single units (TOPS Class 121)

Following the success of the Gloucester Singles, the Western Region took delivery of 16 DMBS and 10 DTS units from Pressed Steel Co Ltd in 1960. They were contemporary with Class 117 sets and reflect all the characteristics of them. Unlike the 117's however, they were AEC powered. DMBS No.W55033 ran for many years with a roof dome at the brake-end similar to Class 122 or 116, presumably as a result of an accident repair (*see page 13*).

Driving Motor Brake Second - DMBS
Seats: as Class 122
Nos.   W55020 - 35   (Lot No. 30518)
Weight: 37 tons 0 cwt.
Drawings: *Fig.201* (except roof domes) and *fig.202*. Plan *fig.203* End views as *fig.225* and *fig.226*.

Driving Trailer Second - DTS
Seats and Weight as Class 122
Nos: W56280 - 9   (Lot No. 30519)
Drawings: *Fig.207* (except roof domes) and *fig.208*. Plan *fig.209* End views as *fig.225* and *fig.228*.

b) Eastern Region 3-car Hydraulic units (TOPS Class 125)

Whilst the Western Region were introducing their units with the standard mechanical transmission into service, the Eastern Region were looking for an arrangement to give them sufficient power to climb the Liverpool Street - Bethnal Green bank with their heavily laden commuter trains on the GE Lea Valley services from Liverpool Street to Cheshunt via Stratford .

The resultant units became TOPS Class 125 and were powered by two Rolls Royce 238 bhp engines on each power car driving through Twin-Disc torque converters. Like the WR units they were 3-car formations with the two power cars having the same layouts as on Class 116. However, the centre cars were truly high-density having seating for 110 second class passengers making them the highest carrying capacity DMU cars of all.

They were, however, the least successful of all the high density sets and the first migration of Class 116 was a number drafted into Finsbury Park to replace failed 125 units. With the electrification of the Kings Cross suburban lines, the Class 125 sets were withdrawn and became the first series of the high-density unit to become extinct.

When new these cars were in unlined green livery with the yellow whiskers. They subsequently carried all the later livery variations being withdrawn whilst running in the Rail Blue livery with the yellow ends. The front end style incorporated the two-digit box and the two lamps.

Driving Motor Brake Second - DMBS
Seats:	65 seconds
Nos.	E51154 - 73 (Lot No. 30464)
Weight:	39 tons 10 cwt.
Drawings:	*Fig.182* and *fig.183* (except that these were never gangway and the roof domes were as shown in *fig.182*)
	End views as *fig.223* and *fig.230*.

Trailer Second - TS
Seats:	110 seconds
Nos:	E59449 - 68 (Lot No. 30463)
Drawings:	*Fig.210* and *fig.211*. Plan *fig.212*
	End views *fig. 228*.

Driving Motor Second - DMS
Seats:	95 second
Nos.	E50988 - 51007 (Lot No. 30462)
Drawings:	*Fig.191* and *fig.192* (see notes for DMBS above) Plan view as *fig.195* End views as *fig.223* and *fig. 230*.
	*Note:*The class used the coupling code, 'Orange Star'.

c) London Midland Region 4-car units

There were two distinct types of 4-car units built for the London Midland Region - the St Pancras and the Marylebone sets.

The St Pancras sets (TOPS Class 127)

Introduced on the Bedford to St Pancras services in 1959, these Derby built four-car sets were developed from the earlier ER Class 125. They were equipped with two Rolls Royce engines, 238bhp per power car and hydraulic torque converter transmission and were extremely powerful units. These were the first high-density four-car sets and their formation included two identical DMBS cars flanking two trailer seconds (one with lavatory). The seating plan of the power cars was similar to that used on the 3-car sets except that each had a guard/luggage area which was smaller giving room for an additional seating bay. No first class accommodation was provided.

They were delivered in the lined dark green livery with the whiskers and had the four-digit box on the roof. The usual yellow panel appeared later and the whole class finished its service life in Rail Blue with the full yellow ends. Electrification of the 'Bedford - St Pancras' services rendered them surplus to requirements and also by then the power cars were worn out so they were withdrawn. Many of the TS & TSL cars were refurbished and fitted with gangways and transferred to the Birmingham area to replace 'asbestos' trailers of both types in the Class 116 units.

Driving Motor Brake Second - DMBS *(two cars per set)*
Seats:	76 seconds
Nos:	M51591 - 650 (Lot No. 30521)
Weight:	40 tons 0cwt.
Drawings:	*Fig. 213* and *fig.214*. Plan *fig.215*.
	End views as *fig.227* and *fig.230*.

Trailer Second - TS
Seats:	106 seconds
Nos:	M59619 - 648 (Lot No. 30523)
Weight:	29 tons 0 cwt.
Drawings:	*Fig.216* and *fig. 217*. Plan *fig.218*.
	End view as *fig.228*.

Trailer Second with Lavatory - TSL
Seats:	90 seconds
Nos:	M59589 - 618 (Lot No. 30522)
Weight:	30 tons 0 cwt.
Drawings :	*Fig.219* and *fig.220*. Plan *fig.221*.
	End views as *fig.228* and *fig.232*.

The Marylebone Sets (TOPS Class 115)

The last series of High Density cars to be built were the 41 four-car sets to Class 115 design for the Marylebone group of services, which were delivered in 1960. Although primarily intended for the LMR commuter services from Marylebone to Aylesbury, High Wycombe and Banbury, six of these sets were allocated to the Liverpool area to work the Liverpool to Manchester (CLC) route.

The general layout of these vehicles was very similar to the Class 127 just described, but the Marylebone sets provided a far superior level of comfort. The lavatory trailer car had first class seating on the 2 + 1 format (with reading lights) which occupied the larger five-bay end which was in contrast to those on the Western region three-car sets. This was because the interiors had been subject to redesign by the BR Design Panel. The interiors of the six Liverpool area sets were similar to the 127 units as built.

Mechanically these cars were unique amongst the high density series in having two Albion 230bhp engines (down-rated to 200bhp in the late 1970's/early 80's to prolong their engine life) in each power car with standard mechanical transmission giving them a good turn of speed. Originally delivered in lined dark green they ultimately wore the Rail Blue livery; refurbished overall white with the broad blue band; the blue and grey livery and then the two shades of Network South East livery until they perished with the arrival of the Chiltern Turbos.

In late 1986/ early 1987 the Liverpool area sets and some of the Marylebone power cars and trailers were transferred to Tyseley Depot to be used on the cross Birmingham services. They were fitted with gangways and used to make up 4-car sets, ie. Class 115 DMBS, TS,TSL, Class 116 DMS or DMBS. The TCL's that had been transferred became TSL's.

As in the case of the Class 127 units, some of the trailer lavatory cars (particularly those from the Merseyside sets) were sent to the Birmingham area to complete the up-grading of the Class 116 sets which lingered in that area.

Driving Motor Brake Second - DMBS (two cars per set)

Seats:	78 second		
Nos:	M51651 - 80	(Lot No. 30530)	*Marylebone*
	M51849 - 60	(Lot No. 30595)	*Liverpool*
	M51861 - 900	(Lot No. 30598)	*Marylebone*
Weight:	38 tons 0 cwt.		
Drawings:	*Fig.213 and fig. 214. Plan fig.215*		
	End views as fig.227 and fig.230.		

Trailer Second - TS

Seats:	106 second		
Nos:	M59649 - 63	(Lot No. 30531)	*Marylebone*
	M59713 - 18	(Lot No. 30596)	*Liverpool*
	M59725 - 44	(Lot No. 30599)	*Marylebone*
Weight:	29 tons 0 cwt.		
Drawings:	*Fig.216 and fig.217. Plan fig.218*		
	End view as fig.228.		

Trailer Composite with Lavatory - TCL

Seats:	30 first, 40 second		
Nos:	M59664 - 78	(Lot No. 30532)	*Marylebone*
	M59719 - 24	(Lot No. 30597)	*Liverpool*
	M59745 - 64	(Lot No. 30600)	*Marylebone*
Weight:	30 tons 0 cwt.		
Drawings:	*Fig. 196 and fig.197 (except gangway connections)*		
	Plan fig. 200. End views as fig.228 and fig.232.		

Note : a) Nos. 51849 - 60, 59713 - 8, 59719 - 24 were the first to be built.
b) Approximately half the fleet was refurbished.
c) Fourteen DMBS's at Marylebone were gangwayed in 1986/87 to run with twelve class 108 DTCL's (one 108 car was replaced by a 101 DTCL following collision damage.)

All the Marylebone cars carried the blue livery, but only a small number of the early refurbished cars wore the 'refurbished white with broad blue band' livery. Later refurbished cars were turned out in the blue and grey, but this livery became the standard for both un- and refurbished cars. All the cars remaining at Marylebone, carried the Network South East livery - 8 were in light blue and the remainder in dark blue. At least 6 of the light blue cars remained in this livery until withdrawn.

BR Derby Class 115 Marylebone unit with car No. 51672 in blue /grey and the remaining cars in Rail Blue seen here at Aylesbury station on 9th September, 1979.

G.Gamble.

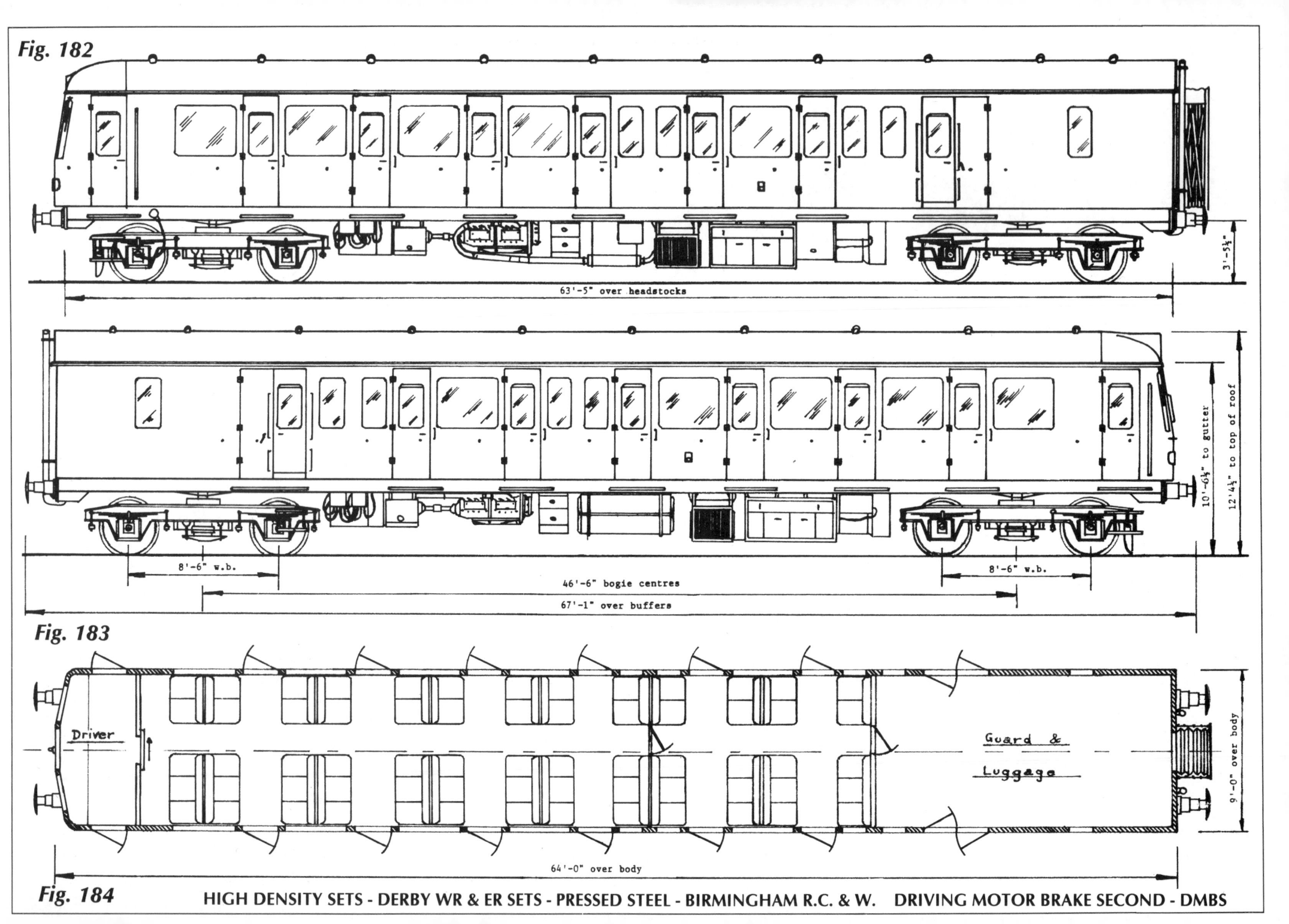

Fig. 182

63'-5" over headstocks

3'-5¼"

Fig. 183

10'-6¼" to gutter

12'-4½" to top of roof

8'-6" w.b.

8'-6" w.b.

46'-6" bogie centres

67'-1" over buffers

Fig. 184

Driver

Guard & Luggage

9'-0" over body

64'-0" over body

HIGH DENSITY SETS - DERBY WR & ER SETS - PRESSED STEEL - BIRMINGHAM R.C. & W.   DRIVING MOTOR BRAKE SECOND - DMBS

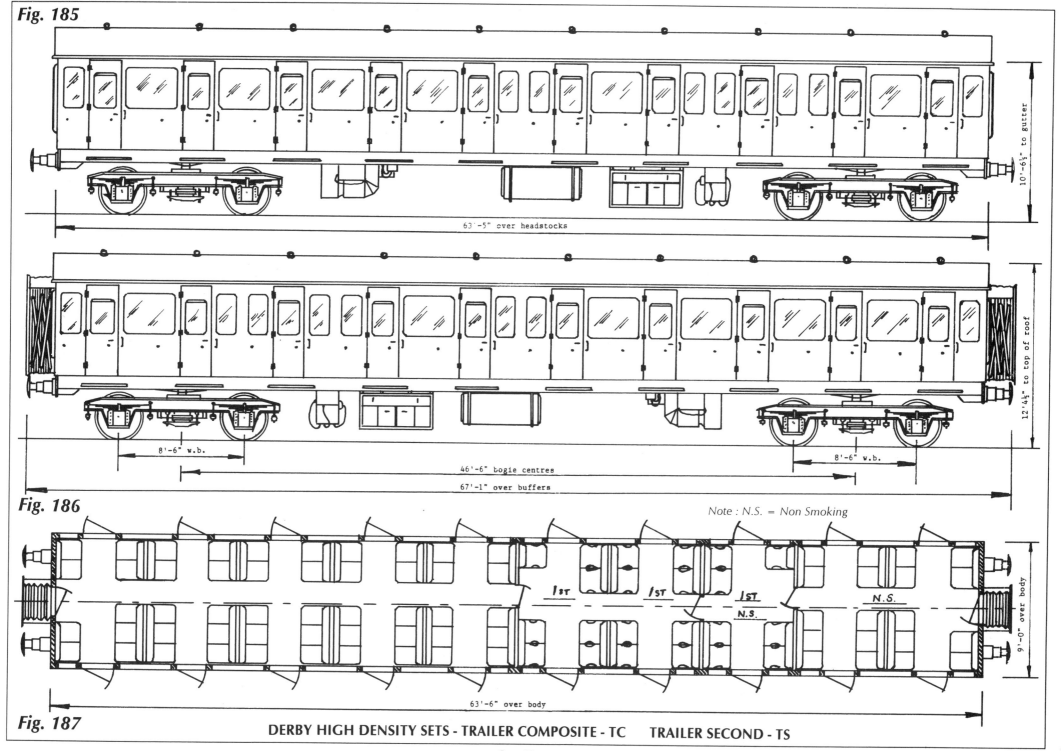

Fig. 185

10'-6½" to gutter

63'-5" over headstocks

Fig. 186

12'-4½" to top of roof

8'-6" w.b.

8'-6" w.b.

46'-6" bogie centres

67'-1" over buffers

Note : N.S. = Non Smoking

Fig. 187

1ST   1ST   1ST   N.S.

N.S.

9'-0" over body

63'-6" over body

DERBY HIGH DENSITY SETS - TRAILER COMPOSITE - TC   TRAILER SECOND - TS

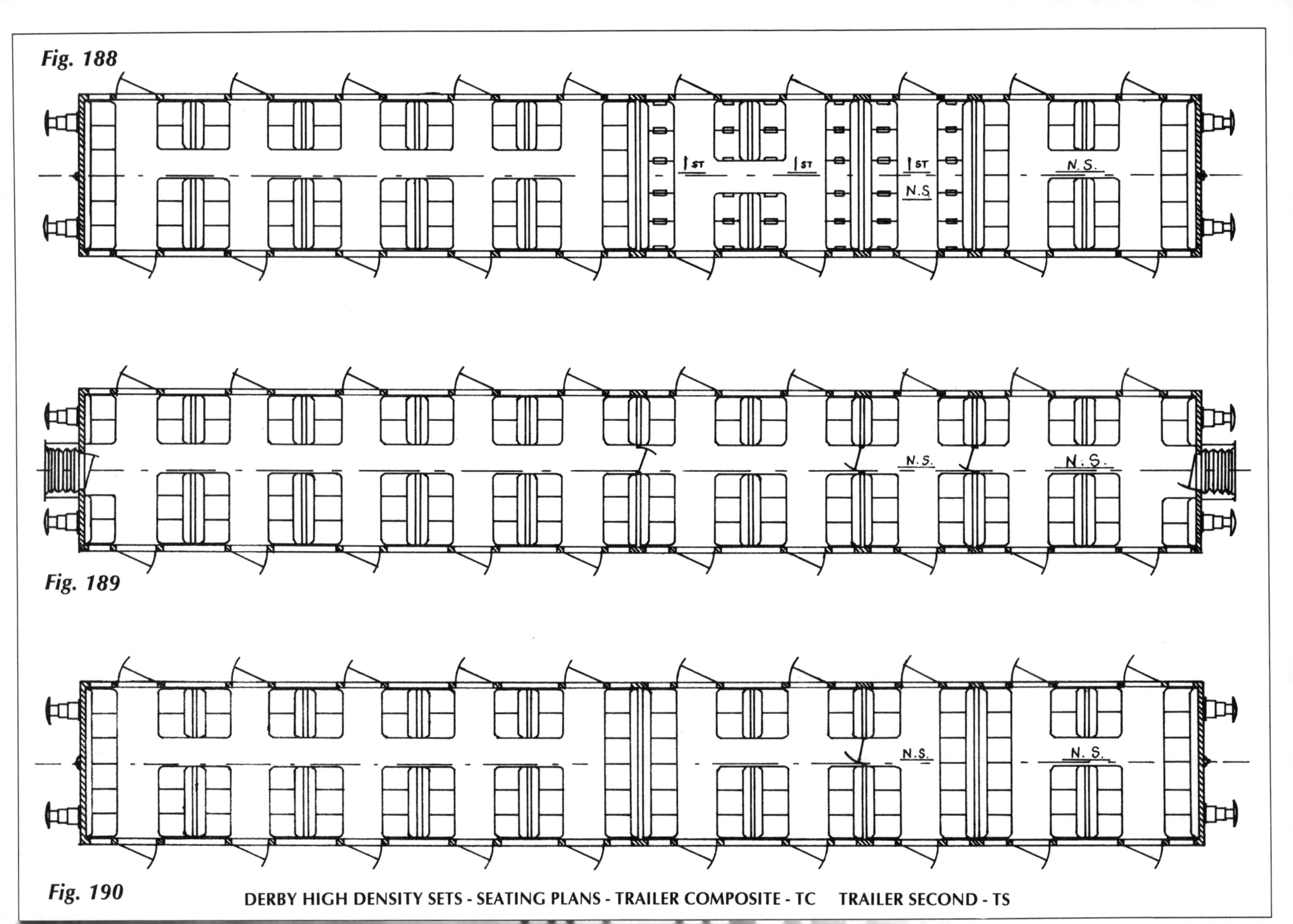

Fig. 188

Fig. 189

Fig. 190

DERBY HIGH DENSITY SETS - SEATING PLANS - TRAILER COMPOSITE - TC   TRAILER SECOND - TS

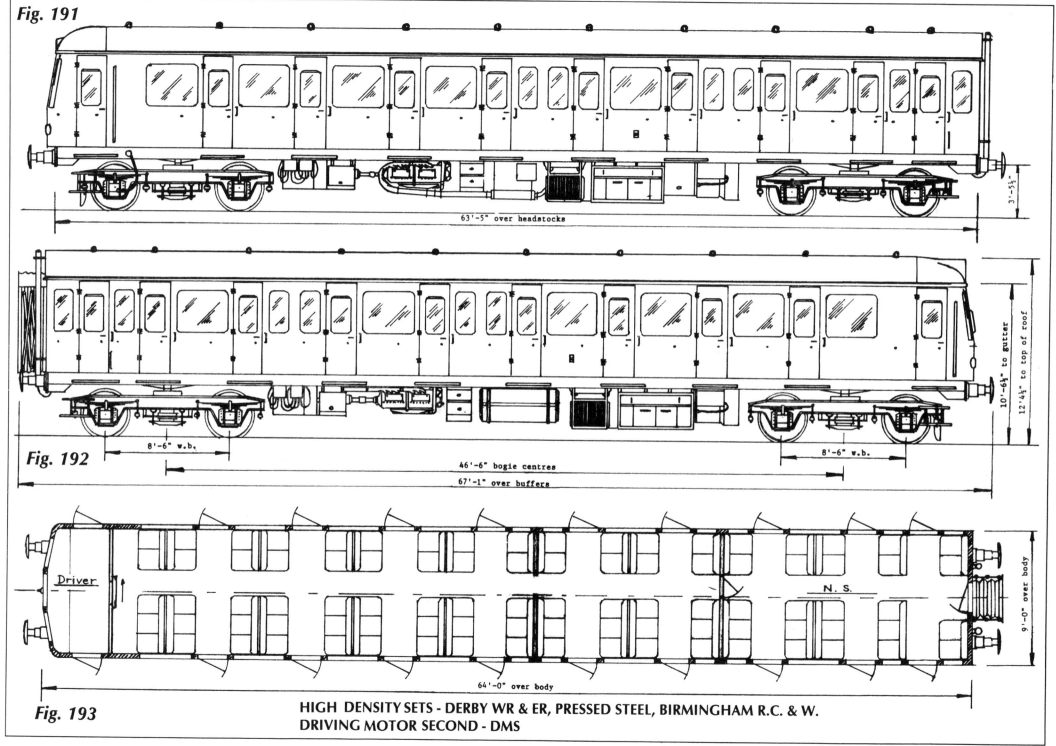

Fig. 191

63'-5" over headstocks

3'-5½"

Fig. 192

8'-6" w.b.

8'-6" w.b.

46'-6" bogie centres

67'-1" over buffers

10'-6¼" to gutter

12'-4¼" to top of roof

Driver

N. S.

9'-0" over body

64'-0" over body

Fig. 193

**HIGH DENSITY SETS - DERBY WR & ER, PRESSED STEEL, BIRMINGHAM R.C. & W.
DRIVING MOTOR SECOND - DMS**

Fig. 194

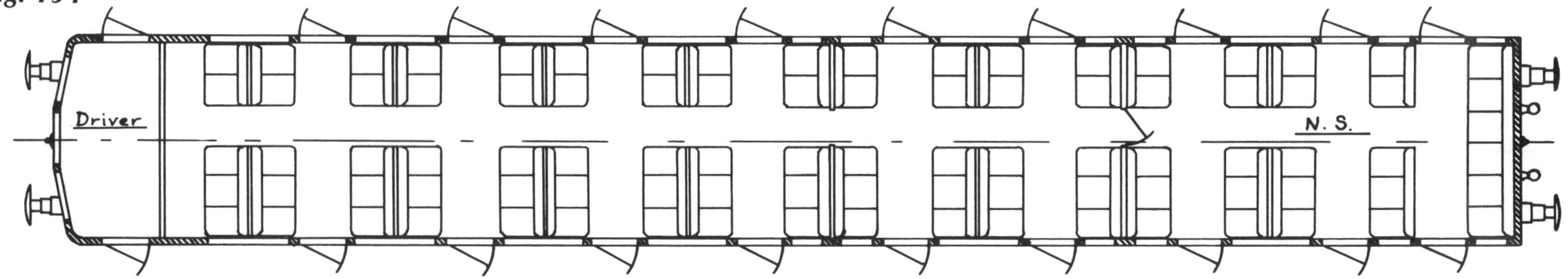

Driver   N. S.

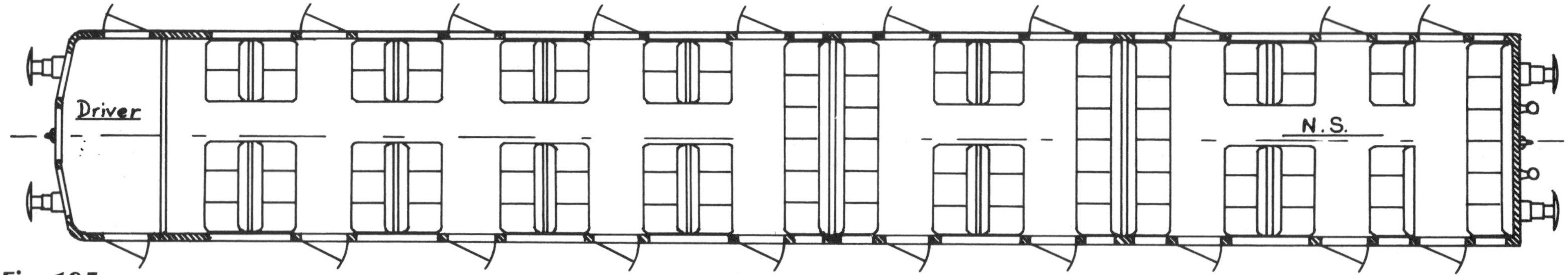

Fig. 195

Driver   N. S.

HIGH DENSITY SETS - SEATING PLANS - DERBY ER & WR , PRESSED STEEL AND BIRMINGHAM R.C. & W. - DRIVING MOTOR SECOND - DMS

A Pressed Steel Class 117 unit L433 in refurbished livery at Oxford with the 16.00 service to Reading on 3rd September, 1978. (The last passenger crosses the track!)

G.Gamble.

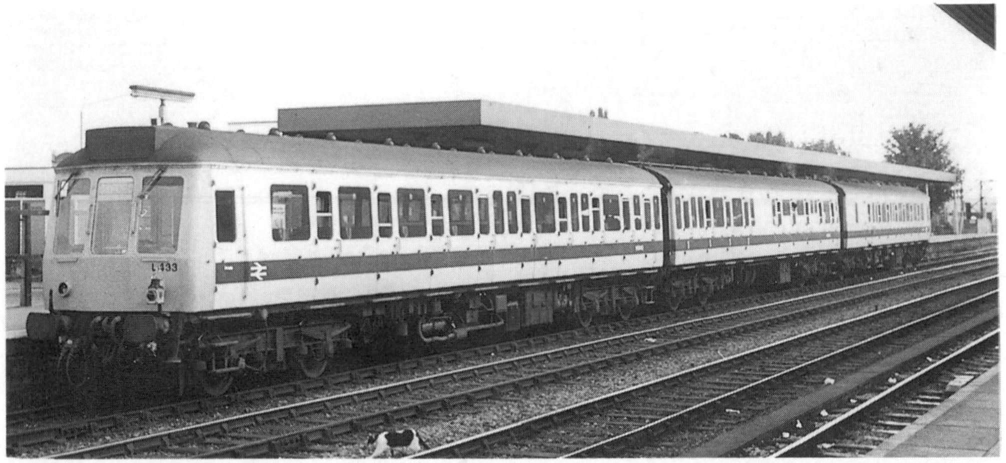

Gloucester RC & W Co. Class 122 single car No. W55019 at Oxford, in green and cream livery with whiskers.

J.Turner.

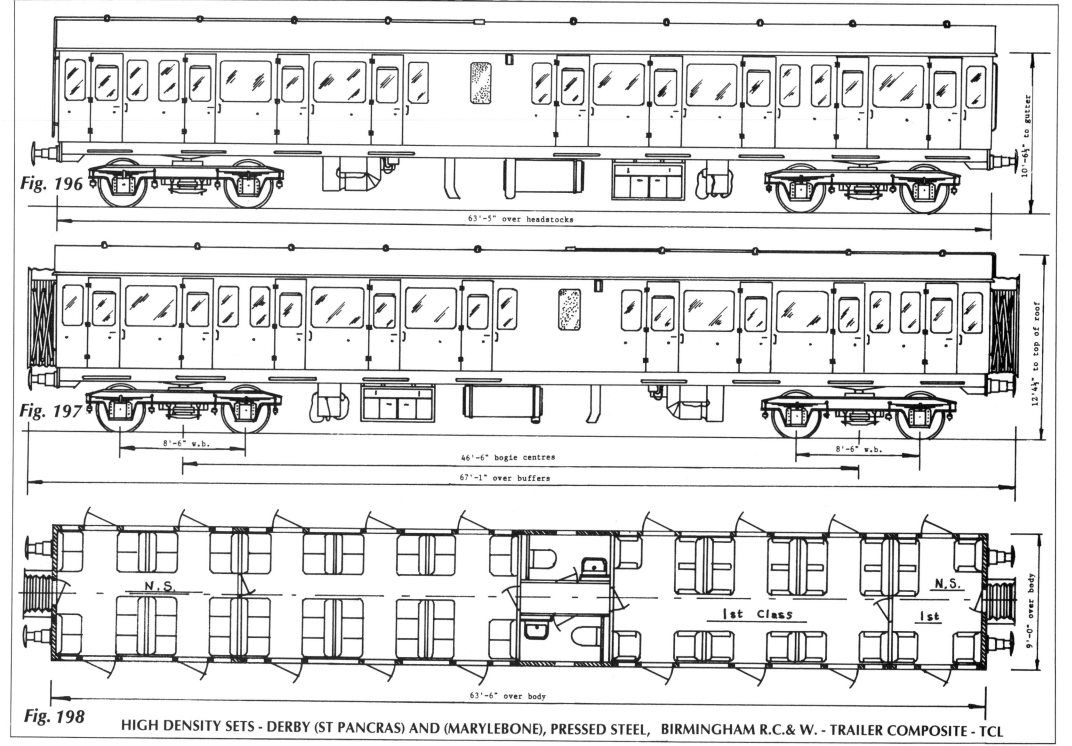

Fig. 196

63'-5" over headstocks

10'-6½" to gutter

Fig. 197

8'-6" w.b.

46'-6" bogie centres

8'-6" w.b.

67'-1" over buffers

12'4½" to top of roof

Fig. 198

N.S.

1st Class

1st

N.S.

9'-0" over body

63'-6" over body

HIGH DENSITY SETS - DERBY (ST PANCRAS) AND (MARYLEBONE), PRESSED STEEL, BIRMINGHAM R.C.& W. - TRAILER COMPOSITE - TCL

Fig. 199

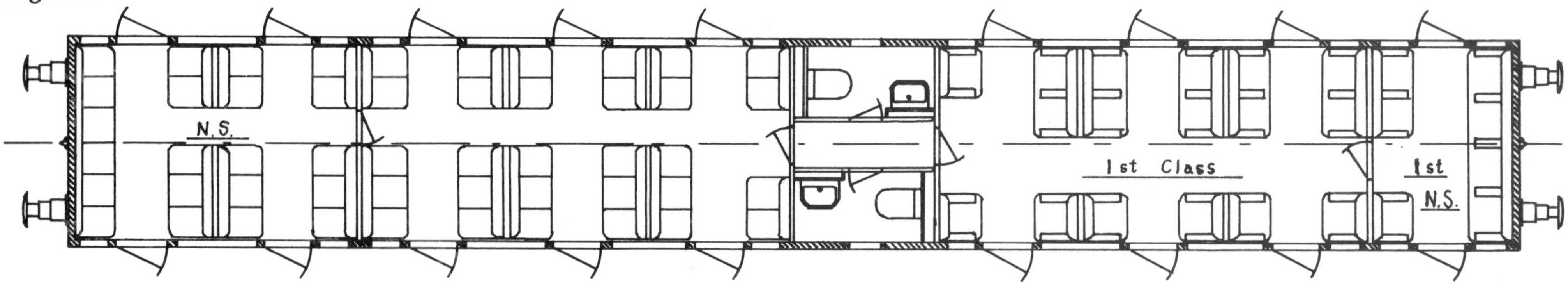

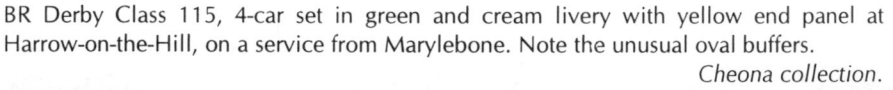

Fig. 200

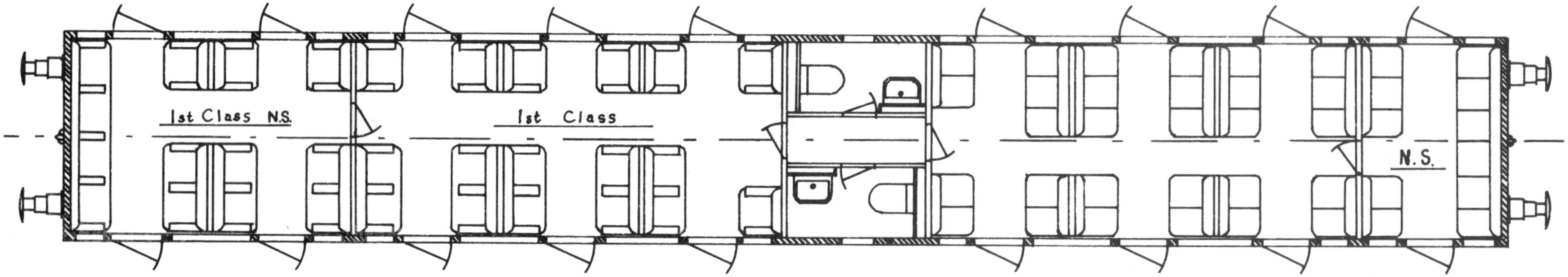

HIGH DENSITY SETS - DERBY (ST PANCRAS) AND (MARYLEBONE), PRESSED STEEL, BIRMINGHAM R.C. & W. - TRAILER COMPOSITE SEATING PLANS

BR Derby Class 115, 4-car set in green and cream livery with yellow end panel at Harrow-on-the-Hill, on a service from Marylebone. Note the unusual oval buffers.

Cheona collection.

BR Derby Class 116, 3-car set at the head of a 6-car train (in light blue livery) at Exeter St Davids, bound for Newton Abbot.

Cheona collection.

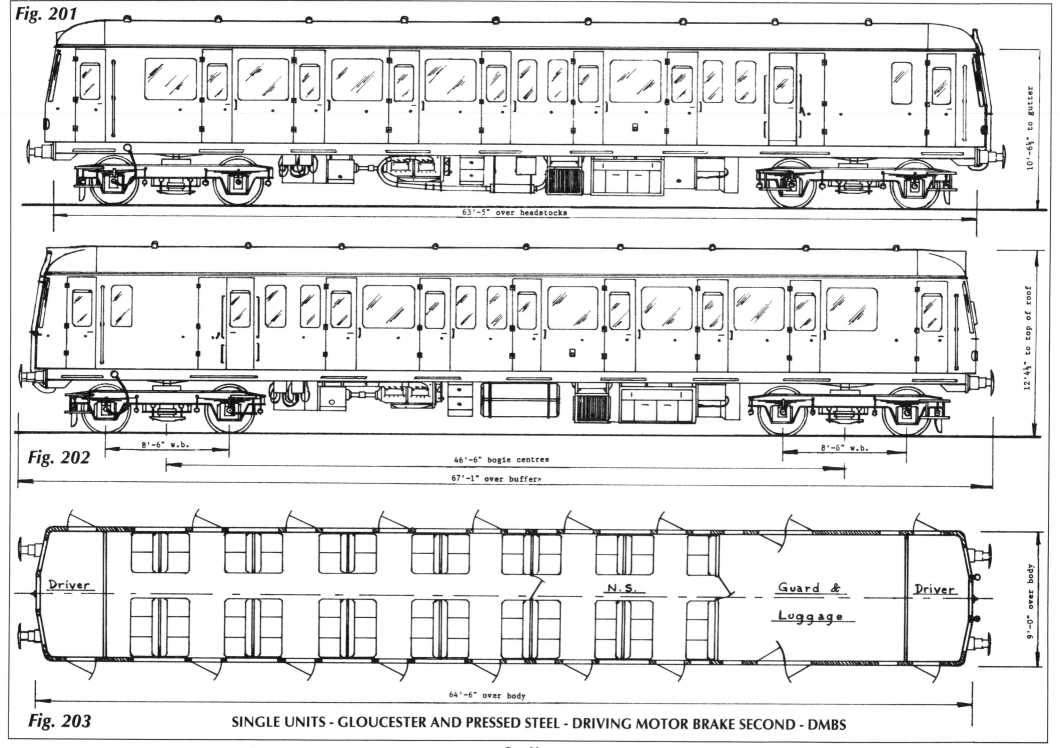

Fig. 201

10'-6¾" to gutter

63'-5" over headstocks

Fig. 202

12'-4¼" to top of roof

8'-6" w.b.

46'-6" bogie centres

8'-6" w.b.

67'-1" over buffers

Driver

N.S.

Guard & Luggage

Driver

9'-0" over body

64'-6" over body

Fig. 203

SINGLE UNITS - GLOUCESTER AND PRESSED STEEL - DRIVING MOTOR BRAKE SECOND - DMBS

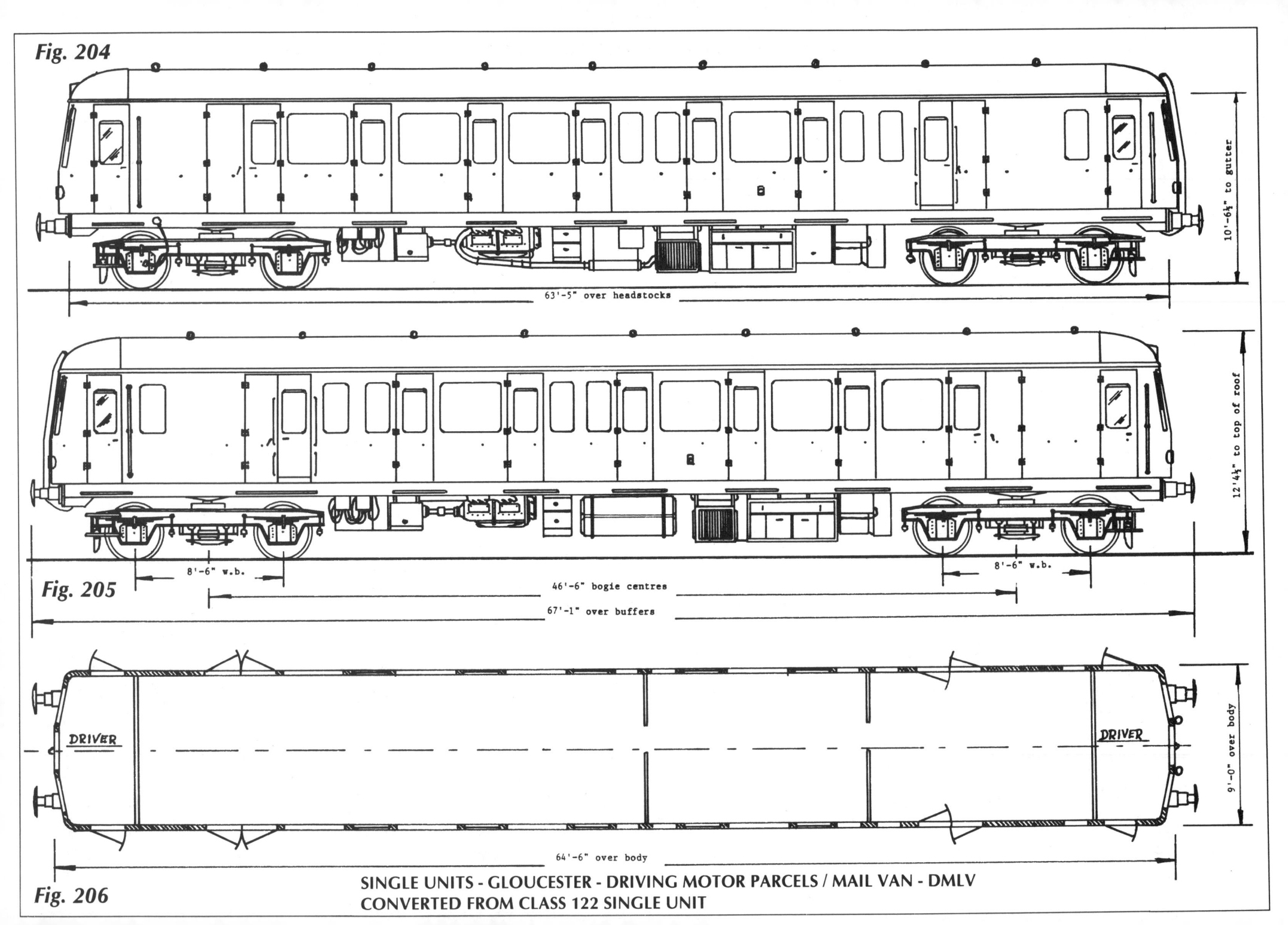

Fig. 204

10'-6½" to gutter

63'-5" over headstocks

Fig. 205

12'-4½" to top of roof

8'-6" w.b.

8'-6" w.b.

46'-6" bogie centres

67'-1" over buffers

DRIVER

DRIVER

9'-0" over body

64'-6" over body

Fig. 206

SINGLE UNITS - GLOUCESTER - DRIVING MOTOR PARCELS / MAIL VAN - DMLV
CONVERTED FROM CLASS 122 SINGLE UNIT

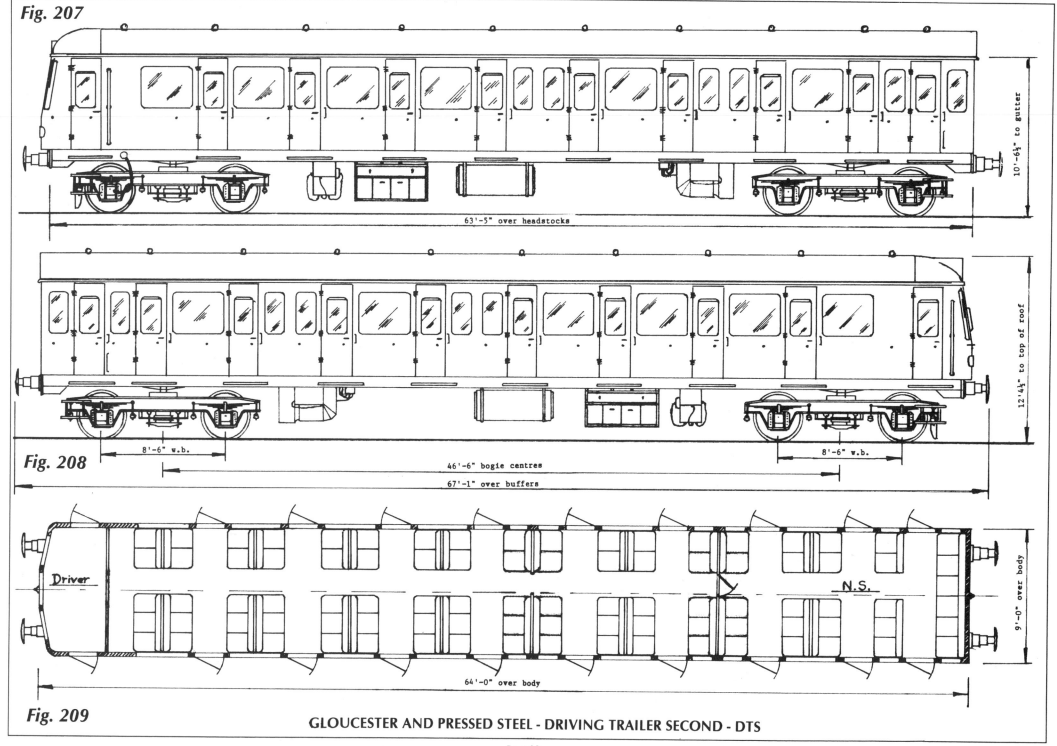

Fig. 207

10'-6¼" to gutter

63'-5" over headstocks

Fig. 208

12'-4¼" to top of roof

8'-6" w.b.

8'-6" w.b.

46'-6" bogie centres

67'-1" over buffers

Driver

N.S.

9'-0" over body

64'-0" over body

Fig. 209

GLOUCESTER AND PRESSED STEEL - DRIVING TRAILER SECOND - DTS

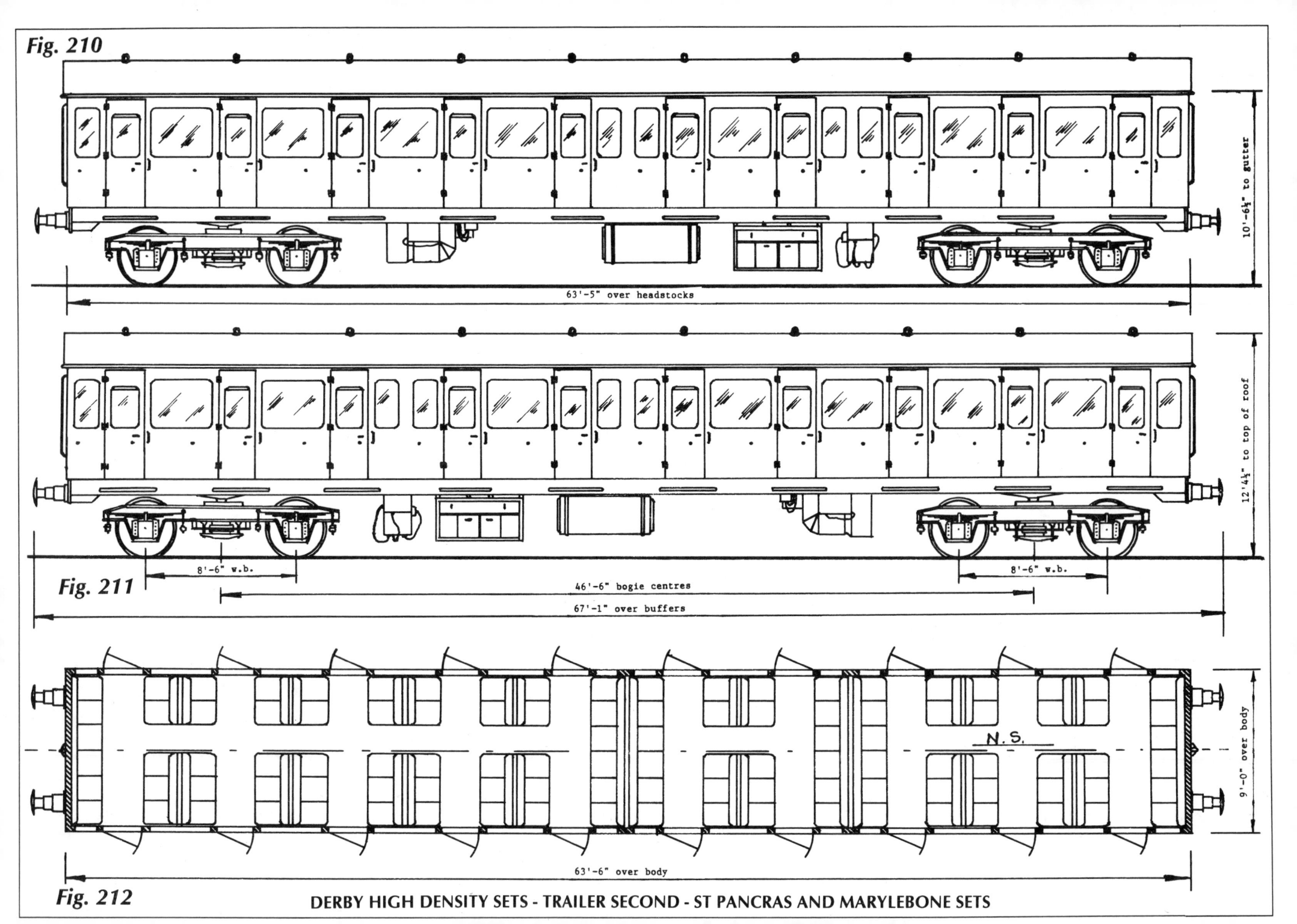

Fig. 210

10'-6½" to gutter

63'-5" over headstocks

Fig. 211

12'-4½" to top of roof

8'-6" w.b.

46'-6" bogie centres

8'-6" w.b.

67'-1" over buffers

N. S.

9'-0" over body

63'-6" over body

Fig. 212

DERBY HIGH DENSITY SETS - TRAILER SECOND - ST PANCRAS AND MARYLEBONE SETS

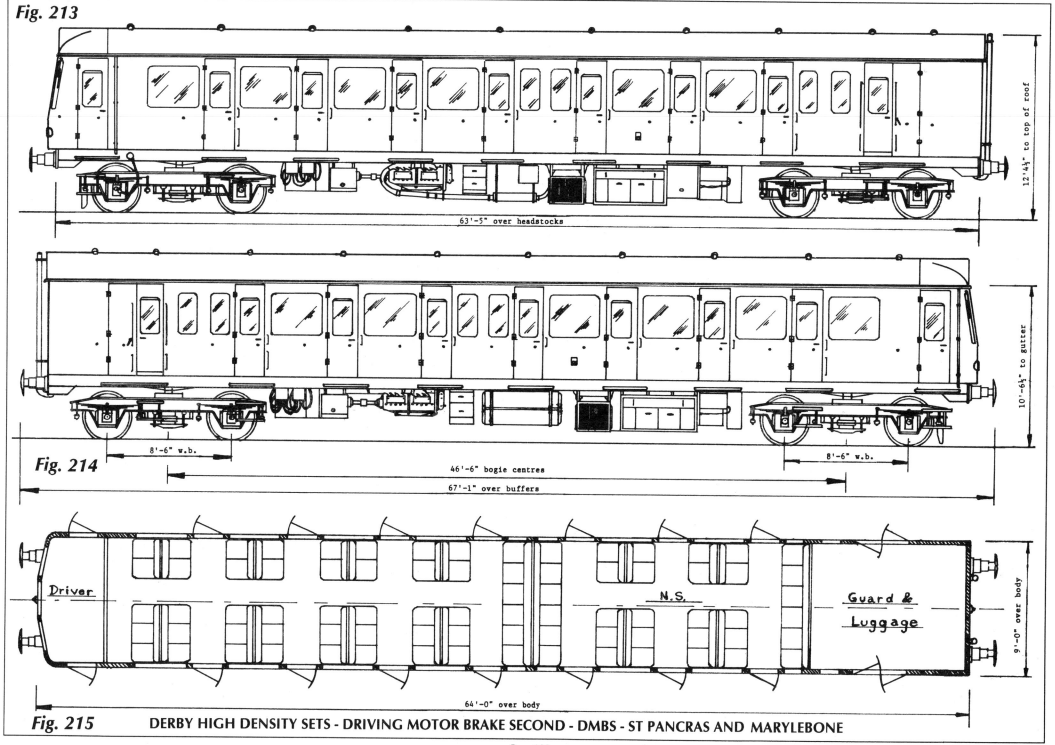

Fig. 213

12'-4½" to top of roof

63'-5" over headstocks

Fig. 214

10'-6½" to gutter

8'-6" w.b.

8'-6" w.b.

46'-6" bogie centres

67'-1" over buffers

Driver

N.S.

Guard & Luggage

9'-0" over body

64'-0" over body

Fig. 215   **DERBY HIGH DENSITY SETS - DRIVING MOTOR BRAKE SECOND - DMBS - ST PANCRAS AND MARYLEBONE**

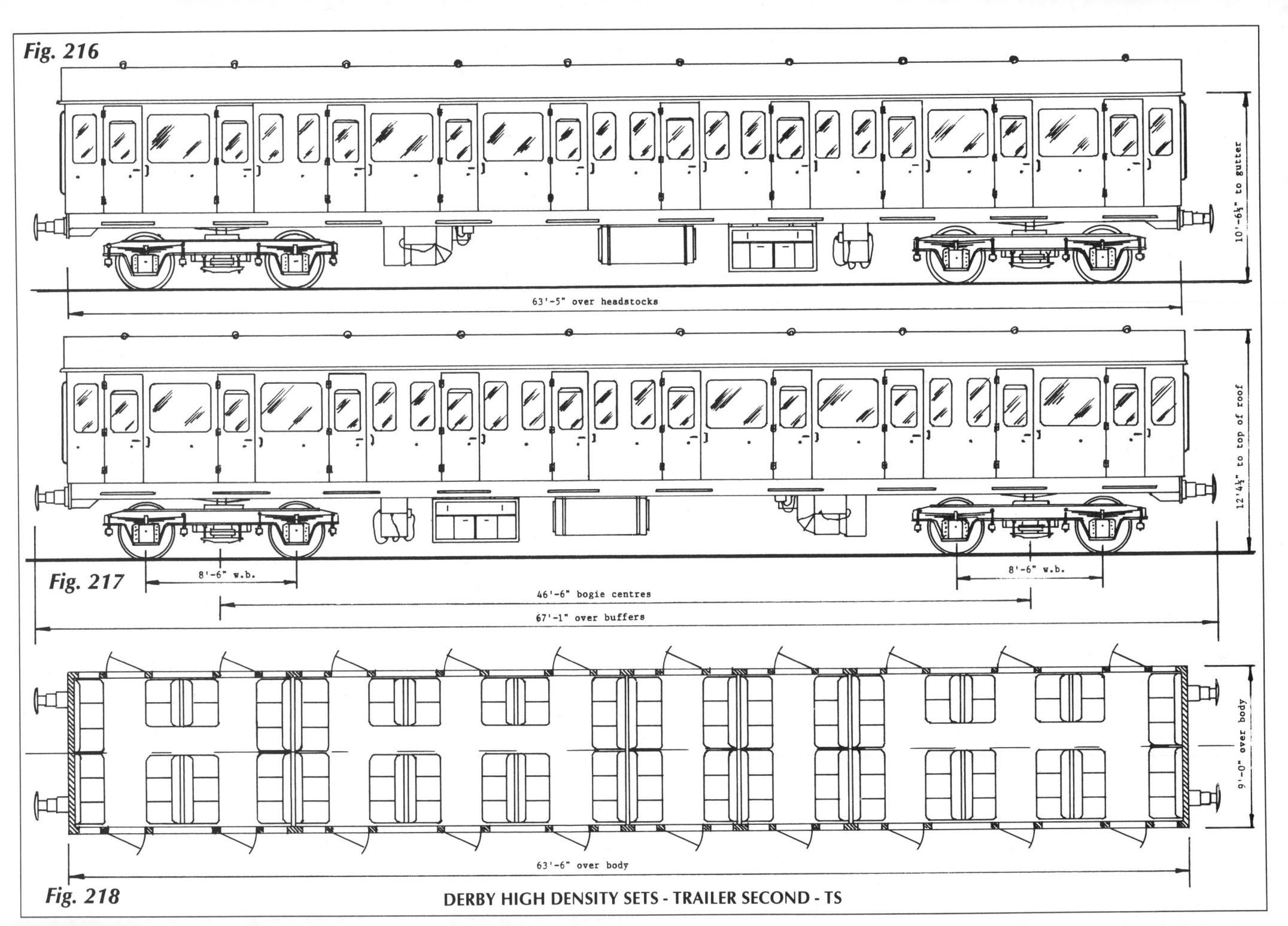

Fig. 216

10'-6¼" to gutter

63'-5" over headstocks

Fig. 217

12'4½" to top of roof

8'-6" w.b.

8'-6" w.b.

46'-6" bogie centres

67'-1" over buffers

Fig. 218

9'-0" over body

63'-6" over body

DERBY HIGH DENSITY SETS - TRAILER SECOND - TS

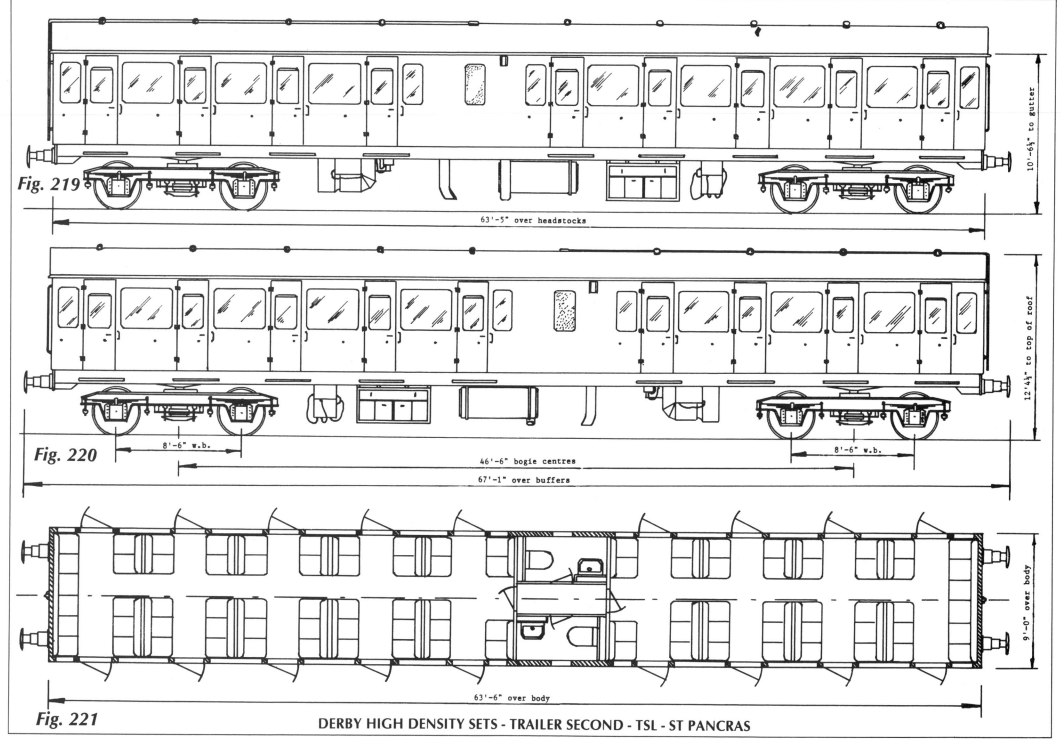

Fig. 219

10'-6½" to gutter

63'-5" over headstocks

Fig. 220

12'-4½" to top of roof

8'-6" w.b.

46'-6" bogie centres

8'-6" w.b.

67'-1" over buffers

Fig. 221

9'-0" over body

63'-6" over body

DERBY HIGH DENSITY SETS - TRAILER SECOND - TSL - ST PANCRAS

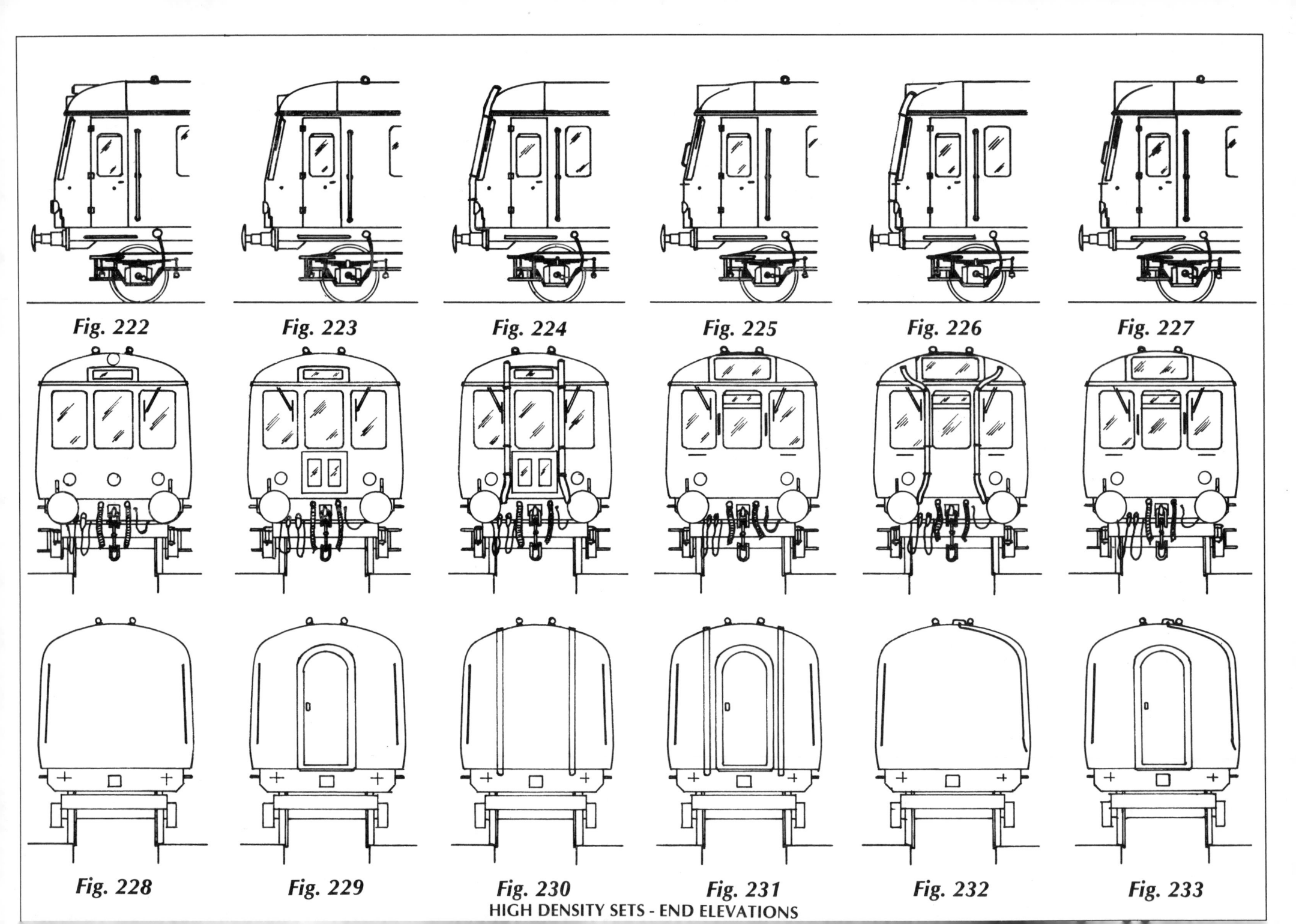

Fig. 222 Fig. 223 Fig. 224 Fig. 225 Fig. 226 Fig. 227

Fig. 228 Fig. 229 Fig. 230 Fig. 231 Fig. 232 Fig. 233

HIGH DENSITY SETS - END ELEVATIONS

CHAPTER ELEVEN

The Swindon Inter-City Units

Whilst Derby Works was developing the low-density and high-density units, Swindon Works was turning its attention to the use of DMU's on the main line for express services. The result was a design of unit with cars resembling the contemporary loco-hauled coaching stock-the standard Mk 1 gangway coach. These new units evolved in four distinct and separate series:-
1) Original three or six car sets for the Western and Scottish Regions.
2) Later developments of the above units for the Scottish Region.
3) Trans-Pennine six car sets for the North Eastern Region.
4) Later four car sets for the Western Region.
The first series entered service in 1956 and the Class 123 sets were the last of the ' Classic ' DMU to be delivered in 1963.
The Inter-City units offered main line standards of comfort and convenience and were well built, sturdy vehicles. Mechanically similar to the standard DMU, they were all built on the longer underframe. The first series were to 'White Circle ' control code and were thus not compatible with other types of DMU. The later survivors were modified when integrated into the Class 126.

Just as the early low-density sets were inspired by the former GWR single railcars, so to some extent were the Inter-Cities based on the GWR twin units which were employed, with an intermediate trailer, on the Birmingham to Cardiff services in their early days. The first BR Inter-City sets saw service on these same routes and through to Swansea. The Scottish Region used them to revitalise the Glasgow to Edinburgh service. Further units were subsequently built for the Scottish Region and the Western sets were transferred north to join them. The experience gained here was put to use when the Trans-Pennine routes were being modernised. The result was the extremely handsome Class 124.

It is unfortunate that the last of the Swindon designs was probably the least successful. The Class 123 for the Western Region incorporated continuous corridors, wrap-round screens and was the only class of DMU mounted on the Swindon designed B4 bogie. Introduced on the busy South Wales to West of England and the South Wales to Portsmouth services, they were later transferred to Old Oak Common Depot for use on the Paddington to Oxford and Newbury services. Finally they moved to the Eastern Region at Botannic Gardens, Hull where they finished their days with the Trans-Pennine cars. In common with all the DMU's the buffet cars were taken out of service fairly early on in their careers and some of the first class accommodation was down graded to second class. Classes 123 and 124 were then treated as one integrated fleet and ran as three and four car sets until withdrawn from service in 1984. The engines were recovered and sent to Bletchley Depot as spares for the similarly powered Marylebone Class 115 high density sets then serviced there.

The Inter-city sets made a considerable contribution to rail services throughout the 1960's and 1970's.

1) Original three and four car sets for the Western and Scottish Regions

Swindon Works produced these early express units in several forms to suit the requirements of both regions. The Western had 18 cars arranged in groups of three, but so designed as to give two nine car formations. There were two types of three car set, one having a Trailer Buffet First flanked by a pair of 'intermediate' Driving Motor Brake Seconds. The other type had a 'leading' DMBSL at the outer end, followed by a trailer corridor first with an 'intermediate' DMBSL at the inner end. The "leading" cars had a full width cab with two windows similar to the later Swindon cross country sets, whilst the 'intermediate' cars had end gangways and a small cab on the left-hand side which was shut off when not in use to enable passengers to pass through the entire train. Thus a nine car train would have a 'leading' car at each end, but could be split down to three or six car units as operations required. In contrast, the Scottish Region formation involved 'leading' DMBS and 'intermediate' Driving Motor Second cars. They had six of these six-car sets arranged - DMBS(L), DMS(L), TFK, TFKRB, DMS(L) and DMBS(L). They also received additional cars sufficient to make up two three-car sets comprising - DMBS(L), TFK, DMS(L) and three spare power cars. The day to day formations of the Scottish sets varied, again to meet traffic requirements.

By the early 1960's all these early Inter-City cars were allocated to the Scottish Region and were operated as one fleet with formations adjusted as required. The Western services reverted to loco-hauled stock or the newer Cross-Country sets.

These Inter-City sets were AEC powered with mechanical transmission to 'white circle' control code. The front ends displayed a single-digit train description stencil positioned centrally under the two cab windows on the fronts of the 'leading' cars or under each of the front windows on the 'intermediate' examples. They carried the lined light green livery with whiskers which were carried across the end gangway covers on the 'intermediate 'cars. From the late 1960's the all-pervading plain blue appeared with the yellow ends and cantrail markings for first class accommodation.

Two-tone blue and grey was the final garb for these sets. The last survivors were eventually modified to conform with the later Class 126 cars and were integrated with them.

Driving Motor Brake Second with Lavatory (Leading) - DMBSL

Seats:	52 second
Nos:	W79091 - 94 (Lot No. 30200)
	SC79096 - 111 (Lot No. 30200)
Weight:	38 tons 0 cwt.
Drawings:	*Fig.234* with *fig.236* showing plan. (shows 'intermediate' cab). End views as *fig.273* and *fig.279*.

Driving Motor Brake Second with Lavatory (Intermediate) - DMBSL

Seats:	52 second
Nos:	W79083 - 90 (Lot No. 30196)
	SC79095 (Lot No. 30196)
Weight:	38 tons 0 cwt.
Drawings:	*Fig.235* with *fig. 236* showing plan.
	End views as shown in *fig.274* and *fig.279*.

Driving Motor Second with Lavatory (Intermediate) - DMSL

Seats:	64 second
Nos:	SC79155 - 68 (Lot No. 30199)
Weight:	38 tons 0 cwt.
Drawings:	*Fig.237* and *fig.238*. Plan *fig.239*.
	End views as *fig.274* and *fig.279*.

Trailer Buffet First with Lavatory - TFKRB

Seats:	18 first, 12 buffet
Nos:	W79440 / 1 (Lot No. 30197)
	SC79442 - 7 (Lot No. 30197)
Weight:	33 tons 0 cwt.
Drawings:	*Fig.240* and *fig.241*. Plan as *fig.242*.
	End view as *fig.281*.

Trailer Corridor First with Lavatory - TFK

Seats:	42 first
Nos:	W79470 - 3 (Lot No. 30198)
	SC79474 - 82 (Lot No. 30198)
Weight:	38 tons 0 cwt.
Drawings:	*Fig.243* and *fig.244* with plan *fig.280*.
	End view as *fig.281*.

2) Later units for Scottish Region - TOPS Class 126

A further series was produced in 1959 and this embodied the experience gained with the pioneer sets. These were all allocated to the Scottish Region for their Glasgow - Edinburgh services. In most respects these new units were similar to the earlier sets. The DMBSL cars were all 'leading' and differed from the earlier ones in having the guard's and luggage accommodation at the inner end of the car. The DMSL's were all 'intermediate' and were identical in appearance to the earlier cars except for the provision of the roller blind indicators in place of the stencils. The cab end of the 'leading' cars had a four-digit roller blind display under the cab windows.

The new delivery comprised a total of 22 three-car sets, 10 of which included a TFK and the other 12 had a trailer composite (TCK) utilising the same body shell as the TFK. By this time all the former Western Region sets were now in Scotland and the earlier ScR sets had been re-formed as three car units. Their fleet then comprised 22 sets DMBSL, TFK, DMSL, 12 sets DMBSL, TCL, DMSL and 8 sets DMBSL, TFKRB and DMSL. It will be recalled that they also had three spare power cars from the original delivery, namely two 'leading' and one 'intermediate' DMBSL. In order to incorporate these spares into working sets the new delivery included one additional 'intermediate' DMSL and two more TFKRB, thereby bringing the buffet sets up to ten. The total Scottish fleet then comprised 44 three-car sets. Controls were made compatible and these sets formed the backbone of the Glasgow - Edinburgh services until displaced by the Class 27/1 powered push-pull formations.

The displaced units were transferred to Ayr where they worked the Glasgow to Ayrshire coast routes, however their numbers diminished and they finally disappeared in 1982. The buffet cars were the first to be scrapped and many of the 'intermediate' cars had their gangways removed and the car ends plated over in their last few years of service.

As with the earlier cars these were also delivered in lined green livery and later carried the usual livery changes.

Driving Motor Second with Lavatory (Intermediate) - DMSL

Seats :	64 second
Nos:	SC50936/51008 - 29 (Lot No. 30413)
Weight:	38 tons 0 cwt.
Drawings:	*Fig.237* and *fig.238*. Plan as *fig.239*
	End views as *fig.276* and *fig.283*.

Trailer Corridor First with Lavatory - TFK

Seats:	42 first
Nos:	SC59391 - 400 (Lot No. 30415)
Weight:	33 tons 0 cwt.
Drawings:	*Fig.243* and *fig.244*. Plan as *fig.245*.
	End view as *fig.280*.

Trailer Corridor Composite with Lavatory - TCK

Seats: 18 first, 32 second
Nos: SC59402 - 12   (Lot No. 30416)
Weight: 33 tons 0 cwt.
Drawings: As TFK SC59391 - 400 (*Note*. Seating plan as TFK
            except that four compartments have eight second
            class seats in lieu of six first class seats).

Trailer Buffet First with Lavatory - TFKRB

Seats: 18 first, 12 buffet
Nos: SC59098/9   (Lot No. 30537)
Weight: 34 tons 0 cwt.
Drawings: As TFKRB, W79440 etc.

Driving Motor Brake Second with Lavatory (Leading) - DMBSL

Seats: 22 second
Nos: SC51030 - 51   (Lot No. 30414)
Weight: 38 tons 0 cwt.
Drawings: *Fig.246* and *fig.247*. Plan as *fig 248*.
            End views as *fig. 275* and *fig. 283*.

3) Trans-Pennine six-car sets - TOPS Class 124

In 1960 Swindon Works produced its masterpiece - the extremely handsome Trans-Pennine sets. These six-car units had four power cars in each giving a total of 1840 hp or the equivalent of a Class 33 diesel locomotive ! The leading end featured a deep three-section, wrap-round screen which, combined with a graceful curved cab, presented a most attractive appearance. These cab ends were manufactured almost entirely in fibre glass by Mickleover Transport who also made similar cab ends for the Glasgow 'Blue' trains.

One unique feature of this class was the inclusion of the only non-driving power car in the entire DMU fleet. Designed for the heavily graded routes across the Pennines from Hull, Leeds and Yorkshire to Liverpool and Manchester, each power car had two Albion 230bhp engines driving through standard mechanical transmission. The standard set formation was DMC, MBSK, TSL, TFKRB, MBSK, DMC and when delivered they were all in the lined dark green livery. The large four-digit display under the cab windows prevented the usual whiskers being added and yellow warning panels arrived fairly soon afterwards. Always classified as main line stock, these units went straight into the blue /grey livery with yellow ends which included the whole area as far back as the leading edge of the cab door.

With the elimination of buffet facilities on the DMU fleet, the TFKRB cars were withdrawn and the class became five-car units, still with 1840 bhp power units installed. In the late 1970's and early 1980's they were supplanted on the principal Trans-Pennine workings by loco-hauled trains (including some of the last workings by Class 55 Deltic diesel locomotives) and began to travel more widely on secondary services. They were all finally based at Hull (Botanic Gardens) and integrated with the survivors of the Class 123 sets from the Western Region. Formations of the combined fleet involved cars of both classes arranged as three and four car sets.

A late modification was the removal of the engines and transmissions from the non-driving Motor Brake Seconds so making them into Trailer cars (51969/73 - 6/8/80/1/3/4 became 59834/41/35/39/38/36/42/33/40/37).

Driving Motor Composite - DMC (two per set)

Seats: 21 first
Nos: E51951 - 67   (Lot No. 30603)
Weight: 40 tons 0 cwt.
Drawings: *Fig.249* and *fig. 250* with plan as *fig.251*.
            End views as *fig.277* and *fig.282*.

Motor Brake Second (non-driving) with Lavatory - MBSK

Seats: 48 second
Nos: E51968 - 84   (Lot No. 30604)
Weight: 41 tons 0 cwt.
Drawings: *Fig.252* and *fig.253*. Plan *fig.254*.
            End views as *fig.283* and *fig.284*.

Trailer Open Second with Lavatory - TSL

Seats: 64 second
Nos: E59765 - 73   (Lot No. 30605)
Weight: 32 tons 0 cwt.
Drawings: *Fig.255* and *fig.256* (Note: *fig.256* shows Class 123
            with a B4 bogie). Plan as *fig.257*.
            End views as *fig.280* and *fig.284*.

Trailer Buffet First with Lavatory - TFKRB

Seats: 18 first, 8 buffet
Nos: E59774 - 81   (Lot No. 30606)
Weight: 34 tons 0 cwt.
Drawings: *Fig.258* and *fig.259*. Plan *fig.260*.
            End view as *fig. 280*.

4) Western Region four-car units - TOPS Class 123

These were the last of the 'Classic' DMU design and were produced at Swindon Works in 1963. There were two varieties of these four-car sets, one incorporating a buffet second and the other with an open second. The principal external features were the provision of end gangways, giving through train access and wrap-round cab windscreens. Basically designed for the regions cross country services, such as Cardiff - Plymouth, Cardiff - Portsmouth etc, they were later used on the Paddington to Oxford route. There were five of each type normally running as eight-car trains, but occasionally they ran as a twelve unit formation. Fitted with Swindon designed B4 bogies, they were otherwise mechanically similar to the earlier Trans-Pennine sets. Unlike those sets however, they had a Driving Motor car at each end and two trailers. One of the power cars had a large guard / luggage area occupying half the length of the body and the other one was virtually a standard Mk1 corridor second class coach with a driving cab at one end. The power cars each had two 230bhp Albion engines and standard mechanical transmission.

When new they presented a striking and not unattractive image in their shiny livery of lined dark green with twin roller blind indicator under each cab window. The gangway covers were painted yellow and the roof domes off-white.

Buffet cars were again withdrawn comparatively early and the common formation was then two three-car units flanking one four-car unit in a train of ten vehicles. The livery later changed to blue and grey, with full yellow ends.

After a spell on the Paddington services they migrated again to the Cardiff area and covered the secondary services from South Wales to Bristol etc. From here they were taken out of service and stored for a while. Ultimately they returned to service and, as already recorded were based at Hull (Botannic Gardens).

Buffet car W59831 had a reprieve, being converted to run with Eastern Region Clacton Electric set No. 309.616 and was renumbered E69108, replacing the original buffet car which had been an accident casualty. It was itself withdrawn on 13th April 1981 following a further accident to the EMU set. W59828 also survived for a few years after conversion to a WR Regional Civil Engineers Staff and Dormitory coach No.DB975327, running with Rail Profiler DX79105.

Driving Motor Brake Second with Lavatory - DMBSL

Seats: 32 second
Nos: W52086 - 95 (Lot No.30703)
Weight: 41 tons 0 cwt.
Drawings: Fig.261 and fig.262. Plan fig.263. End views as fig.278 and fig.283.

Trailer Corridor Composite with Lavatory - TCK

Seats: 24 first, 24 second
Nos: W59818 - 27 (Lot No. 30705)
Weight: 32 tons 0 cwt.
Drawings: Fig.264 and fig.265. Plan as fig.266. End view as fig.280.

Trailer Open Second with Lavatory - TSL

Seats: 64 second
Nos: W59235 - 39 (Lot No. 30706)
Weight: 31 tons 0 cwt.
Drawings: Fig.255 and fig.256 (Note: Fig.255 shows class124 with the mark 1 bogie). Plan as fig.257. End views as fig.280 and fig.284.

Trailer Buffet Second with Lavatory - TSLRB

Seats: 32 second, 8 buffet
Nos: W59828 - 32 (Lot No. 30707)
Weight: 35 tons 0 cwt.
Drawings: Fig.267 and fig.268. Plan as fig.269. End view as fig.280.

Driving Motor Second with Lavatory - DMSK

Seats: 56 second
Nos: W52096 - 105 (Lot No. 30704)
Weight: 41 tons 0 cwt.
Drawings: Fig.270 and fig.271. Plan as fig .272. End views as fig.278 and fig .283.

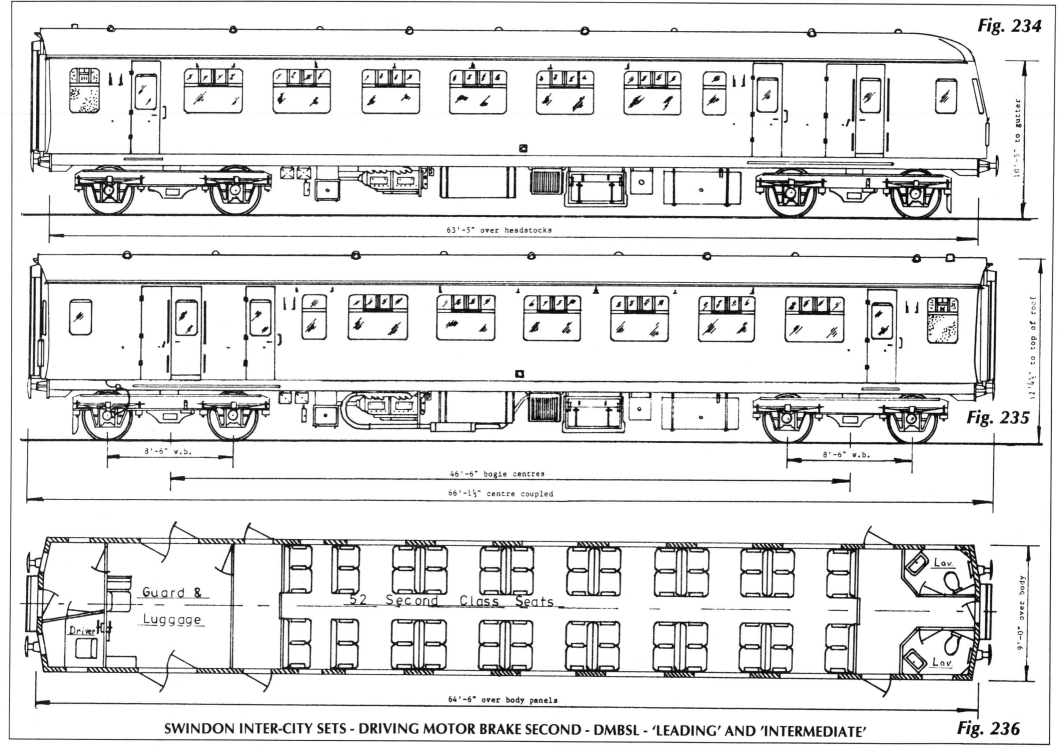

Fig. 234

Fig. 235

Fig. 236

63'-5" over headstocks

10'-5" to gutter

12'-4½" to top of roof

8'-6" w.b.

46'-6" bogie centres

66'-1½" centre coupled

8'-6" w.b.

Guard & Luggage

Driver

52 Second Class Seats

Lav.

Lav.

9'-0" over body

64'-6" over body panels

SWINDON INTER-CITY SETS - DRIVING MOTOR BRAKE SECOND - DMBSL - 'LEADING' AND 'INTERMEDIATE'

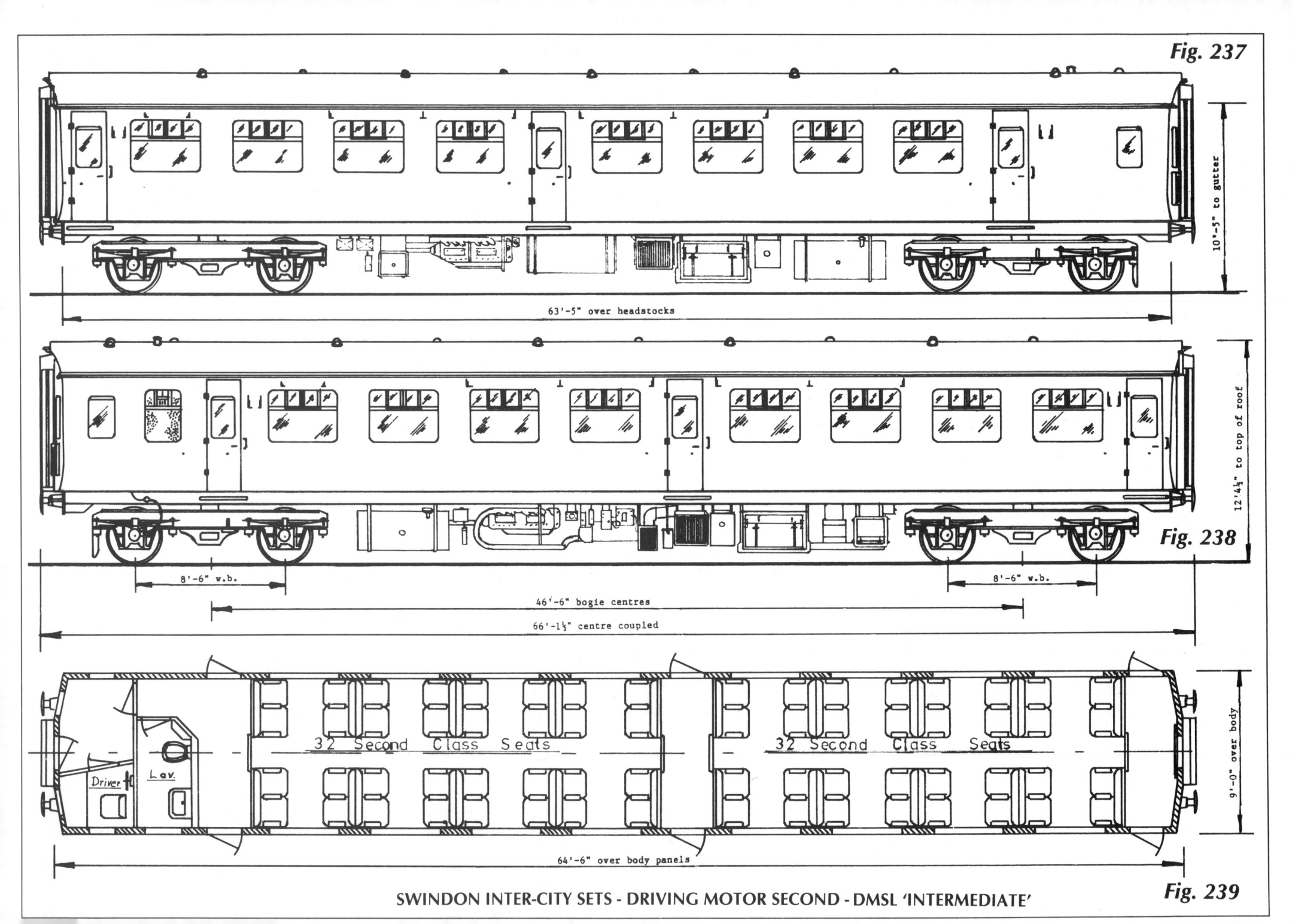

Fig. 237

10'-5" to gutter

63'-5" over headstocks

Fig. 238

12'-4¼" to top of roof

8'-6" w.b.

8'-6" w.b.

46'-6" bogie centres

66'-1½" centre coupled

9'-0" over body

Driver

Lav.

32 Second Class Seats

32 Second Class Seats

64'-6" over body panels

Fig. 239

SWINDON INTER-CITY SETS - DRIVING MOTOR SECOND - DMSL 'INTERMEDIATE'

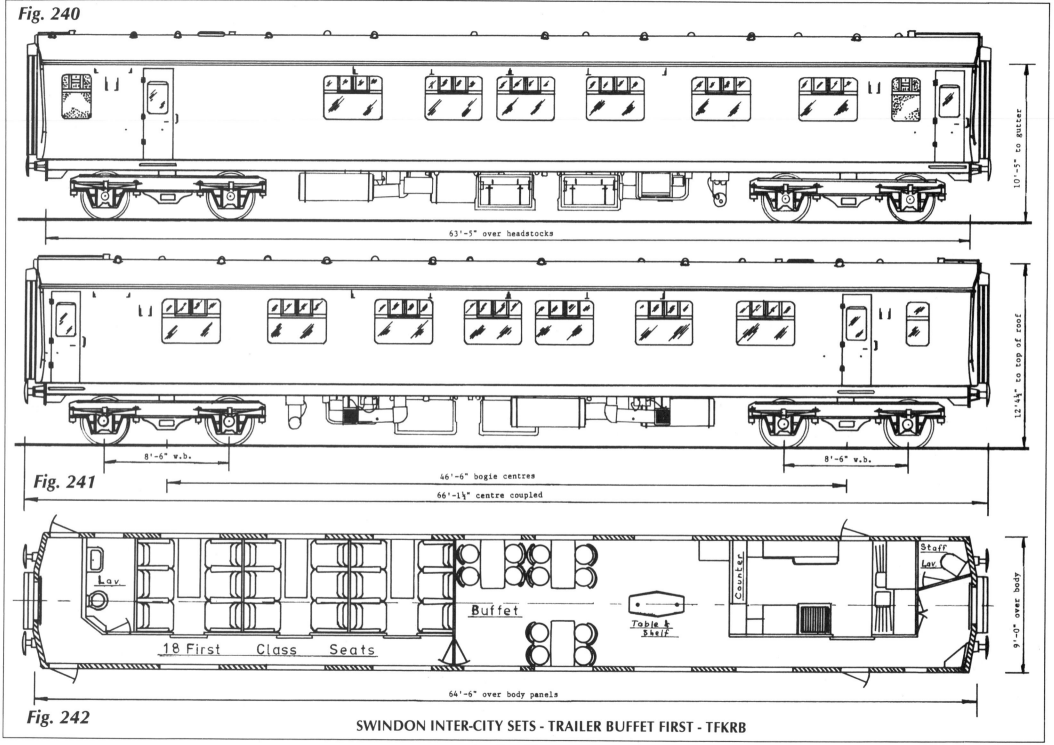

Fig. 240

10'-5" to gutter

63'-5" over headstocks

Fig. 241

12'-4½" to top of roof

8'-6" w.b.

8'-6" w.b.

46'-6" bogie centres

66'-1½" centre coupled

Lav.

18 First Class Seats

Buffet

Table & Shelf

Counter

Staff Lav.

9'-0" over body

64'-6" over body panels

Fig. 242

SWINDON INTER-CITY SETS - TRAILER BUFFET FIRST - TFKRB

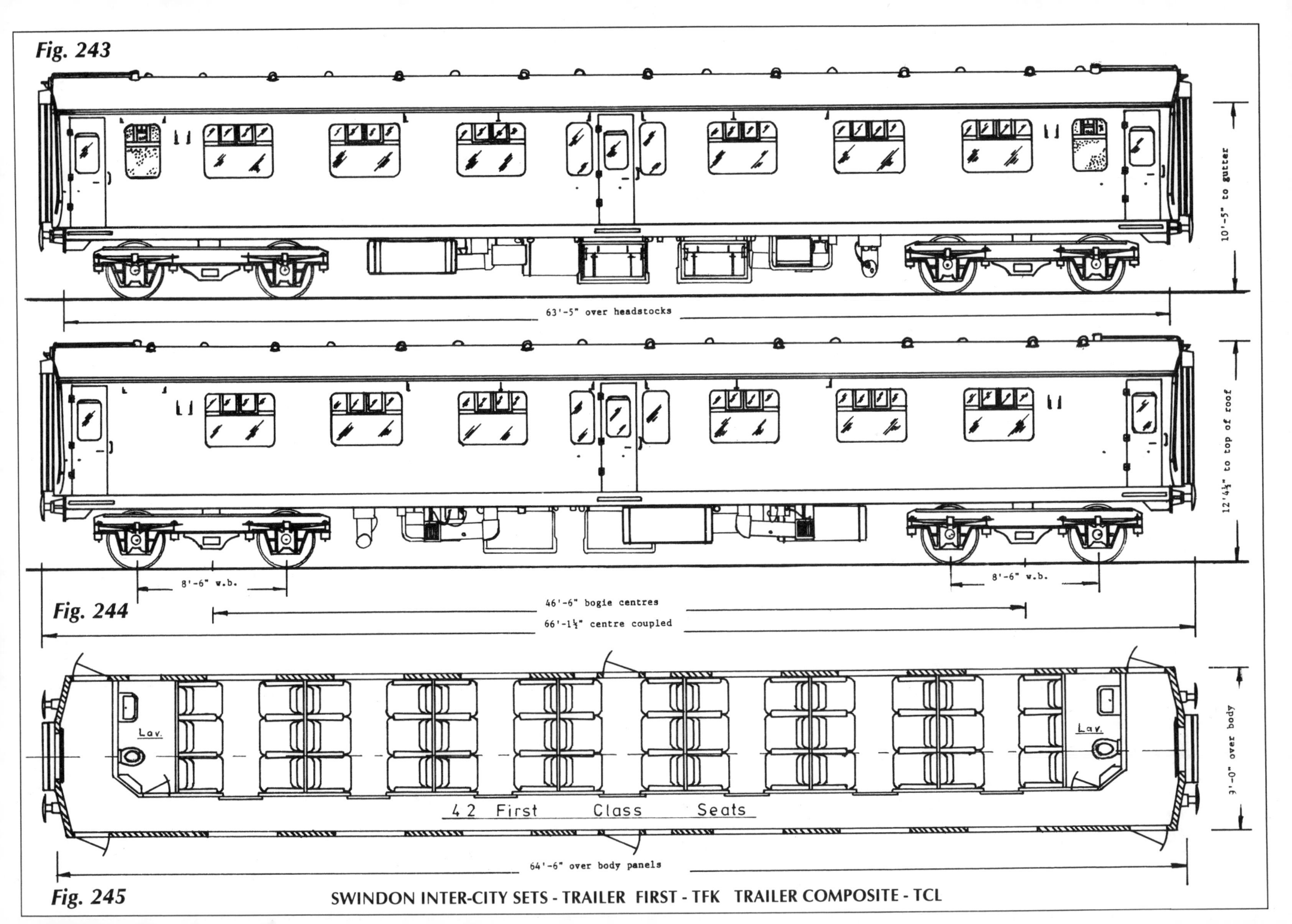

Fig. 243

10'-5" to gutter

63'-5" over headstocks

Fig. 244

12'-4½" to top of roof

8'-6" w.b.

8'-6" w.b.

46'-6" bogie centres

66'-1½" centre coupled

Fig. 245

Lav.

Lav.

42 First Class Seats

3'-0" over body

64'-6" over body panels

SWINDON INTER-CITY SETS - TRAILER FIRST - TFK   TRAILER COMPOSITE - TCL

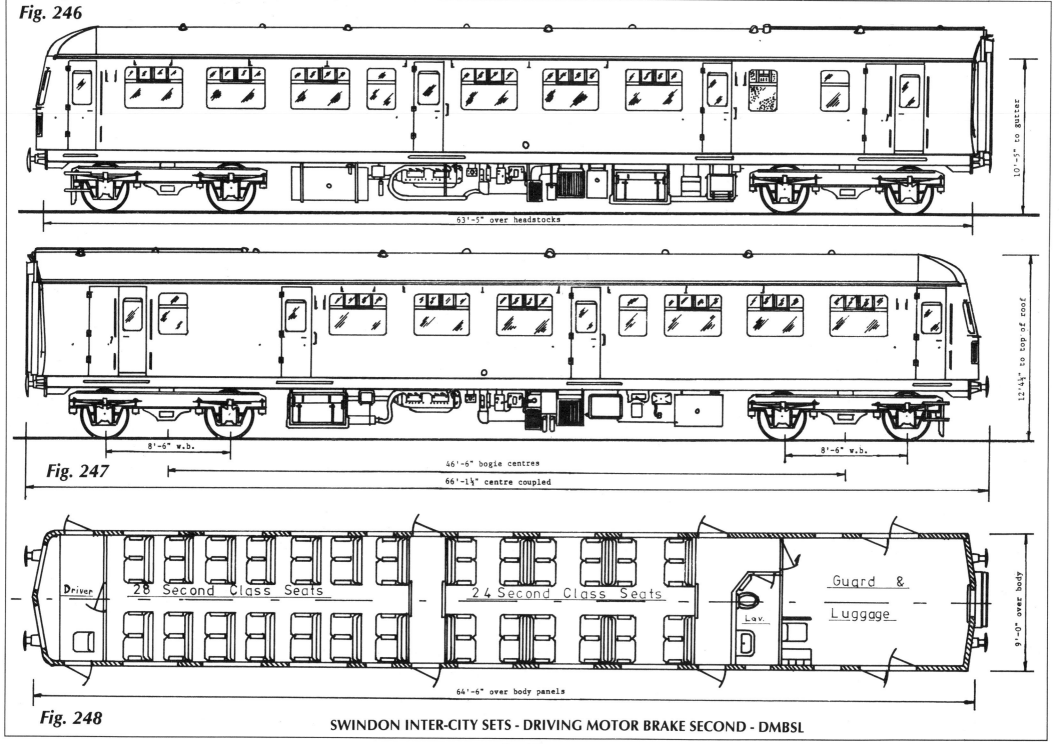

Fig. 246

10'-5" to gutter

63'-5" over headstocks

Fig. 247

12'4½" to top of roof

8'-6" w.b.

8'-6" w.b.

46'-6" bogie centres

66'-1½" centre coupled

Driver

28 Second Class Seats

24 Second Class Seats

Lav.

Guard & Luggage

9'-0" over body

64'-6" over body panels

Fig. 248

SWINDON INTER-CITY SETS - DRIVING MOTOR BRAKE SECOND - DMBSL

Fig. 249

10'-5" to gutter

63'-5" over headstocks

Fig. 250

12'-4¼" to top of roof

8'-6" w.b.

8'-6" w.b.

46'-6" bogie centres

67'-1" over buffers (extended)

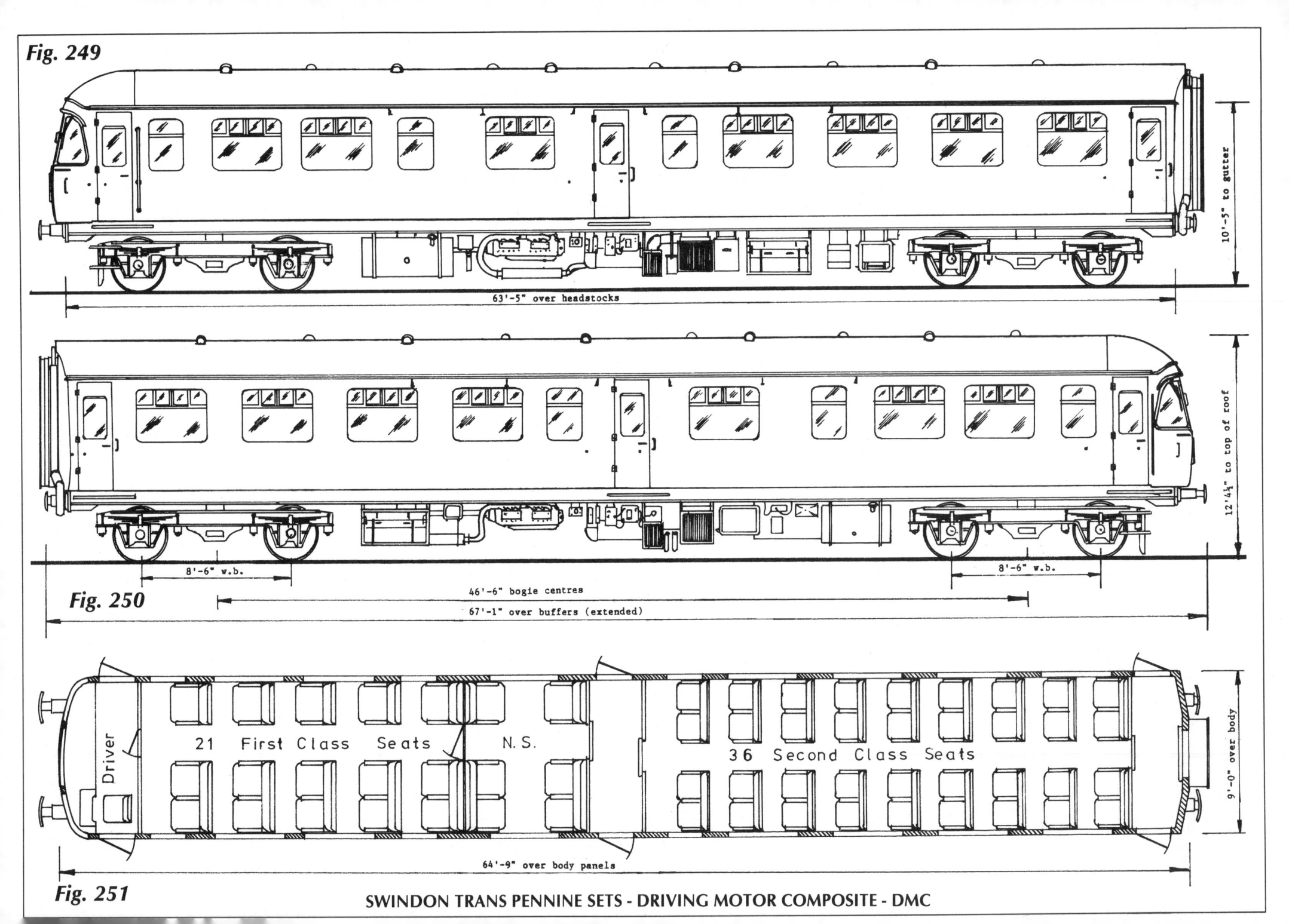

Driver

21 First Class Seats

N.S.

36 Second Class Seats

9'-0" over body

64'-9" over body panels

Fig. 251

SWINDON TRANS PENNINE SETS - DRIVING MOTOR COMPOSITE - DMC

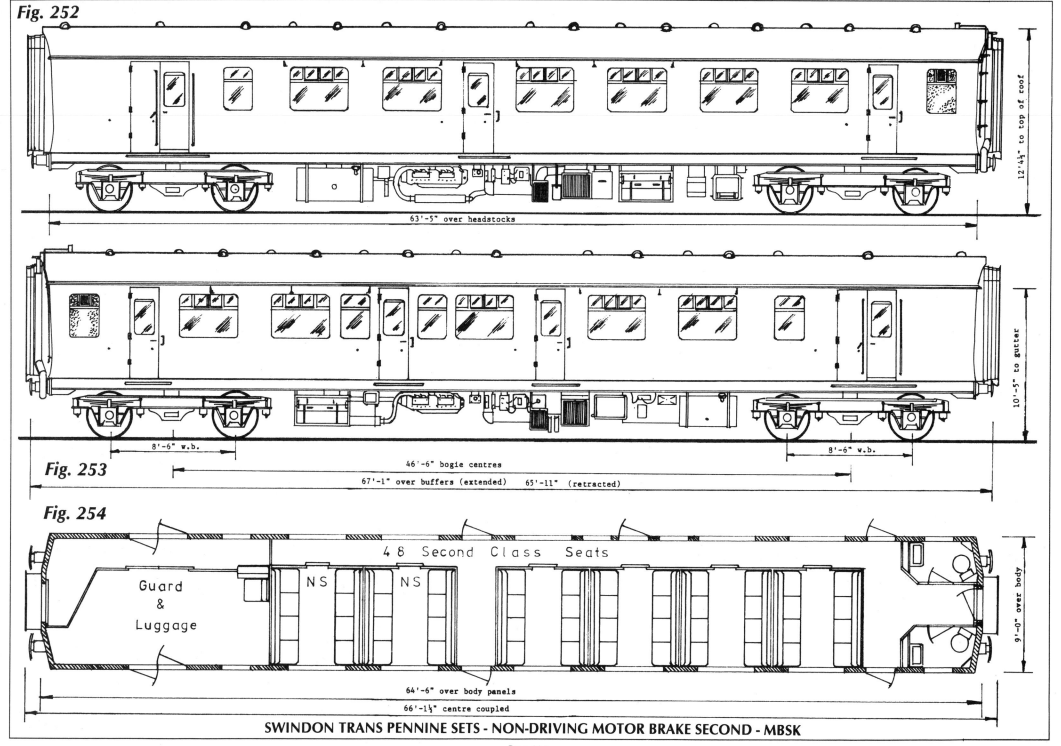

Fig. 252

12'-4¼" to top of roof

63'-5" over headstocks

Fig. 253

10'-5" to gutter

8'-6" w.b.

46'-6" bogie centres

8'-6" w.b.

67'-1" over buffers (extended)   65'-11" (retracted)

Fig. 254

48 Second Class Seats

Guard & Luggage

NS   NS

9'-0" over body

64'-6" over body panels

66'-1½" centre coupled

SWINDON TRANS PENNINE SETS - NON-DRIVING MOTOR BRAKE SECOND - MBSK

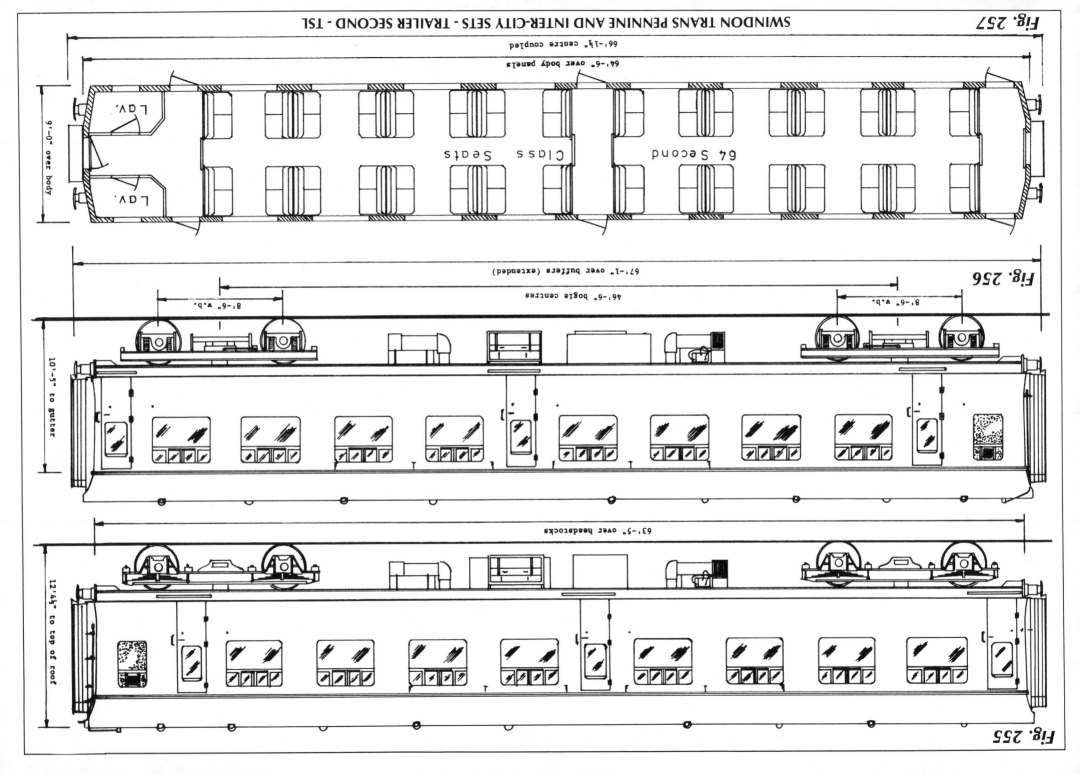

Fig. 257

66'-1¼" centre coupled

64'-6" over body panels

LAV.

LAV.

64 Second Class Seats

9'-0" over body

Fig. 256

67'-1" over buffers (extended)

46'-6" bogie centres

8'-6" w.b.

8'-6" w.b.

10'-5" to gutter

Fig. 255

63'-5" over headstocks

12'-4¼" to top of roof

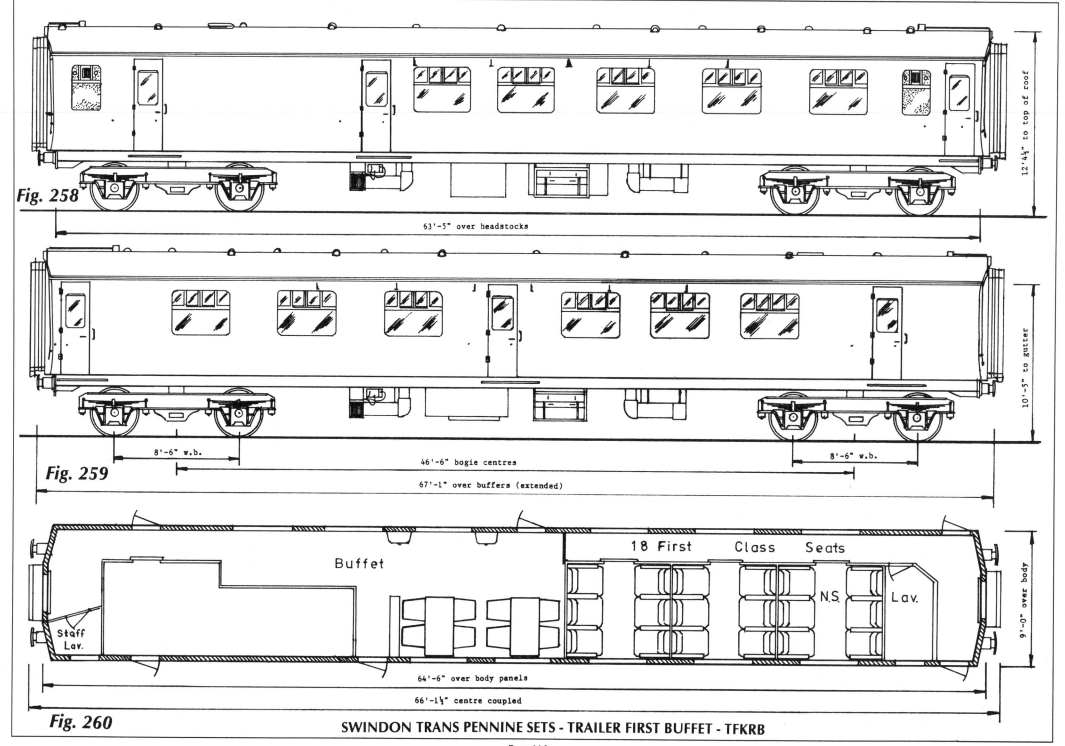

Fig. 258

12'4¼" to top of roof

63'-5" over headstocks

Fig. 259

10'-5" to gutter

8'-6" w.b.

46'-6" bogie centres

8'-6" w.b.

67'-1" over buffers (extended)

Fig. 260

Buffet

18 First Class Seats

Staff Lav.

N.S.

Lav.

9'-0" over body

64'-6" over body panels

66'-1½" centre coupled

SWINDON TRANS PENNINE SETS - TRAILER FIRST BUFFET - TFKRB

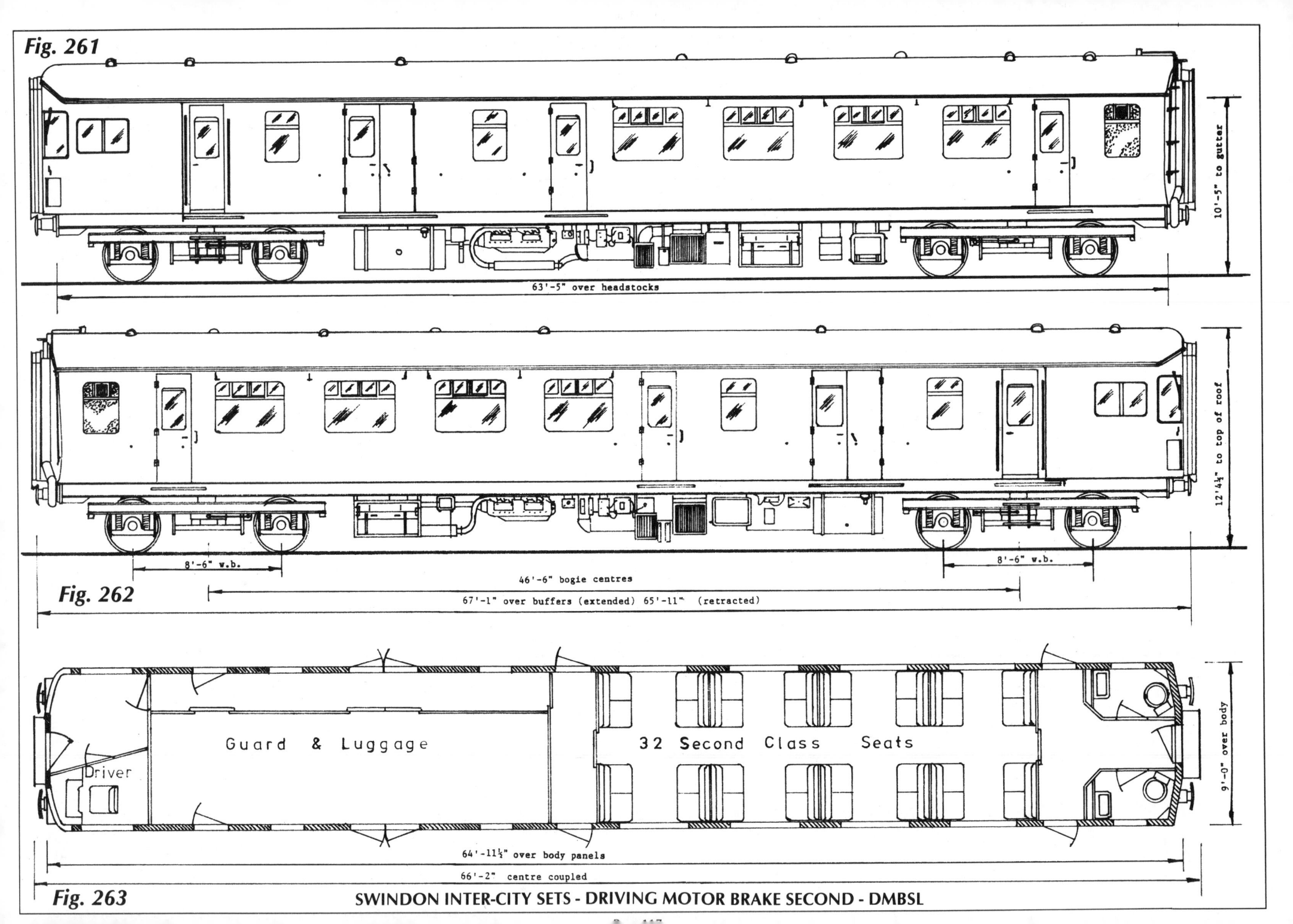

Fig. 261

10'-5" to gutter

63'-5" over headstocks

Fig. 262

12'4½" to top of roof

8'-6" w.b.

46'-6" bogie centres

8'-6" w.b.

67'-1" over buffers (extended) 65'-11" (retracted)

Driver

Guard & Luggage

32 Second Class Seats

9'-0" over body

64'-11½" over body panels

66'-2" centre coupled

Fig. 263　　SWINDON INTER-CITY SETS - DRIVING MOTOR BRAKE SECOND - DMBSL

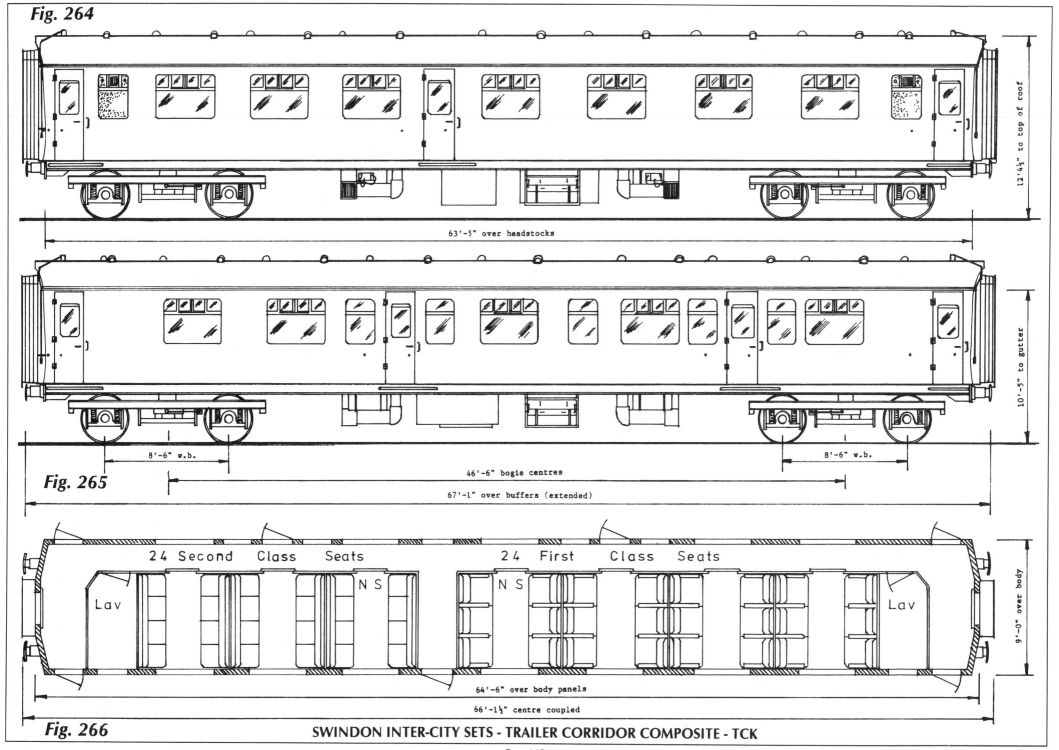

Fig. 264

12'4¾" to top of roof

63'-5" over headstocks

Fig. 265

10'-5" to gutter

8'-6" w.b.

8'-6" w.b.

46'-6" bogie centres

67'-1" over buffers (extended)

Lav 24 Second Class Seats N S N S 24 First Class Seats Lav

9'-0" over body

64'-6" over body panels

66'-1½" centre coupled

Fig. 266

SWINDON INTER-CITY SETS - TRAILER CORRIDOR COMPOSITE - TCK

Fig. 267

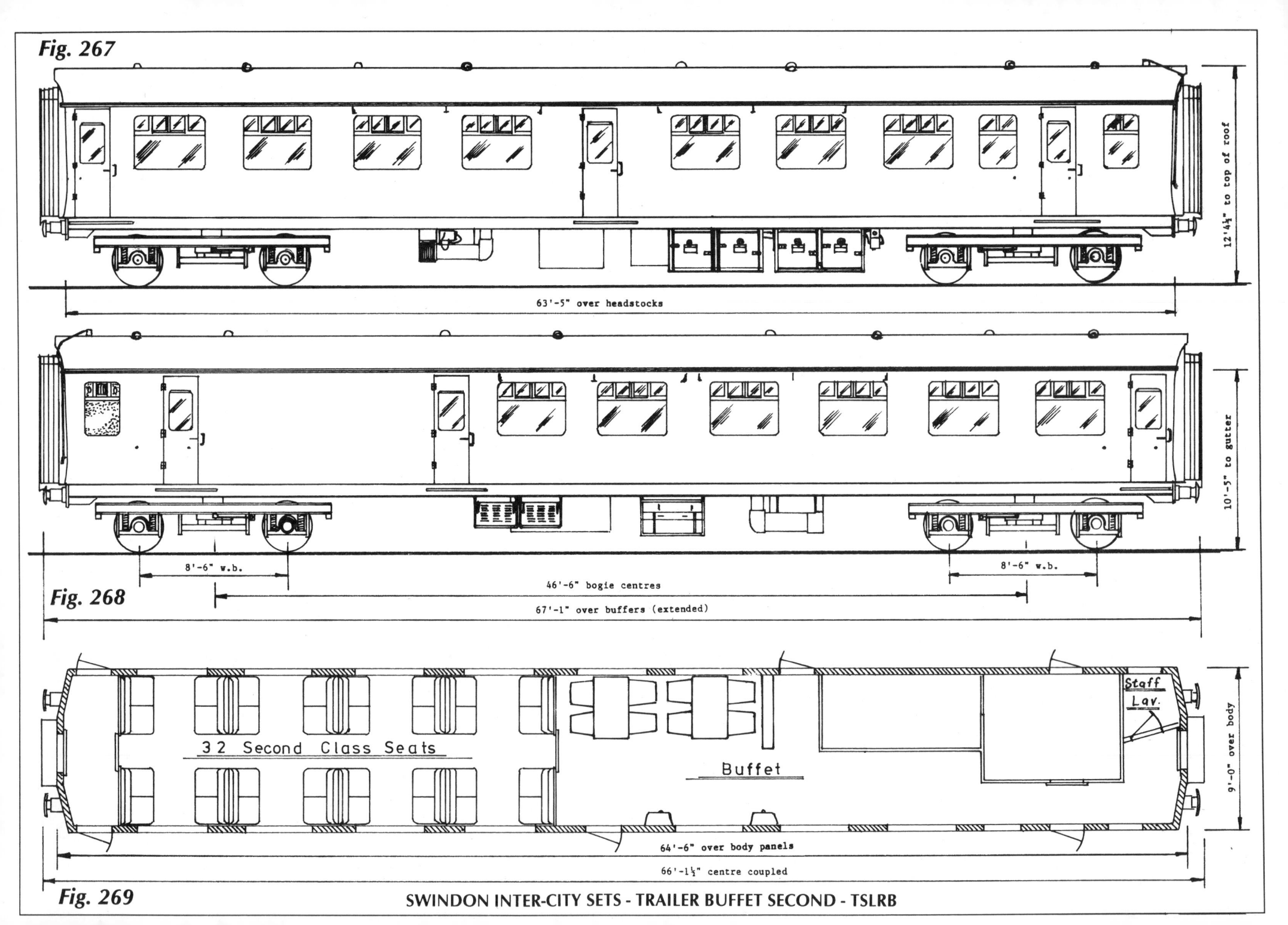

12'4¼" to top of roof

63'-5" over headstocks

Fig. 268

10'-5" to gutter

8'-6" w.b.

8'-6" w.b.

46'-6" bogie centres

67'-1" over buffers (extended)

Fig. 269

32 Second Class Seats

Buffet

Staff Lav.

9'-0" over body

64'-6" over body panels

66'-1½" centre coupled

SWINDON INTER-CITY SETS - TRAILER BUFFET SECOND - TSLRB

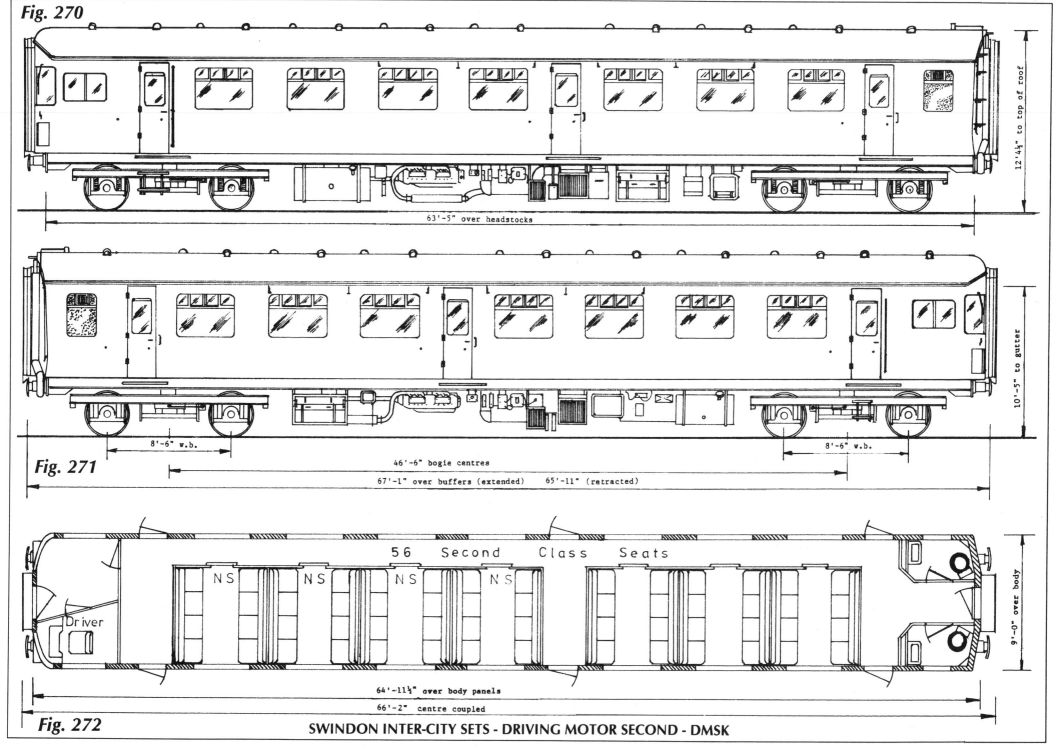

Fig. 270

12'4½" to top of roof

63'-5" over headstocks

Fig. 271

10'-5" to gutter

8'-6" w.b.

46'-6" bogie centres

8'-6" w.b.

67'-1" over buffers (extended)   65'-11" (retracted)

56 Second Class Seats

NS   NS   NS   NS

Driver

9'-0" over body

64'-11½" over body panels

66'-2" centre coupled

Fig. 272

SWINDON INTER-CITY SETS - DRIVING MOTOR SECOND - DMSK

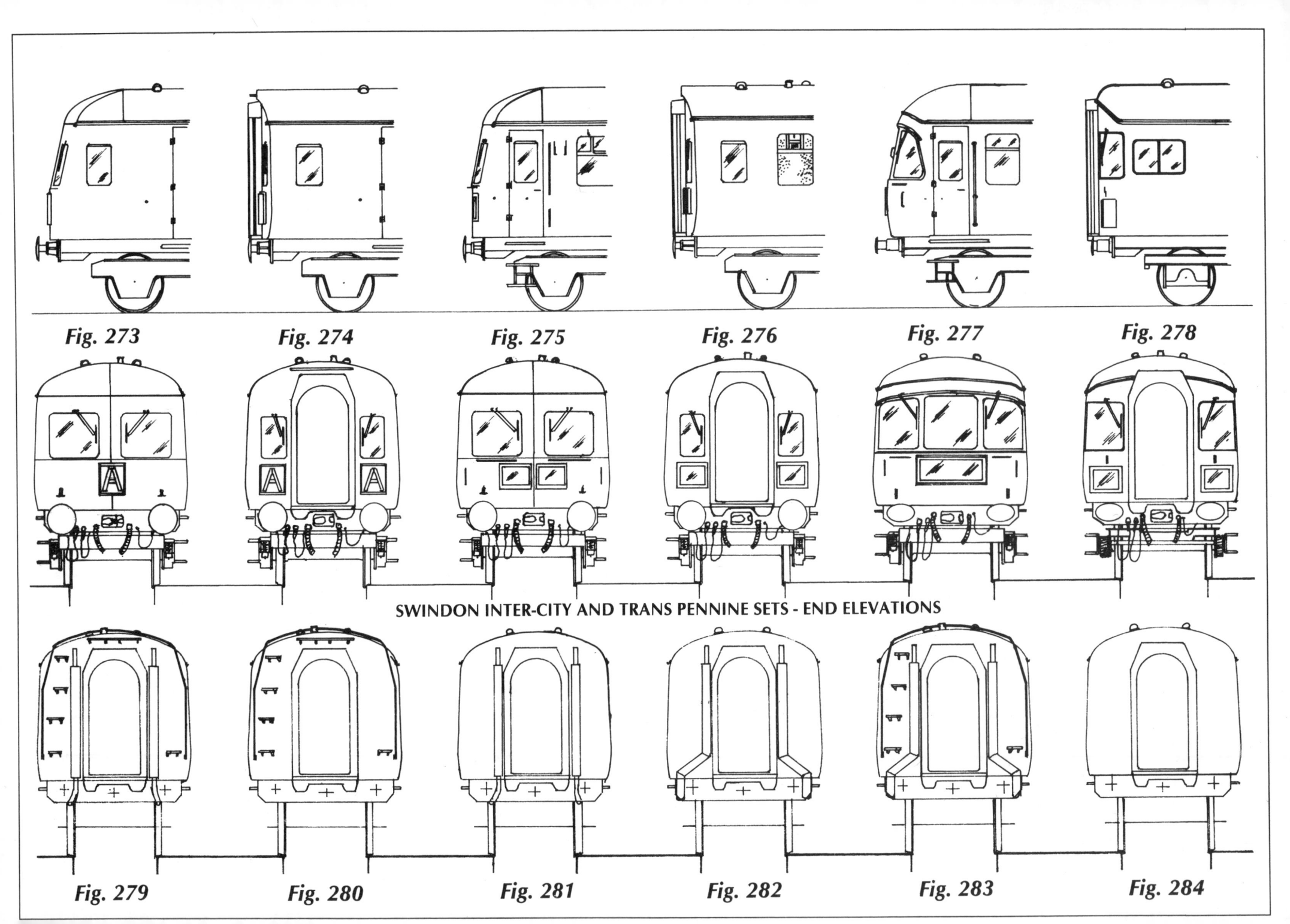

Fig. 273   Fig. 274   Fig. 275   Fig. 276   Fig. 277   Fig. 278

SWINDON INTER-CITY AND TRANS PENNINE SETS - END ELEVATIONS

Fig. 279   Fig. 280   Fig. 281   Fig. 282   Fig. 283   Fig. 284

CHAPTER TWELVE

As the Modernisation Plan gathered momentum, the Western Region identified a need for a self-contained DMU set that had first and second class accommodation, plenty of luggage space and catering facilities: thus was born the Cross Country Unit. As the name suggests they were developed for those secondary routes that snaked their way between the major trunk routes, often with lengthy journey times.

All these units were built on the long underframe and were arranged with maximum comfort for both classes of traveller. In essence they were superior low-density types and, indeed were officially described as 'low density'. Designed at Swindon Works, they were tailor-made for the Western Region, although a small batch was produced for the Scottish Region to be used on services around Inverness. The initial batch emerged from Swindon in 1958 and was soon followed later in the year, by a delivery from the Gloucester Railway, Carriage and Wagon Co. Ltd. at Gloucester. The Swindon sets had a very severe front end with two rather small cab windows in a shallow pointed front which bore a passing resemblance to the final GWR railcars (see photographs page 31 and page 132). The Gloucester sets followed on from their Single unit design and employed the same front end grafted onto the basic design. This marriage of the Derby front end and the excellent Swindon Cross Country car produced one of the most attractive designs of British Rail DMU's.

Swindon produced a series of seven sets for the Scottish Region and these were identical to the first batch. The final units were built by Swindon in 1961 for the Western Region, however these omitted the buffet section from the centre cars. This batch also featured a four-digit number box which was located below the cab windows. The earlier Swindon units had a four-lamp style of front whilst the Gloucester sets had a two-digit indicator and a head / tail lamp either side. Some of the earlier sets later had a four-digit box installed, but these were fitted slightly higher and the original lamp arrangement was retained.

Each power car was fitted with two AEC 150 bhp engines driving through standard mechanical transmission.

The Scottish Region modified four of their DMBC cars to increase the luggage space, by removing the two second class seating bays and fitting a pair of double doors in place of the second window each side in this area. A side corridor was installed running on the right hand side and the remaining window on the left hand side was blanked off, the cars being reclassified as DMBF. The buffets were not used after the mid-1970's, but were left in situ. Most of the Scottish sets were transferred to the South Wales area of the Western Region in the early 1980's, although one set remained to be withdrawn in Scotland.

A later modification was carried out on some of the Gloucester units based at Reading. These were modified for use on the Reading-Gatwick Airport services and had the buffets replaced by luggage racks. These sets were branded "For Passengers' Luggage" lettered in white on a flame red or black panel placed on the former buffet section and on the luggage van.

Both types were delivered in lined green (early cars of Class 120 and all Class 119 were light green, all later dark green) and apart from the last Swindon batch, had the whiskers on the front ends with the yellow warning panels to follow. The Scottish units carried the overall Rail Blue with full yellow ends until withdrawn or transferred away. The Western Swindon units wore the interim blue livery with the small yellow panels until succumbing to the corporate blue. Later the blue and grey livery followed and the Gloucester units were seen in Network South East livery.

Mention must be made of the three Hawksworth ex-GWR corridor composite coaches which were converted to run with the Cross Country sets and which were painted multiple unit dark green with cream lining. They were marshalled within the sets to strengthen them to form four-car sets. The three coaches concerned were:- W7254W, W7804W and W7813W (see next page).

Swindon built units (TOPS Class120)
1958 series. 49 sets (47 trailers) for the Western Region.
1959 series. 7 sets for the Scottish Region.
1961 series. 9 sets for the Western Region (10 trailers without buffet)

Driving Motor Brake Composite - DMBC
Seats:	18 first, 16 second
Nos:	W50696 - 744 (Lot No. 30335)
	W51582 - 90 (Lot No. 30516)
	SC51781 - 7 (Lot No. 30559)
Weight:	36 tons 0 cwt.
Drawings:	Fig.285 (1958/59 series and fig.286 (1961 series). Plan fig.287. End views ; fig.310 (1958/9) and fig.311 (1961).

Trailer Second with Lavatory and Buffet - TSLRB
Seats:	60 second (4 buffet)
Nos:	W59255 - 301 (Lot No. 30336)
	SC59679 - 85 (Lot No. 30561)
Weight:	31 tons 0 cwt.
Drawings:	Fig.288 and fig.289. Plan as fig.290.

Trailer Second with Lavatory - TSL

Seats: 68 second
Nos: W59579 - 88 (Lot No. 30517)
Weight: 31 tons 0 cwt.
Drawings: *Fig.294* and *fig.295*. Plan *fig.296*.

Driving Motor Second with Lavatory - DMSL

Seats: 68 seconds
Nos: W50647 - 95 (Lot No. 30334)
W51573 - 81 (Lot No. 30515)
SC51788 - 94 (Lot No. 30560)
Weight: 36 tons 0 cwt.
Drawings: *Fig.291* (1958 /9 series) and *fig.292* (1961 series)
Plan view as *fig.293*.
End views, *fig.310* (1958 /9) and *fig.311* (1961).

Driving Motor Brake First - DMBF (converted from DMBC)

Seats: 18 first
Nos: SC51783 - 6 (Lot No. 30559)
Weight: 36 tons 0 cwt.
Drawings: *Fig.297* and *fig.298*. Plan view as *fig.299*.
End view as *fig.310*.

Gloucester RC & W. Co. Ltd. Units (TOPS Class 119)

Apart from the obvious difference of the cab ends there was one other distinctive point of identification for these units compared with the Swindon built units. On the Gloucester cars the rain gutters turned down over the last four inches at the extreme ends of the units. 28 sets (with only 25 trailers) were built in 1958 for the Western Region.

Driving Motor Brake Composite - DMBC

Seats: 18 first, 16 second
Nos: W51052 - 79 (Lot No. 30421)
Weight: 37 tons 0 cwt.
Drawings: *Fig.300* and *fig.301*. Plan view as *fig.302*.
End view as *fig.309*.

Trailer Second with Lavatory and Buffet - TSLRB

Seats: 60 second, 4 buffet
Nos: W59413 - 37 (Lot No. 30423)
Weight: 31 tons 0 cwt.
Drawings: *Fig.303* and *fig.304*. Plan as *fig.305*.

Driving Motor Second with Lavatory - DMSL

Seats: 68 second
Nos: W51080 - 51107 (Lot No.30422)
Weight: 37 tons 0 cwt.
Drawings: *Fig.306* and *fig.307*. Plan as *fig.308*.
End view as *fig.309*.

Car No.W7804W - one of 3 Hawksworth ex-GWR corridor composite coaches converted to run with the cross-country diesel multiple units. Livery is dark multiple unit green with cream lining. *Cheona collection.*

Swindon built Class 120 unit (car No. 50665 nearest the camera) in blue and grey livery, crosses Water Orton Junction with the 12.15 service from Birmingham New Street to Leicester on 15th April, 1982. *G.Gamble.*

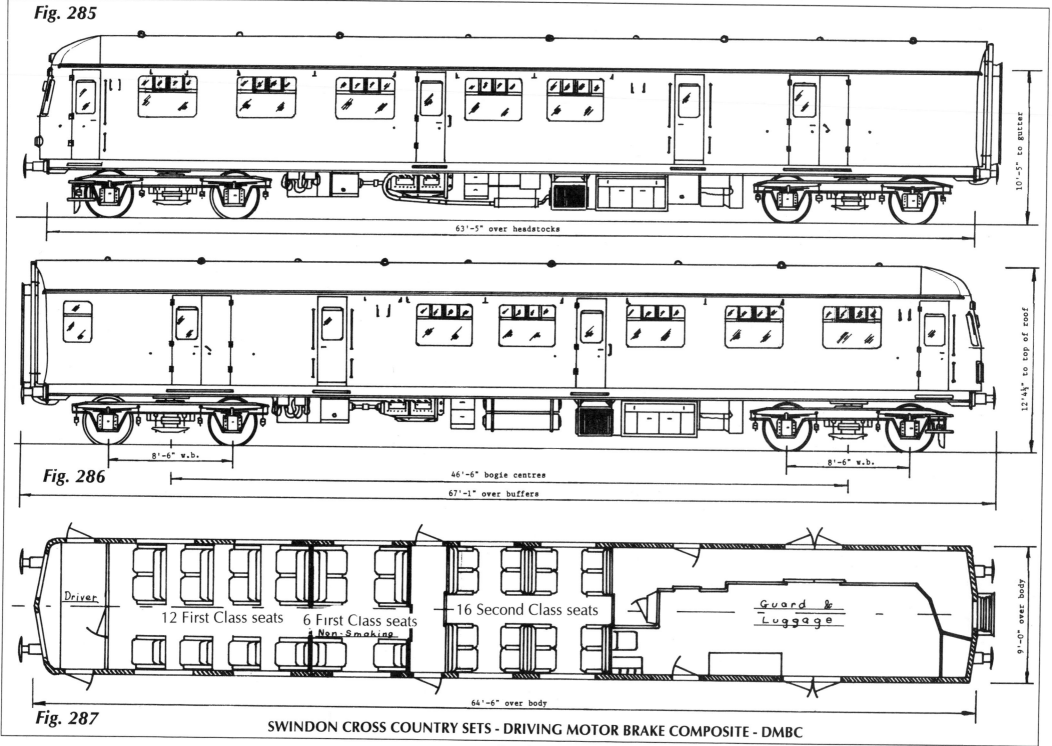

Fig. 285

10'-5½" to gutter

63'-5" over headstocks

Fig. 286

12'-4½" to top of roof

8'-6" w.b.

46'-6" bogie centres

8'-6" w.b.

67'-1" over buffers

Driver

12 First Class seats

6 First Class seats
Non-Smoking

16 Second Class seats

Guard & Luggage

9'-0" over body

64'-6" over body

Fig. 287

SWINDON CROSS COUNTRY SETS - DRIVING MOTOR BRAKE COMPOSITE - DMBC

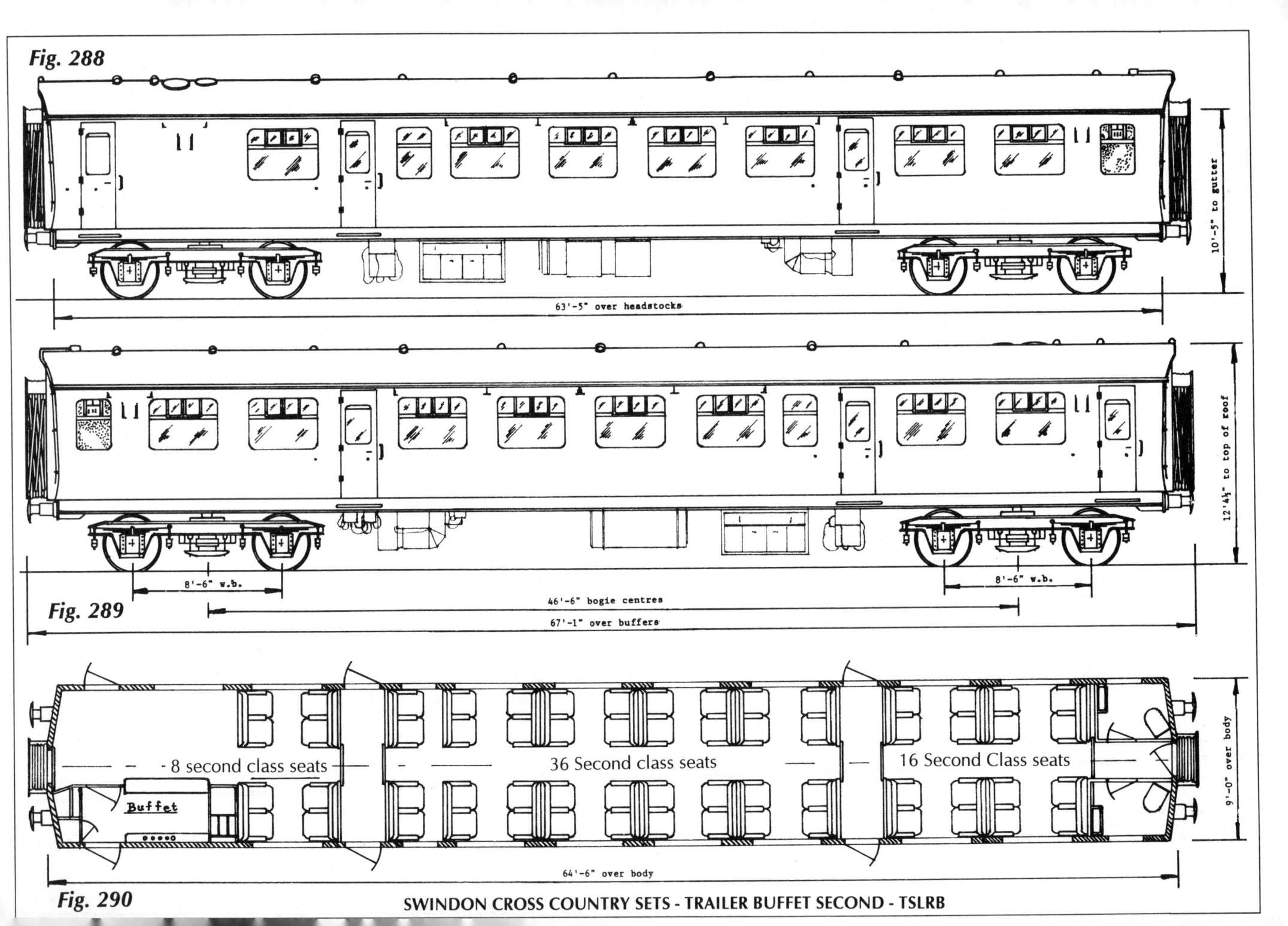

Fig. 288

10'-5" to gutter

63'-5" over headstocks

Fig. 289

8'-6" w.b.

8'-6" w.b.

12'-4½" to top of roof

46'-6" bogie centres

67'-1" over buffers

8 second class seats — 36 Second class seats — 16 Second Class seats

Buffet

9'-0" over body

64'-6" over body

Fig. 290   SWINDON CROSS COUNTRY SETS - TRAILER BUFFET SECOND - TSLRB

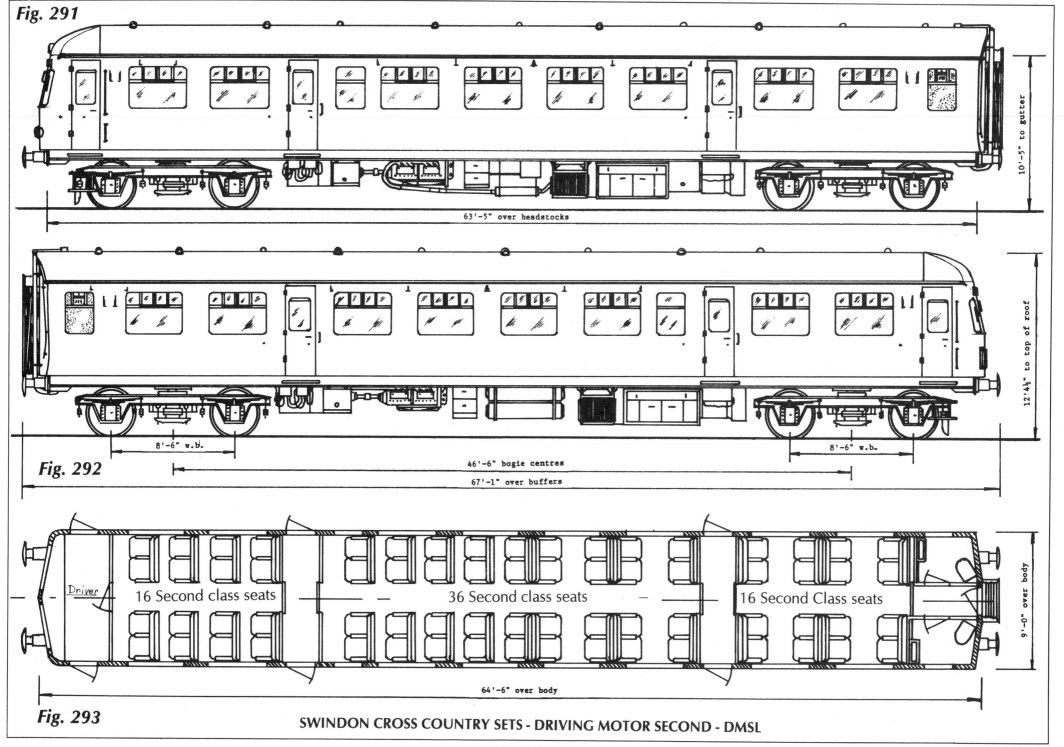

Fig. 291

10'-5" to gutter

63'-5" over headstocks

Fig. 292

12'4½" to top of roof

8'-6" w.b.

46'-6" bogie centres

8'-6" w.b.

67'-1" over buffers

Driver

16 Second class seats

36 Second class seats

16 Second Class seats

9'-0" over body

64'-6" over body

Fig. 293

SWINDON CROSS COUNTRY SETS - DRIVING MOTOR SECOND - DMSL

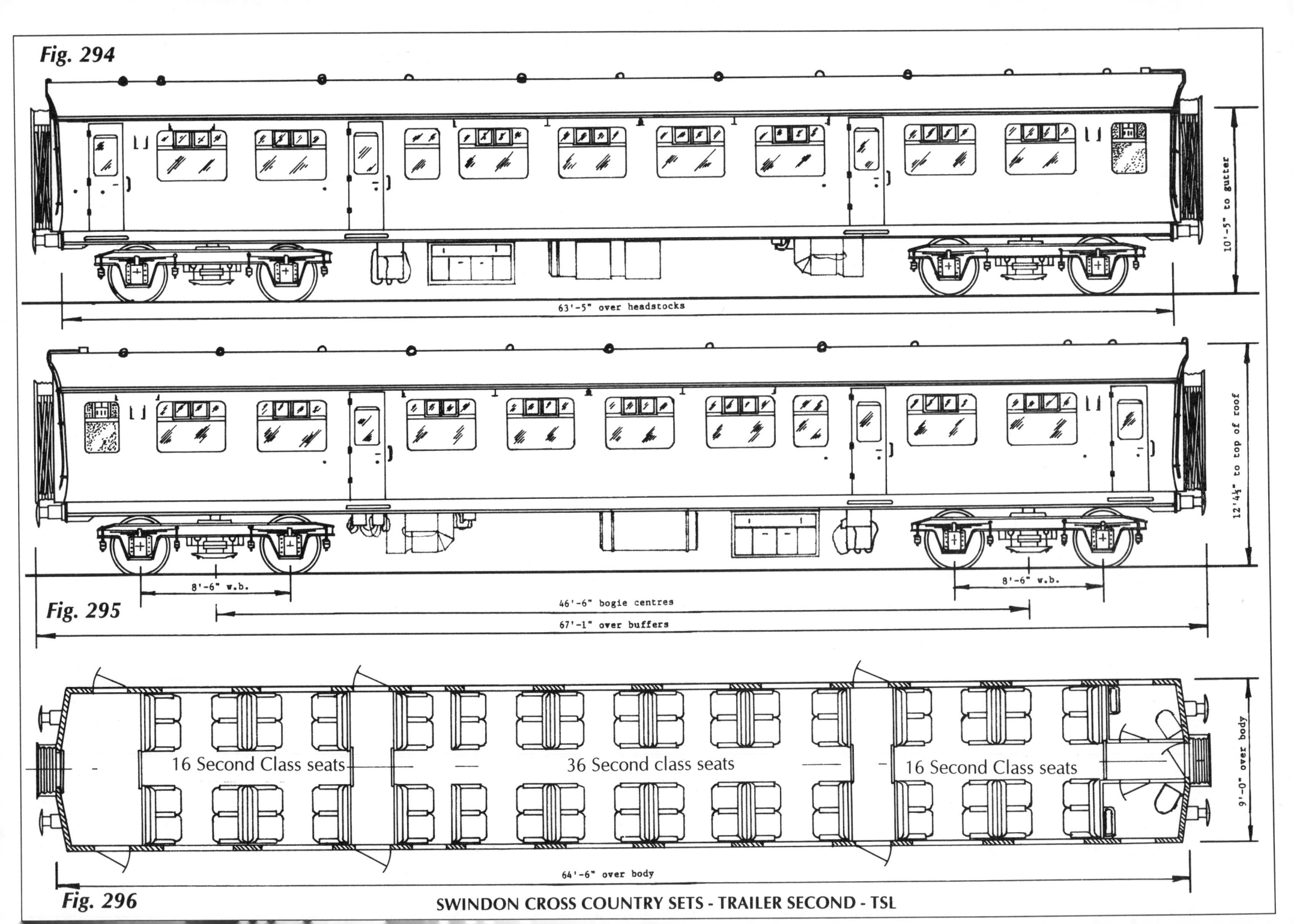

Fig. 294

10'-5" to gutter

63'-5" over headstocks

Fig. 295

12'-4½" to top of roof

8'-6" w.b.

8'-6" w.b.

46'-6" bogie centres

67'-1" over buffers

16 Second Class seats   36 Second class seats   16 Second Class seats

9'-0" over body

64'-6" over body

Fig. 296

SWINDON CROSS COUNTRY SETS - TRAILER SECOND - TSL

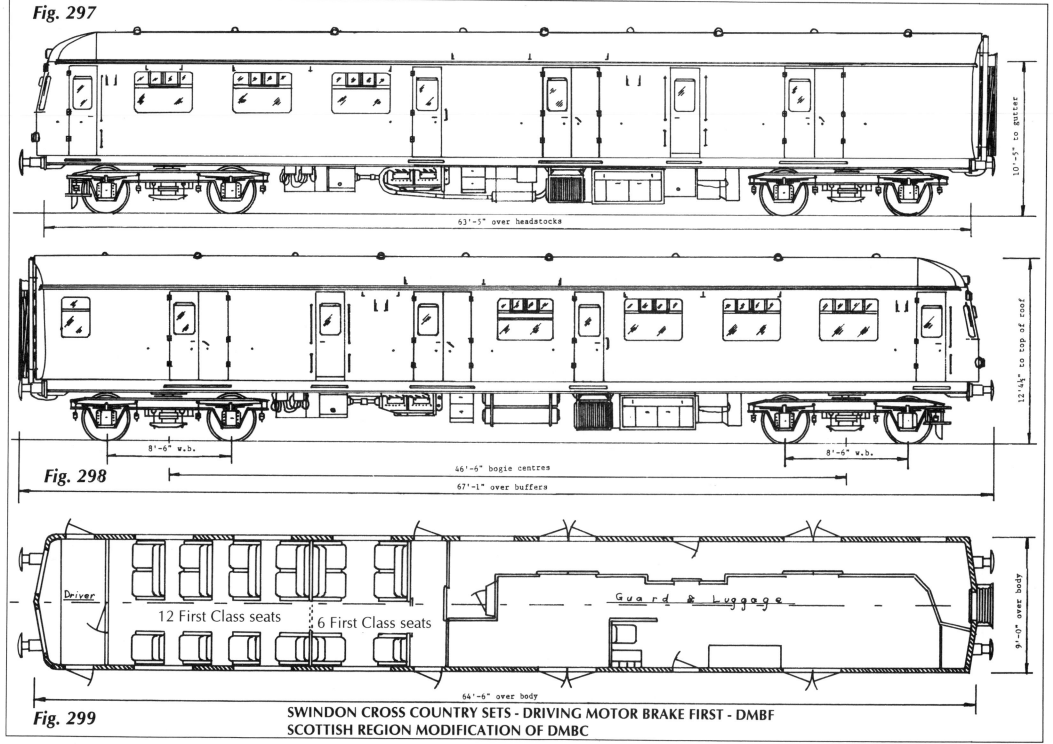

Fig. 297

10'-5" to gutter

63'-5" over headstocks

Fig. 298

12'-4½" to top of roof

8'-6" w.b.

8'-6" w.b.

46'-6" bogie centres

67'-1" over buffers

Driver

12 First Class seats

6 First Class seats

Guard & Luggage

9'-0" over body

64'-6" over body

Fig. 299

SWINDON CROSS COUNTRY SETS - DRIVING MOTOR BRAKE FIRST - DMBF
SCOTTISH REGION MODIFICATION OF DMBC

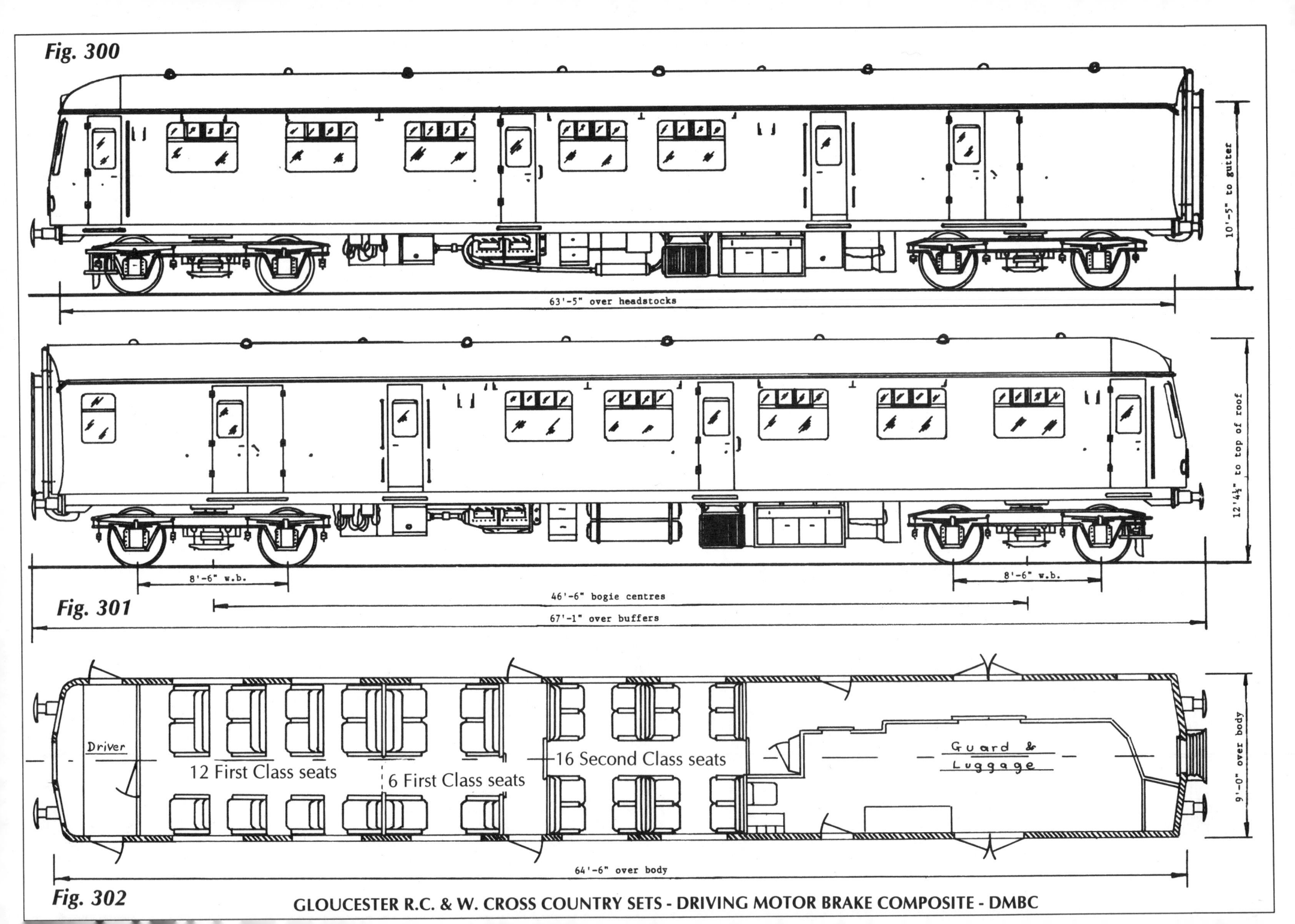

Fig. 300

10'-5" to gutter

63'-5" over headstocks

Fig. 301

12'-4½" to top of roof

8'-6" w.b.

46'-6" bogie centres

8'-6" w.b.

67'-1" over buffers

Fig. 302

Driver

12 First Class seats

6 First Class seats

16 Second Class seats

Guard & Luggage

9'-0" over body

64'-6" over body

GLOUCESTER R.C. & W. CROSS COUNTRY SETS - DRIVING MOTOR BRAKE COMPOSITE - DMBC

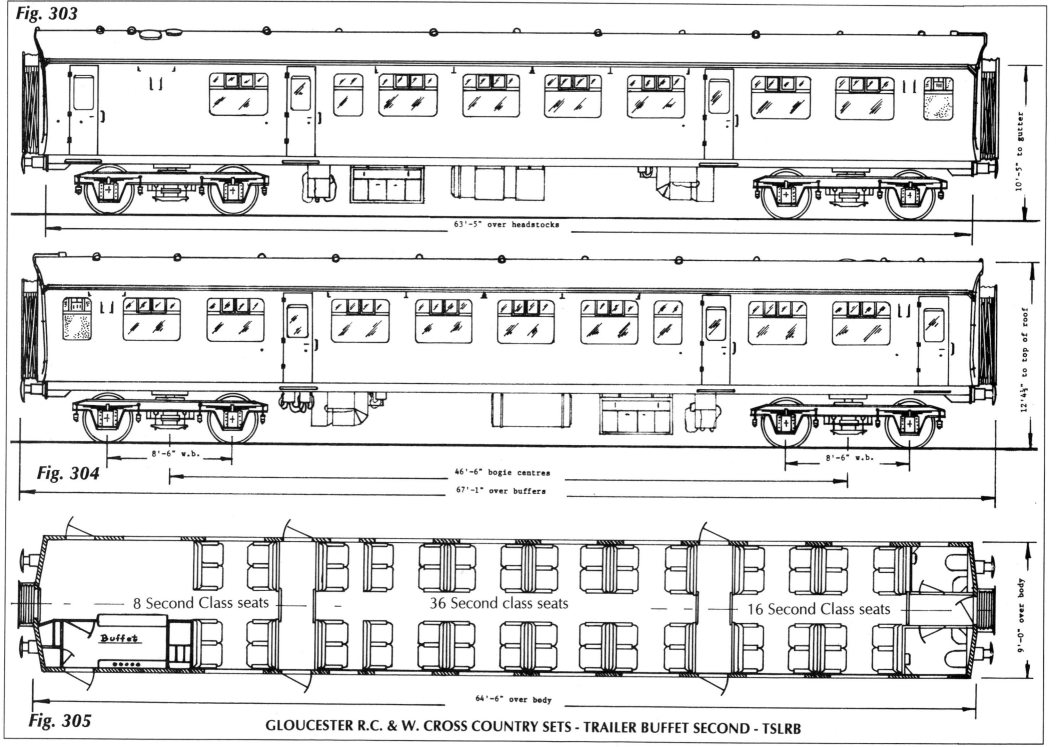

Fig. 303

10'-5" to gutter

63'-5" over headstocks

Fig. 304

12'4½" to top of roof

8'-6" w.b.

8'-6" w.b.

46'-6" bogie centres

67'-1" over buffers

9'-0" over body

8 Second Class seats

36 Second class seats

16 Second Class seats

Buffet

64'-6" over body

Fig. 305

GLOUCESTER R.C. & W. CROSS COUNTRY SETS - TRAILER BUFFET SECOND - TSLRB

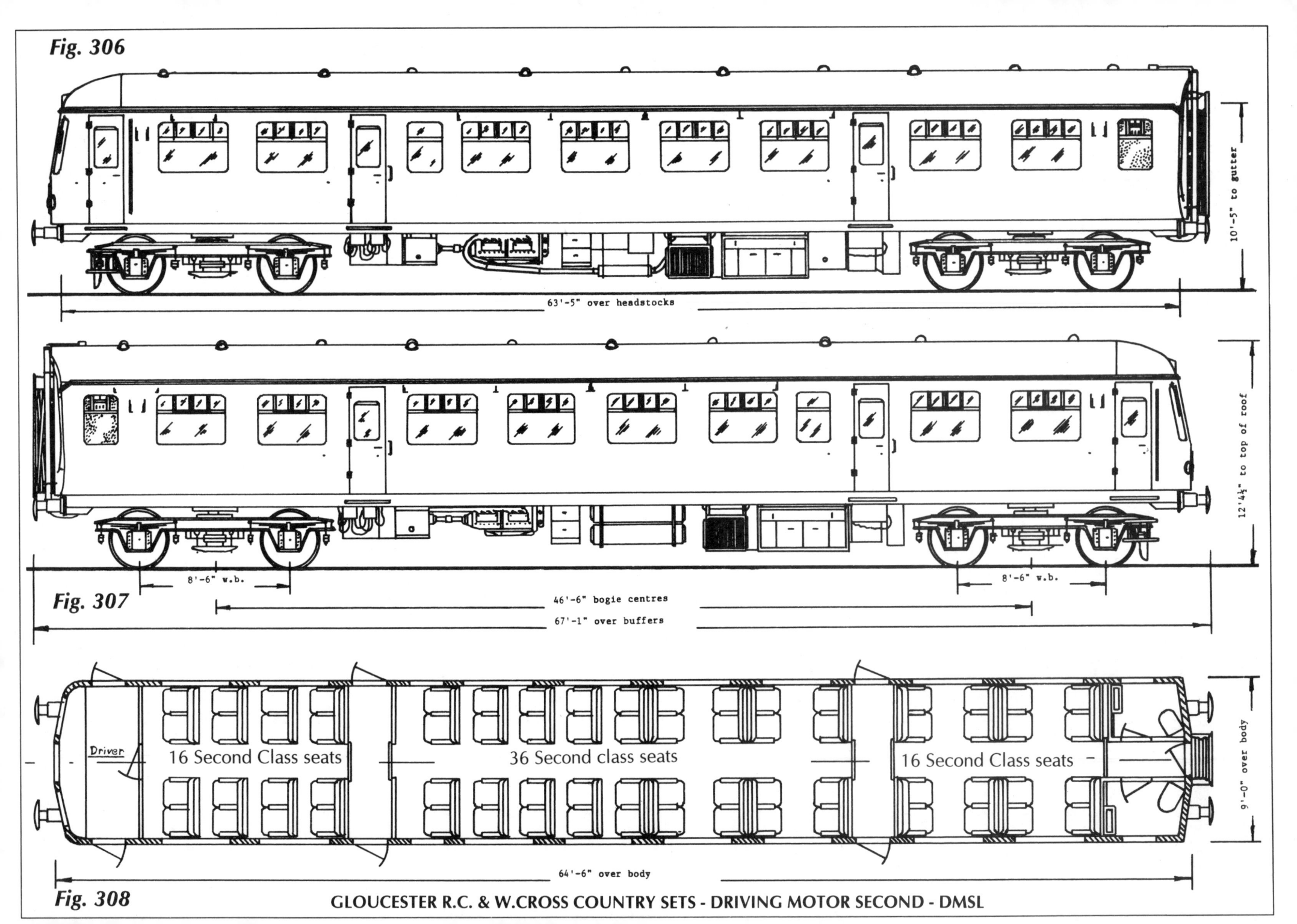

Fig. 306

10'-5" to gutter

63'-5" over headstocks

Fig. 307

12'-4½" to top of roof

8'-6" w.b.

8'-6" w.b.

46'-6" bogie centres

67'-1" over buffers

Driver

16 Second Class seats

36 Second class seats

16 Second Class seats

9'-0" over body

64'-6" over body

Fig. 308

GLOUCESTER R.C. & W. CROSS COUNTRY SETS - DRIVING MOTOR SECOND - DMSL

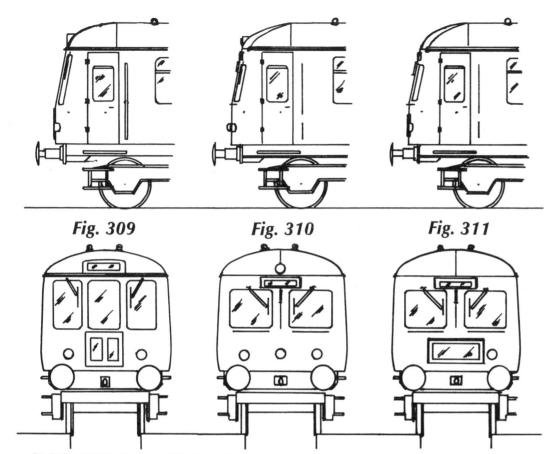

Fig. 309   Fig. 310   Fig. 311

GLOUCESTER R.C.& W. AND SWINDON CROSS COUNTRY SETS - CAB ENDS

End detail of Swindon Class 120 DMBC No. 50703 seen at Matlock, with the 14.17 service from Derby on 11th August, 1981.

G.Gamble.

The corridor connection between two Gloucester RC & W Co. Class 119 cars. The exhaust pipe can be seen on the rear of the DMBC car on the left and the toilet tank overflow pipe and toilet waste pipe are visible on the TS car on the right.

Cheona collection.

CHAPTER THIRTEEN

Parcels Cars

1) The Gloucester Cars - TOPS Class 128

We have already dealt with the Parcels Cars which were converted from the Gloucester single units, but we are now going to take a look at those built as such.

Once again we draw a comparison with the former GWR railcar development* and in particular with Express Parcels cars 17 and 34. These were each based on their contemporary passenger cars and proved very successful. In consequence the Western Region looked to extend this traffic as a part of the dieselisation of their London and Birmingham suburban services. Six cars were ordered from the Gloucester RC & W. Co. Ltd. and entered service in 1959. They were fitted with end gangways and had their cabs off-set, as in the 'intermediate' Inter-City cars, so that they could run in multiple and allow parcels to be sorted in transit. Three pairs of sliding doors were fitted on each side giving excellent accessibility. A two-digit indicator blind was situated under each windscreen enabling the full four character headcode to be shown on the leading car. The engine exhausts were carried up to roof level beside the gangway connection at one end.

At the same time the London Midland Region identified a requirement for a similar type of car for the Manchester area. The four cars delivered did not have end gangways, but were otherwise identical. In place of the connection a third window was placed in the centre of each end and a full four-digit display was centred under the cab windows at each end. The exhausts followed the same arrangement as the Western cars.

With the transfer of the Western Region's Birmingham area to the London Midland Region the four WR cars operating there became LMR property. The gangways were not used thereafter and, in later years, they were removed and some cars of both types lost their route indicator boxes. The only obvious difference then was the lack of central end windows on the former WR cars. The two cars which remained in the London area retained their gangways.

When new these cars all carried the lined dark green livery with the words 'PARCELS SERVICE' flanking the centre pair of doors on each side. They later carried the all-blue with yellow ends style and the legend then appeared in smaller white letters to the left of the centre doors. The extent of the yellow varied over the years. Initially it covered the entire end right round to the leading edge of the driver's doors but later it stopped some four inches ahead of the doors.

All these cars were built on the long underframe and each was powered by two Albion horizontally mounted 230 bhp engines with standard mechanical transmission. Coupling code was 'Blue Square'.

Driving Motor Luggage Van - DMLV (originally classified)
Driving Motor Parcels and Mail Van - DMPMV

Nos.	M55987 - 90 (non-gangway)	(Lot No. 30552)
Weight:	40 tons 0 cwt.	
Nos:	W55991 - 6 (gangway)	(Lot No. 30551)
Weight:	41 tons 0 cwt. (W55991/2 remained with WR)	
Drawings:	*Fig.312* shows the gangway version and *fig.313* the non-gangway type. The plan view *fig.314.* shows the gangway version and *fig.315* shows the alternative cab arrangement on the non-gangway cars. The end views *(fig.316)* are self explanatory.	

2) The Cravens Cars (TOPS Class 129)

When the Class 128 cars arrived on the LMR they joined three other Parcels Cars which the Region had received from Cravens in the previous year. These were on the short chassis and were based on that manufacturer's successful low density cars. The standard Cravens cab was fitted at each end and a guard's section was located at one end. The exhaust stacks were carried to the roof internally via trunking against the internal bulkhead in the same way as in their low density units. Three pairs of hinged doors were fitted on each side and the cars were in lined green with whiskers. They carried the coaching stock crest on each side. They were withdrawn in 1972/73 and finished their careers in the blue livery.

Powered by two AEC 150 bhp engines with standard transmission, they were coupling coded 'Yellow Diamond' in order to be able to run in multiple with the original Derby Lightweight Units in the North West.

Car No. M55997 had a more useful existence after being withdrawn from revenue service as it became the Railway Technical Centre's 'Laboratory 9 - HYDRA ' numbered RDB975385 in the Departmental series and was used in research into hydro-static drive systems.

Driving Motor Luggage Van - DMLV

Nos:	M55997 - 9	
Weight:	30 tons 0 cwt.	
Drawings:	*Fig.317* shows the plan and both side elevations of these cars. The end views can be taken from the appropriate drawing in the low density section.	

---

* See **Great Western Railcars** by C. W. Judge published by Oxford Pub Co.

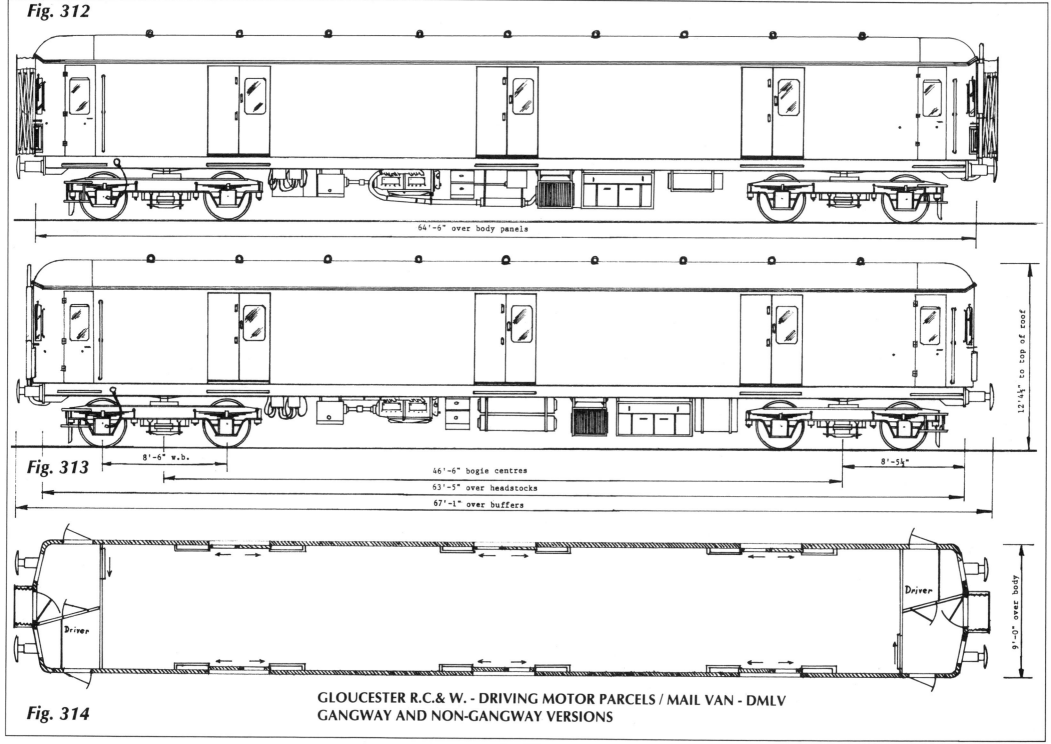

Fig. 312

64'-6" over body panels

Fig. 313

8'-6" w.b.

46'-6" bogie centres

63'-5" over headstocks

67'-1" over buffers

12'-4¼" to top of roof

8'-5¼"

Driver

Driver

9'-0" over body

GLOUCESTER R.C.& W. - DRIVING MOTOR PARCELS / MAIL VAN - DMLV
GANGWAY AND NON-GANGWAY VERSIONS

Fig. 314

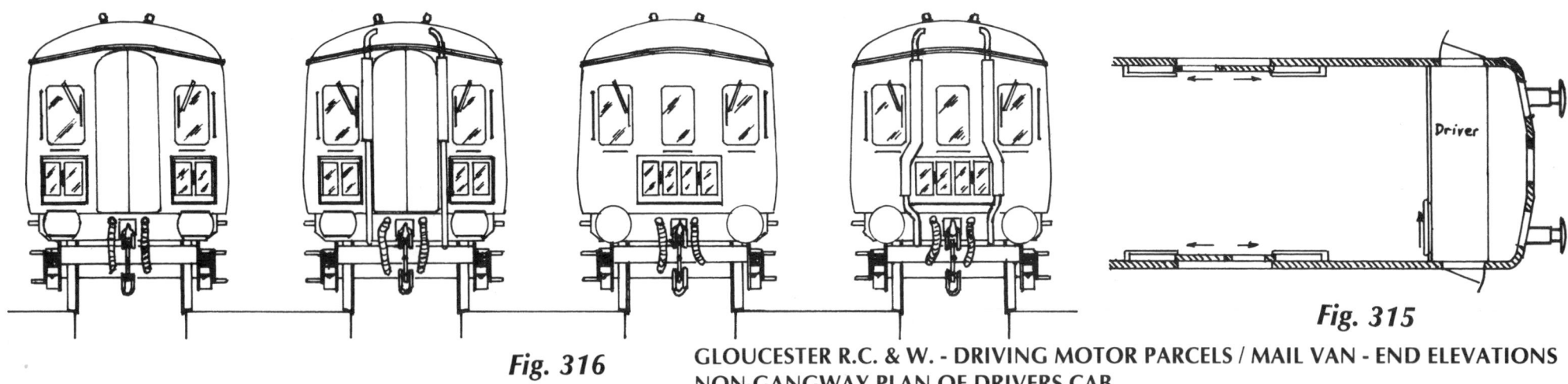

Fig. 316

Fig. 315

GLOUCESTER R.C. & W. - DRIVING MOTOR PARCELS / MAIL VAN - END ELEVATIONS
NON-GANGWAY PLAN OF DRIVERS CAB

Gloucester C & W Co. Class 128, DMLV in green and cream livery seen here at Tyseley Goods Yard sidings in September, 1966.   *R.S.Carpenter.*

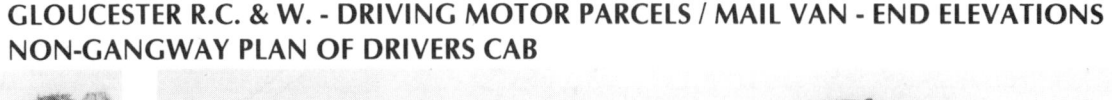

Gloucester C & W Co. Class 128, DMLV No. W55991 in green and cream livery, with whiskers on the corridor connection.   *M.Smith/Kelland collection.*

Cravens Class 129, DMPV No. M55998 in green and cream livery with whiskers seen at Birmingham New Street on 1st September, 1960.   *R.S.Carpenter.*

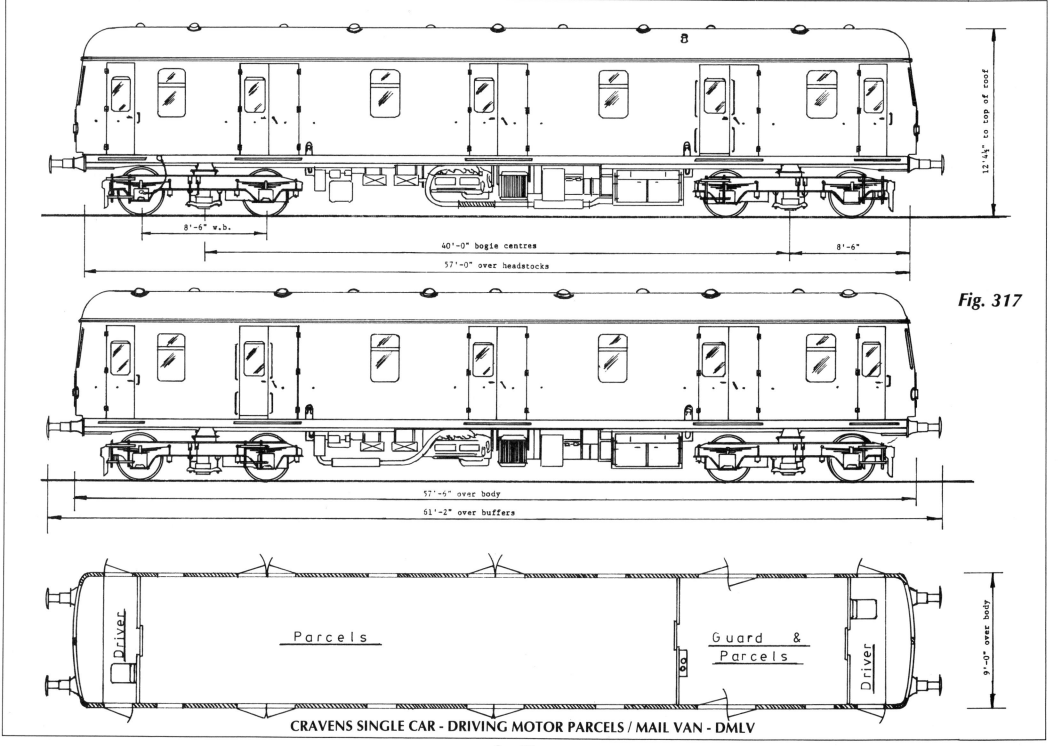

12'4½" to top of roof

8'-6" w.b.

40'-0" bogie centres

8'-6"

57'-0" over headstocks

Fig. 317

57'-6" over body

61'-2" over buffers

9'-0" over body

Driver

Parcels

Guard & Parcels

Driver

CRAVENS SINGLE CAR - DRIVING MOTOR PARCELS / MAIL VAN - DMLV

CHAPTER FOURTEEN

The Four Wheeled Railbuses

1) 1952 BUT Units

As a private venture the BUT Company (an AEC / Leyland joint venture) built a series of eleven four-wheeled railbuses to three designs and after a period of evaluation BR took them into stock. The basic unit was the Driving Motor Brake Second which could operate as a self-contained 'train ' having driving controls at each end and guard's / luggage accommodation. This type could operate in multiple with the Driving Motor Second which also had controls at each end but had no guard's van. Both types could be strengthened to a three car train by the insertion of the Trailer Second. Each power car was fitted with an AEC 6-cylinder 125 bhp engine with the standard mechanical transmission.

All three types had the same 37' 6" bodyshell and when built had full depth skirts covering underframes.

Driving Motor Brake Second - DMBS

Seats:	28 second
Nos:	M79742 (Lot No. 30128)
	M79743/4 (Lot No. 30174)
	M79750 (Lot No. 30216)
Weight:	15 tons 0 cwt.
Drawings:	*Fig.318*. Plan view as *fig.319*
	End view as *fig.320*.

Trailer Second - TS

Seats:	48 second
Nos:	M79741 (Lot No. 30128)
	M79746/7 (Lot No. 30176)
	M79749 (Lot No. 30215)
Weight:	10 tons 0 cwt.
Drawings:	*Fig.321*. Plan as *fig.322*.
	End view as *fig.320*.

Driving Motor Second - DMS

Seats:	34 second
Nos:	M79740 (Lot No. 30128)
	M79745 (Lot No. 30175)
	M79748 (Lot No. 30214)
Weight:	15 tons 0 cwt.
Drawings:	*Fig.323*. Plan as *fig. 324*.
	End view as *fig.320*.

2) The 1958 Units

In 1958 British Rail placed twenty two four-wheeled railbuses into service on rural lines as a last attempt to avoid their complete threatened closure. In most cases the attempt failed and the railbuses had a comparatively short working life. The fleet came from five different builders and each had its own distinctive character.

a) Bristol - ECW cars

This well known combination of state owned companies supplied virtually all the 'buses and coaches of the BTC 'bus operating concerns. They built two railbuses which incorporated considerable quantities of standard 'bus items, particularly seats and windows. The motif on the ends of the cars was the same as that on the front of the Bristol MW 'buses and coaches built around the same time. Power was supplied by a single Gardner 6HLW six-cylinder horizontal 'bus engine of 112 bhp driving through a five speed epicyclic gearbox manufactured by Self-Changing Gears Ltd. The overall length was 42' 4"and they seated 56 second class passengers.

Nos:	SC79958 / 9	(Lot No. 30483)
Weight:	13 tons 0 cwt.	
Drawing:	*Fig.325*	

b) Waggon und Maschinenbau Units

The only units supplied from outside the UK were these five cars. They were constructed to the manufacturer's standard design adapted to the requirements of British Rail. Unlike the other railbuses, these were fitted with buffers and drawgear and could be coupled to other vehicles, so hauling freight or an extra coach. They were also the only railbuses fitted with MV connections and control gear, but could only be coupled to others of the same type. Of the five built, four found their way onto Preserved Railways - a high survival rate ! The standard engine was the Buessing 150 bhp bus engine driving through a cardan shaft to a ZF electro-magnetic six-speed gearbox. Unit E79963 was fitted with an AEC A220X engine and used for performance comparison purposes. These 56 seat second class vehicles were 41' 10" long.

Nos:	E19960 - 4	(Lot No. 30482)
Weight:	15 tons 0 cwt.	
Drawings:	*Fig.326*.	

c) D.Wickham & Co Ltd. Units

This company built five railbuses on similar principles to the low-density units which have already been described and were later involved with constructing experimental railcars derived from the Leyland National 'bus.

Their railbuses were each powered by a Meadows six-cylinder type 6HDT500 engine of 105bhp with transmission via a Freeborn-Wickham disc-and- ring coupling, driving a Self-Changing Gears Ltd. four-speed gearbox and cardan shaft to the final drive. The 38' 0" long vehicle had 44 second class seats.

Wickham did construct one other four-wheeled vehicle in 1959 and this was very similar (bodily) to the railbus, but had a special chassis and was a Track Recording Vehicle. An excellent article on this vehicle by *P. Entwist* appeared in the November 1959 issue of *Model Railway News*. Because of the similarity in the body design, this vehicle was often mistaken for one of the railbuses.

Nos:	SC79965 - 9	(Lot No. 30481)
Weight:	11 tons 5 cwt.	
Drawing:	*Fig.327.*	

d) Park Royal units

Another well established 'bus body builder, Park Royal Vehicles Ltd built five handsome railbuses drawing heavily on their 'bus building experience. Being an associate of AEC within the ACV Group they (naturally) selected an AEC 150 bhp engine which had a similar drive train to the other railbuses. It contained 50 second class seats within its 42' 0" body length.

Nos:	M79970 - 4	(Lot No. 30480)
Weight:	15 tons 0 cwt.	
Drawing:	*Fig.328.*	

e) AC Cars units

Quite how AC Cars came to be involved in the Railbus project is something of a mystery since they were famous for building invalid cars and high performance sports and racing cars. However they built five units using AEC 150 bhp engines with standard transmission. The bodies were 36' 0" long and provided second class seating for 46.

Nos:	W79975 - 9	(Lot No, 30479)
Weight:	11 tons 0cwt.	
Drawing:	*Fig.329.*	

General

As the various lines closed these units became redundant and they all migrated to the Scottish Region and their running numbers carried the SC prefix. The livery throughout their short service lives was the standard green with cream lining and they eventually received small yellow panels below the cab windscreens. An interesting experiment which was only partially successful. Seven of the twenty two passed into railway preservation, but these only represented two types - the German and AC Cars. No.79979 was scrapped in 1992 so that only six now remain.

Car No. 79979 was the first vehicle actually completed and had the horns mounted on the top of the roof whereas all the others had their warning horns mounted below the buffer beams.

Two views of the retractable steps fitted to the Wickham railbuses. *Left* - shown in the raised position and *right* - in the down position. *Railway Gazette.*

AC Cars railbus No. SC79975 in smart green and cream livery with whiskers at Swindon shed on 27th September, 1959.

Merchant Navy Loco. Pres. Soc. Ltd.

Park Royal railbus No. SC79970 in green and cream livery with yellow end panel.

C.Reid.

Wickham railbus No. SC79969 in green and cream livery with whiskers.

M.Smith/Kelland collection.

Bristol - ECW railbus No. SC79958 in green livery. Note the Bristol MW 'bus style motif on the end.

Railway Gazette.

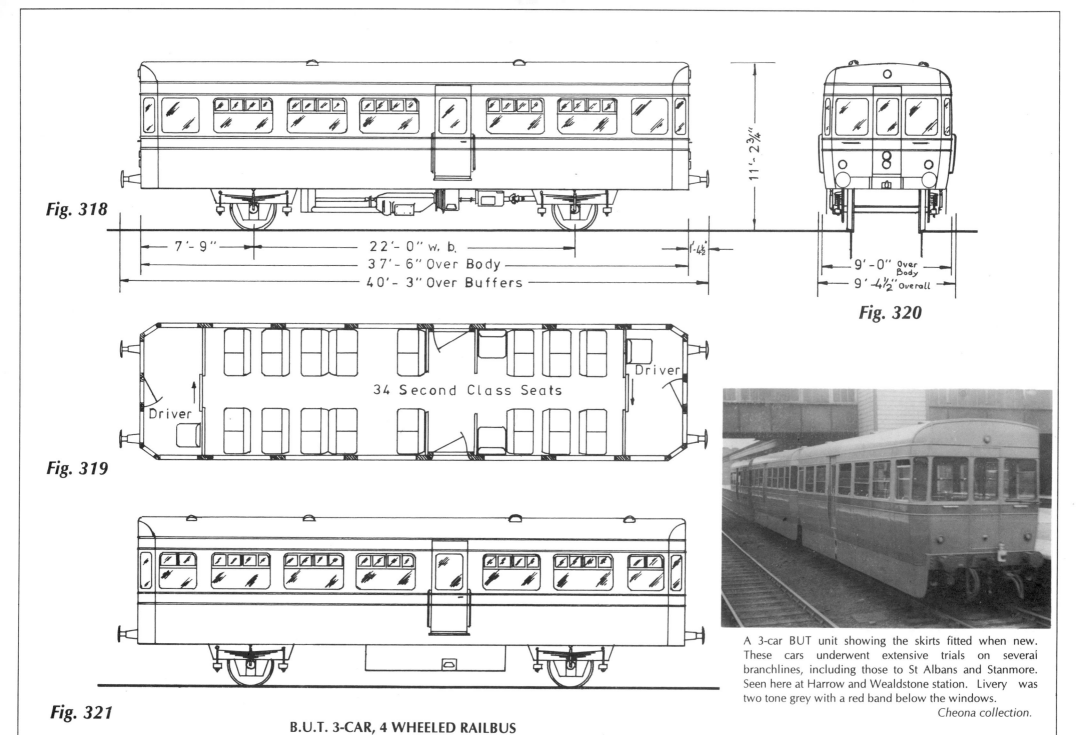

Fig. 318

11'- 2 3/4"

7'- 9"   22'- 0" w. b.   1'-4½"

37'- 6" Over Body

40'- 3" Over Buffers

9'- 0" Over Body

9'- 4½" Overall

Fig. 320

Driver

34 Second Class Seats

Driver

Fig. 319

A 3-car BUT unit showing the skirts fitted when new. These cars underwent extensive trials on several branchlines, including those to St Albans and Stanmore. Seen here at Harrow and Wealdstone station. Livery was two tone grey with a red band below the windows.

Cheona collection.

Fig. 321

B.U.T. 3-CAR, 4 WHEELED RAILBUS

Fig 322

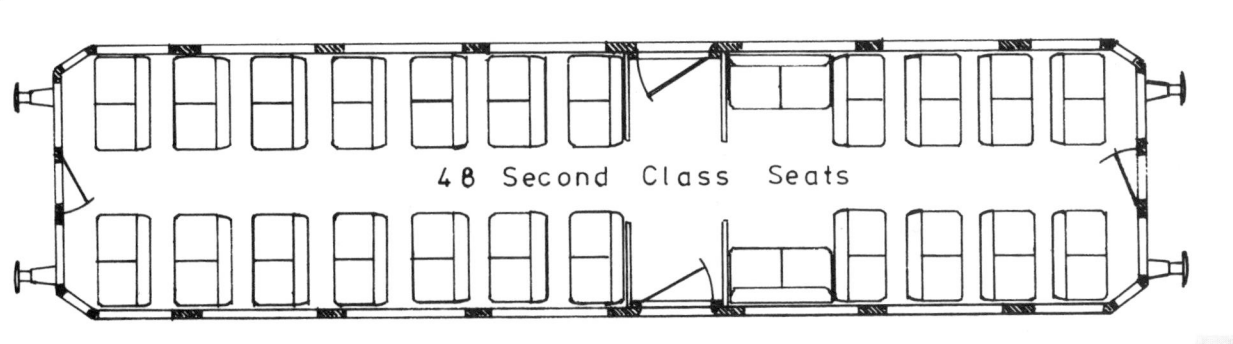

48 Second Class Seats

Fig. 323

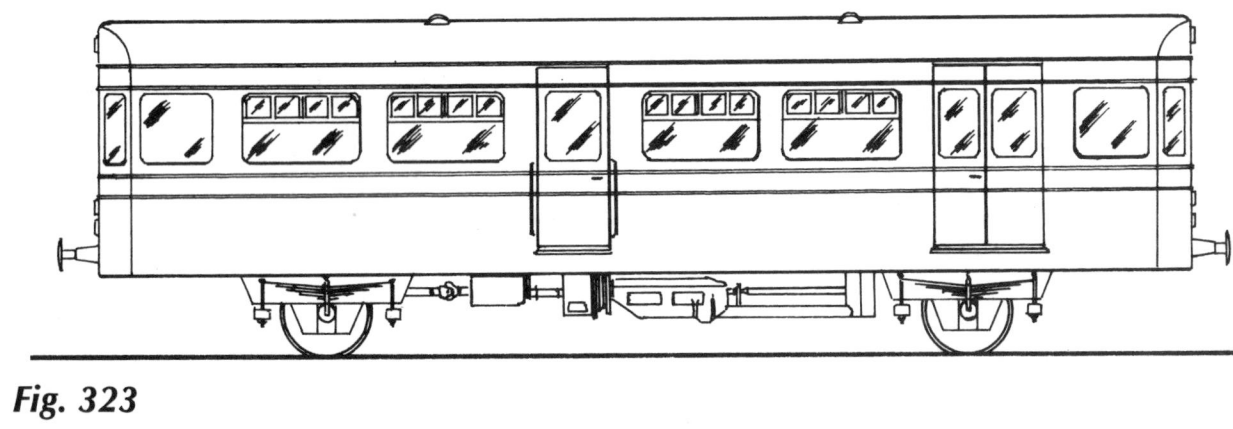

BUT 4-wheeled railcars seen here in 1961 stored at Derby Friargate Goods yard, minus their skirts but still wearing the green and cream livery.   *R.S. Carpenter.*

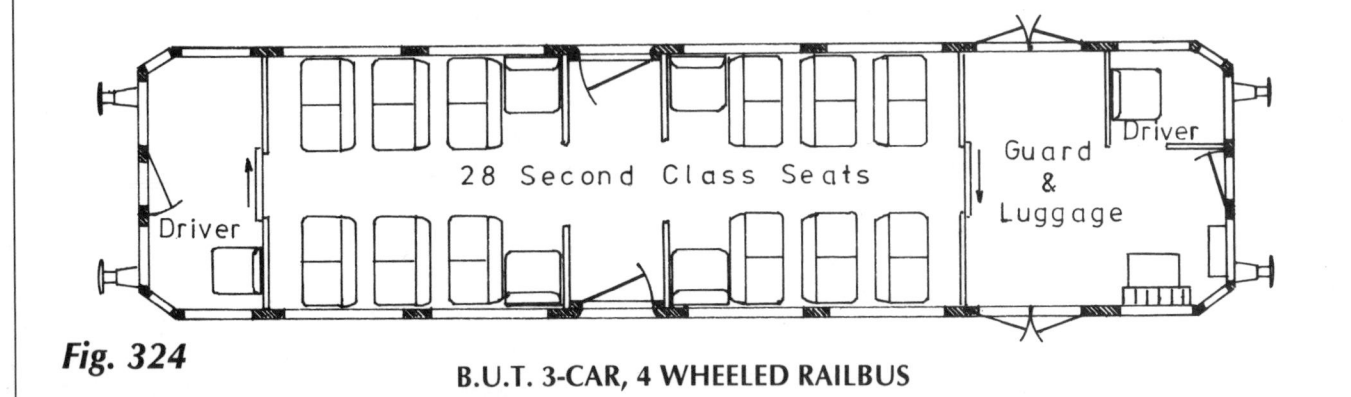

Driver

28 Second Class Seats

Guard & Luggage

Driver

Fig. 324

B.U.T. 3-CAR, 4 WHEELED RAILBUS

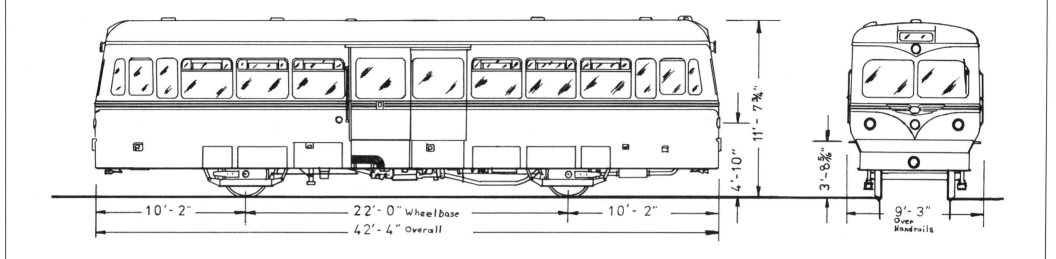

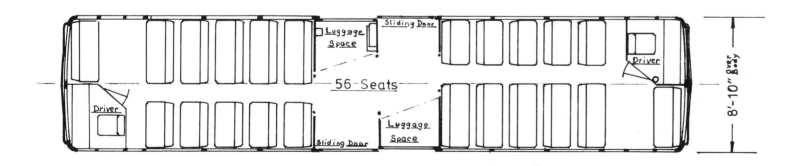

BRISTOL - E.C.W. 4 WHEELED RAILBUS

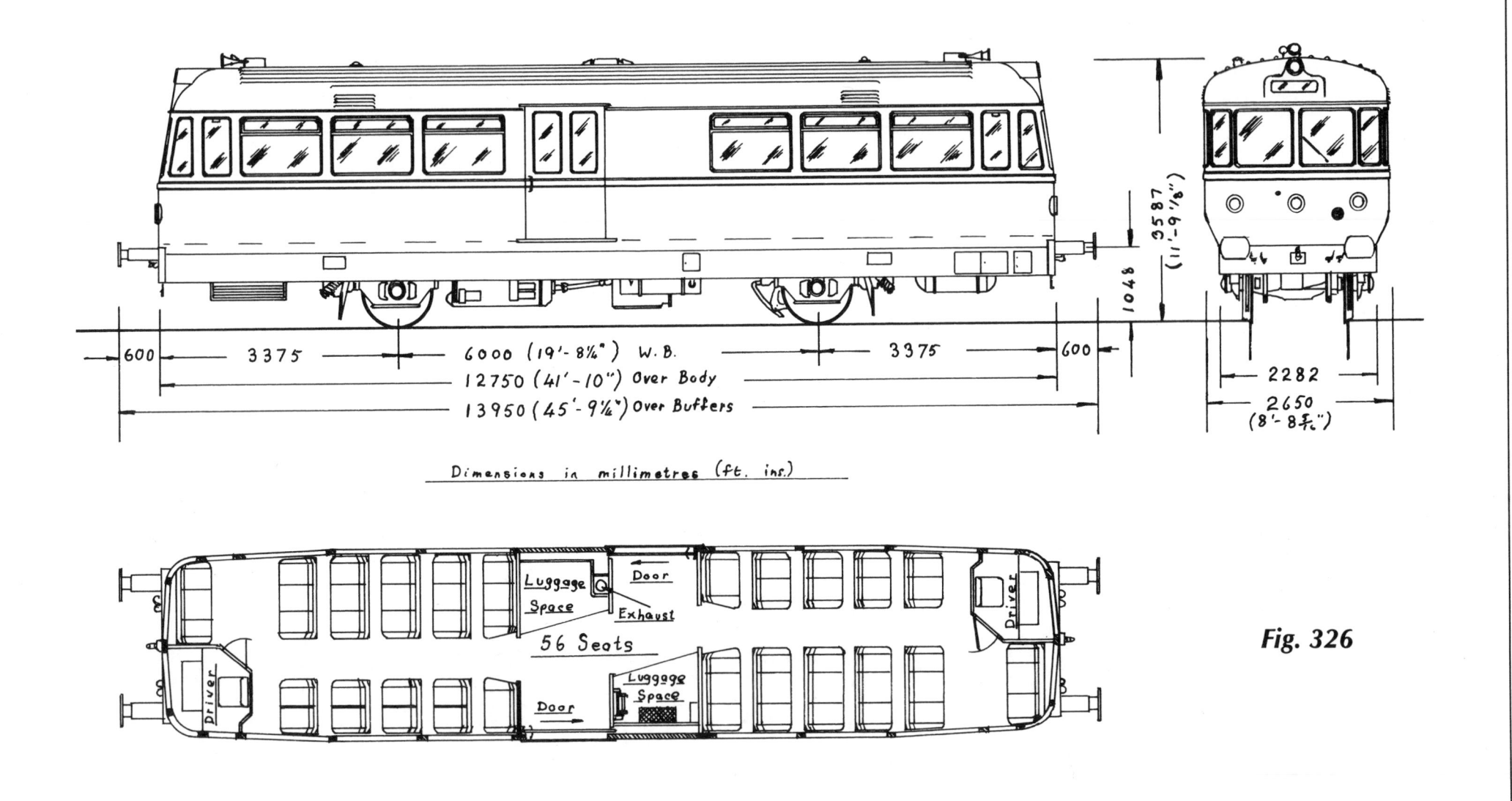

600 | 3375 | 6000 (19'-8¼") W.B. | 3375 | 600

12750 (41'-10") Over Body

13950 (45'-9¼") Over Buffers

3587 (11'-9⅛")

1048

2282

2650 (8'-8¾")

Dimensions in millimetres (ft. ins.)

Luggage Space

Door

Exhaust

56 Seats

Door

Luggage Space

Driver

Driver

Fig. 326

WAGGON UND MASCHINEN A.G. 4 WHEELED RAILBUS

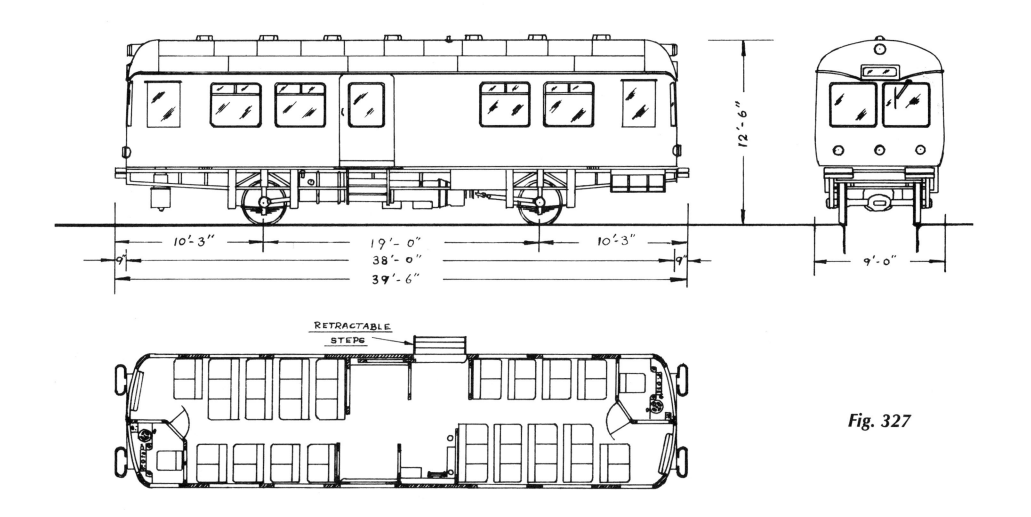

12'-6"

10'-3"   19'-0"   10'-3"
9"   38'-0"   9"
39'-6"

9'-0"

RETRACTABLE
STEPS

Fig. 327

WICKHAM 4 WHEELED RAILBUS

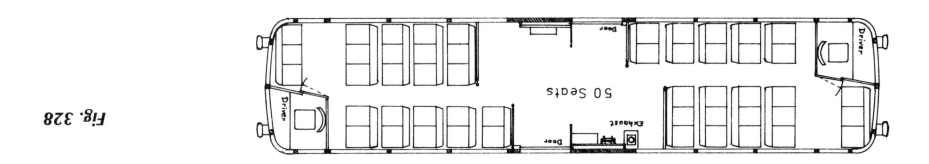

50 Seats

Fig. 328

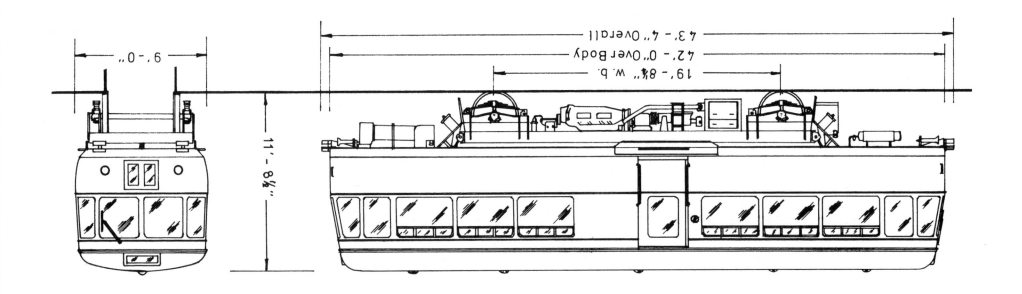

9'-0"

43'-4" Overall

42'-0" Over Body

19'-8¾" w.b.

11'-8½"

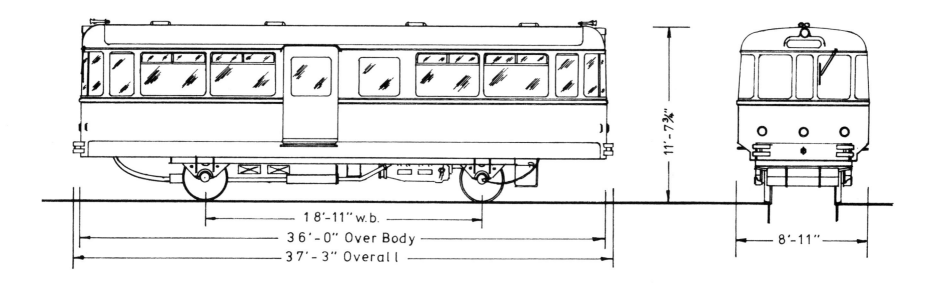

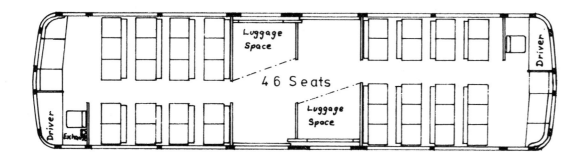

18'-11" w.b.

36'-0" Over Body

37'-3" Overall

11'-7¾"

8'-11"

Luggage Space

Luggage Space

46 Seats

Driver

Driver

Exhaust

Fig. 329

A.C.CARS 4 WHEELED RAILBUS

CHAPTER FIFTEEN

Hastings Main Line Units

As we have seen the Classic DMU saw service on all the regions except the Southern. The reason for this was that the Southern already had the most intensely developed network of electrified lines and it was logical to develop these even further in the Modernisation Plan. This led to the Kent Coast Electrification scheme and a number of other local extensions and eventually to the later Bournemouth and Weymouth schemes. The stock for the Modernisation Plan schemes was derived from the designs of the Southern Railway using British Rail Mk 1 standard coach components.

The Region was left with a number of lines on which it was not possible at that time to install the third rail. Notable amongst these was the Charing Cross to Hastings line. To serve this group of services and other feeder and cross country routes, the Southern developed a series of DEMU sets following the style of the contemporary EMU's.

In all the DEMU sets each power car had an English Electric four-cylinder type 4SRKT Mk 2 diesel engine of 500 bhp (600bhp in two and three car sets). The engine was coupled to a generator in the same manner as in the conventional diesel-electric locomotive. Engine and generator were mounted above the floor in a large engine room with removable hatches in the roof to facilitate removal of the complete power plant for major overhauls.

1) 1957 short bodied units - TOPS Class 201

The units for the Hastings line were distinctive due to restricted clearances which resulted in very narrow bodies. The first deliveries in 1957 were a batch of seven six-car units (with slab sides) only 8' 2½" wide. The style of the windows and general appearance was in line with the new EMU stock for the Kent Coast Line as far as the restricted dimensions would allow. These early cars were built on the shorter (57') underframe being 58' overall. The formations were fixed in common with the established SR practice and the units were allocated set Nos: 1001 - 1007. The formation was DMBSO, TSOL, TFK, TSOL, TSOL and DMBSO.

Driving Motor Brake Open Second - DMBSO

Seats:	22 second
Nos:	S60000 - 13 (Lot No. 30329)
Weight:	54 tons 0 cwt.
Drawings:	*Fig.330*. End view as *fig.349*.

Trailer Open Second with Lavatory - TSOL

Seats:	52 second
Nos:	S60500 - 20 (Lot No. 30331)
Weight:	28 tons 0 cwt.
Drawing:	*Fig.331*

Trailer Corridor First with Lavatory - TFK

Seats:	42 first
Nos:	S60700 - 6 (Lot No. 30330)
Drawing:	*Fig.332.*

In the later years the TFK cars were downgraded to composite seating (36 first and 6 second). In 1965 sets 1002 - 1004 were disbanded and the trailer cars used as spares whilst the power cars became the basis of the 'Tadpoles 'or 3-R sets. In 1981 sets 1002 and 1004 were reformed and the two power cars from 1003 set became spares.

2) 1957 built long framed units - TOPS Class 202

These sets proved successful and later the same year (1957) nine more were built, but on the longer frames. The original units were classified 6-S prior to the TOPS system and the second series were 6-L indicating six-car short or long framed cars. They were to the same layout as the earlier examples with an additional seating bay or compartment. Set Nos: were 1011 - 1019

Driving Motor Brake Open Second - DMBSO

Seats:	30 second
Nos:	S60014 - 19 (Lot No. 30395)
	S60020 - 31 (Lot No. 30391)
Weight:	55 tons 0 cwt.
Drawings:	*Fig.333*. End view as *fig.349*.

Trailer Open Second with Lavatory - TSOL

Seats:	60 second
Nos:	S60521 - 29 (Lot No. 30397)
	S60530 - 47 (Lot No. 30394)
Weight:	29 tons 0 cwt.
Drawing:	*Fig.334.*

Trailer Corridor First with Lavatory - TFK

Seats:	48 first
Nos:	S60707 - 09 (Lot No. 30396)
	S60710 - 15 (Lot No. 30392)
Weight:	29 tons 0 cwt.
Drawing:	*Fig.335.*

Like the earlier sets these had their TFK vehicle downgraded to composite with 36 first and 12 second class seats in later years.

3) 1958 built long framed Buffet units - TOPS Class 203

Seven additional sets were introduced in 1958, again constructed on long frames, but with a trailer buffet car in place of one of the trailer seconds. In all other respects they were identical to the 6-L sets being given the classification 6-B (six-car buffet set). The normal formation for the principal trains on the Hastings line was a 6-L coupled to a 6-B. However, since the sets had no end gangways the buffet facilities were only available to half the train's passengers.

These sets were numbered 1031 - 1037.

Driving Motor Brake Open Second - DMBSO

Seats:	30 second
Nos:	S60032 - 45 (Lot No. 30391)
Weight:	55 tons 0 cwt.
Drawings:	*Fig.333.* End view as *fig.349.*

Trailer Open Second with Lavatory - TSOL

Seats:	60 second
Nos:	S60548 - 61 (Lot No. 30394)
Weight:	29 tons 0 cwt.
Drawing:	*Fig.334.*

Trailer Corridor First - TFK

Seats:	48 first
Nos:	S60716 - 22 (Lot No. 30392)
Weight:	29 tons 0 cwt.
Drawing:	*Fig.335.*

Trailer Buffet - TRB

Seats:	21 buffet
Nos:	S60750 - 56 (Lot No. 30393)
Weight:	34 tons 0 cwt.
Drawing:	Fig.336.

Once again the TFK cars were later downgraded to TCK with 36 first and 12 second class seats. However, more fundamental changes affected these sets over the years. First of all sets 1031 & 1032 were reformed as 6-L units by the transfer of TSOL car No. S60551 from 1032 to 1031 and the inclusion of downgraded TFK's S60701 & S60702 as TSK from the disbanded sets 1002 and 1003. This released TRB's S60750 (which became RDB975386 'Hastings' and was used by the Railway Technical Centre as an APT tilt test vehicle) and S60755 (which became RDB975025 - the Southern Region General Manager's saloon).

In 1980 the remaining TRB's were withdrawn and sets 1034 - 1037 were reclassified 5-L (five-car long framed sets). Further remarshalling also occurred with the withdrawal of set 1033.

General

When new these cars carried the BR livery version of SR Malachite Green with no lining and power cars carried the coaching stock crest. Later the first class and buffet cars carried the identifying colour bands at cantrail level in cream (first class) and red (buffet) respectively. Small yellow warning panels appeared on some of the sets before the standard blue and grey livery with the full yellow ends engulfed the entire Hastings fleet.

Class 202 Hastings unit No.1016 in green livery at Battle.   *Cheona collection.*

Class 203 Hastings unit No.1034 in green livery with DMBSO nearest the camera at Tonbridge.

The late R.Mack.

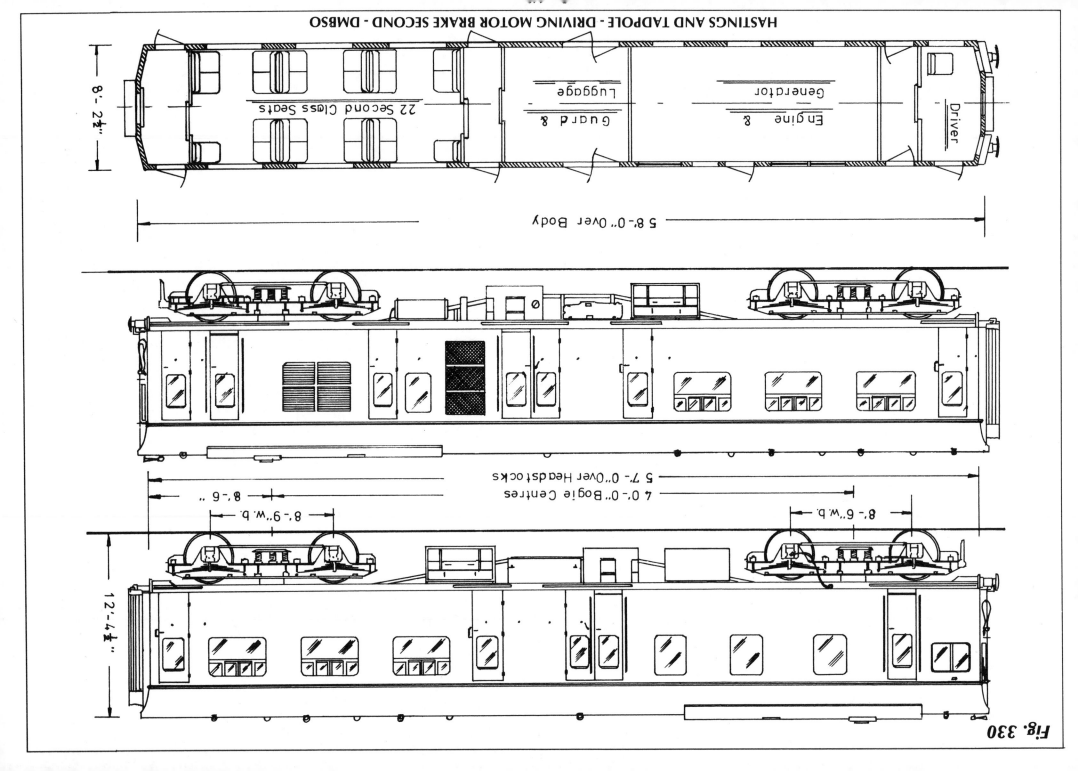

HASTINGS AND TADPOLE - DRIVING MOTOR BRAKE SECOND - DMBSO

Driver

Engine & Generator

Guard & Luggage

22 Second Class Seats

8'- 2½"

5 8'-0" Over Body

5 7'-0" Over Headstocks

4 0'-0" Bogie Centres

8'-6" w.b.

8'-6"

8'- 9" w.b.

12'-4½"

Fig. 330

Fig. 331

12'- 4½"

8'- 6'w.b.

8'- 6''

40'- 0'' Bogie   Centres

57'- 0'' Over   Headstocks

58'- 0'' Over   Body

Lav.

Lav.

8'- 2½"

22 Second Class Seats

30 Second Class Seats

HASTINGS AND TADPOLE - TRAILER OPEN SECONDS - TSOL

Class 201 DMBSO No. S60005 leads this early Hastings unit on the 57' chassis. Livery is the BR version of malachite green.

Railway Gazette

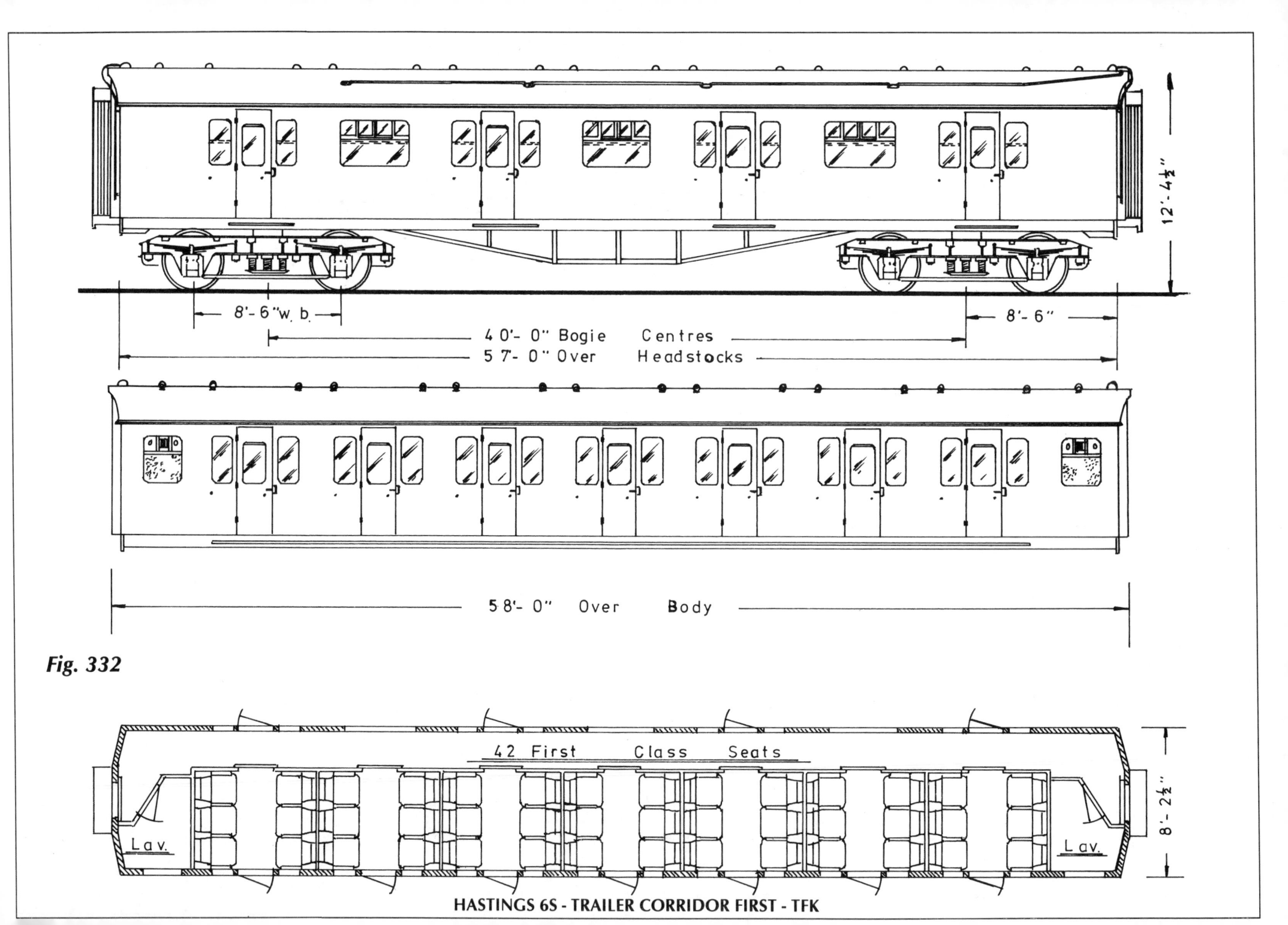

12'-4½"

8'-6" w.b.

40'-0" Bogie Centres

57'-0" Over Headstocks

8'-6"

58'-0" Over Body

Fig. 332

42 First Class Seats

8'-2½"

Lav.

Lav.

HASTINGS 6S - TRAILER CORRIDOR FIRST - TFK

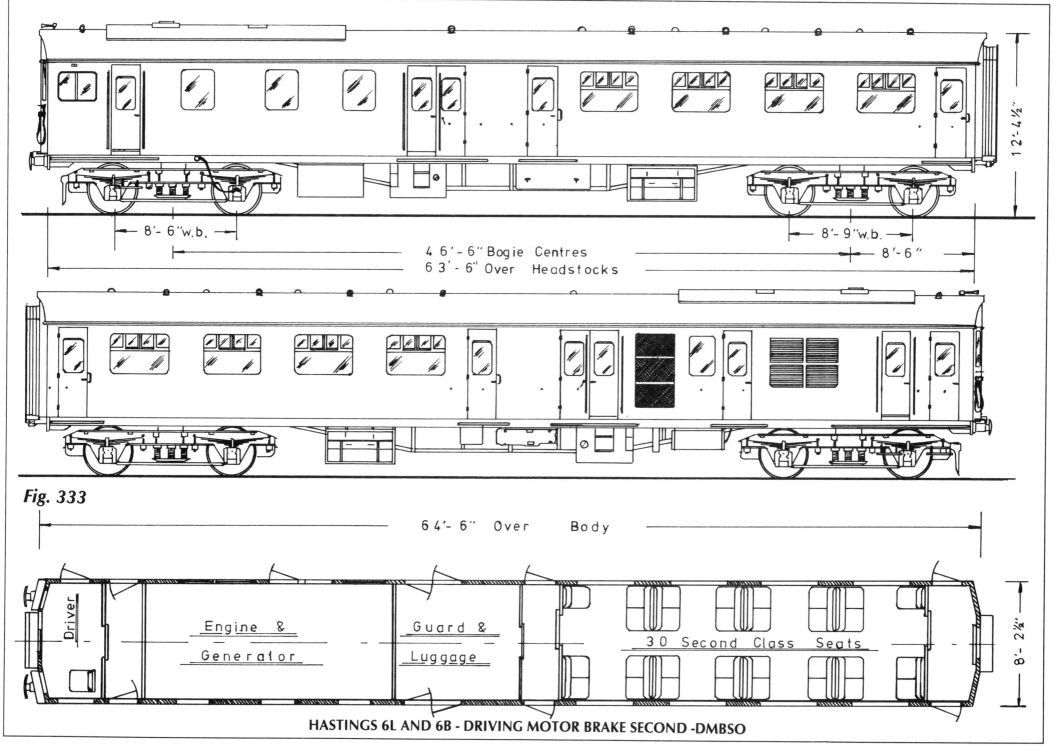

Fig. 333

4 6'– 6" Bogie Centres

6 3'– 6" Over Headstocks

8'– 6" w.b.

8'– 9" w.b.

8'– 6"

12'– 4½"

64'– 6" Over Body

8'– 2½"

Driver

Engine & Generator

Guard & Luggage

30 Second Class Seats

HASTINGS 6L AND 6B - DRIVING MOTOR BRAKE SECOND -DMBSO

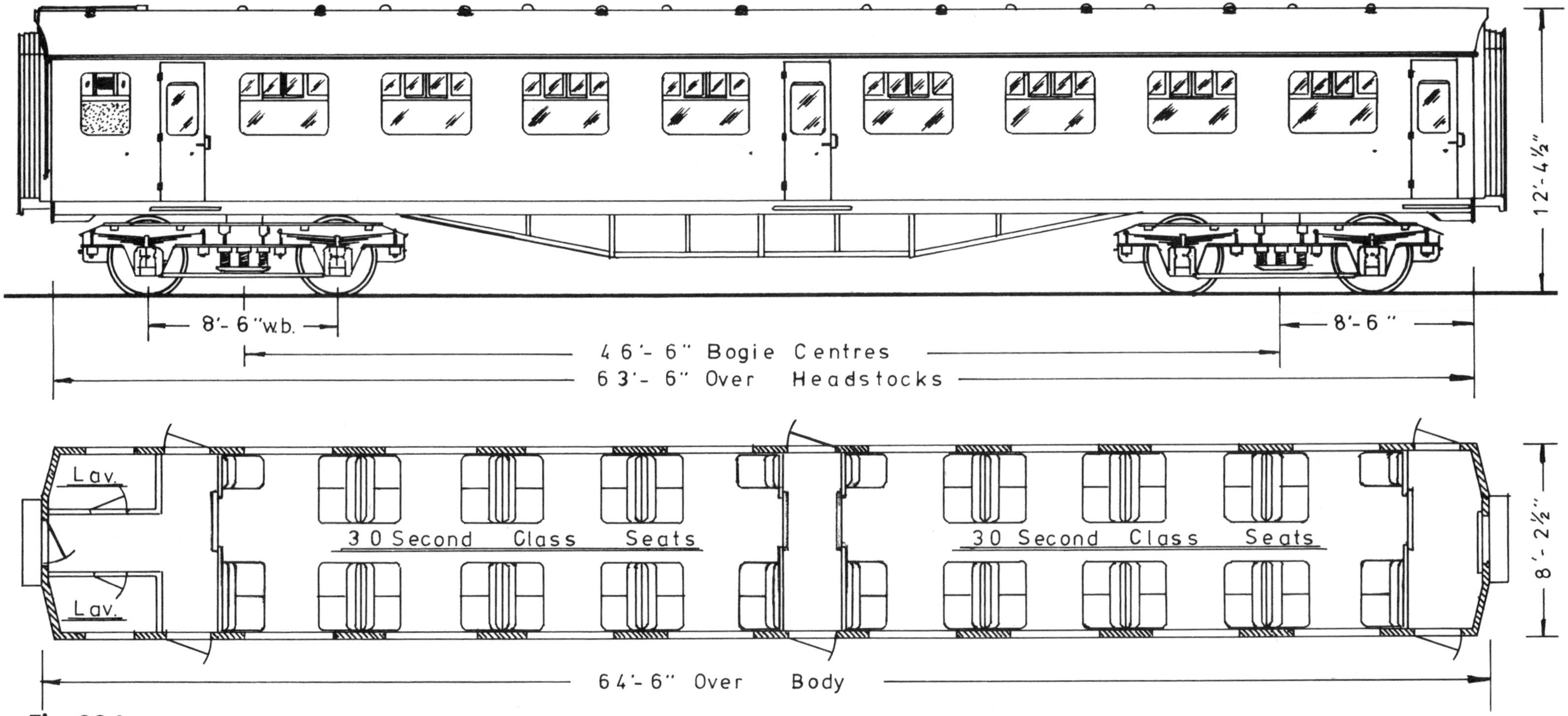

12'- 4½"
8'- 6"w.b.
8'- 6"
4 6'- 6" Bogie Centres
6 3'- 6" Over Headstocks
Lav.
Lav.
3 0 Second Class Seats
3 0 Second Class Seats
8'- 2½"
6 4'- 6" Over Body

Fig. 334

HASTINGS 6L AND 6B - TRAILER OPEN SECOND - TSOL

1007
13

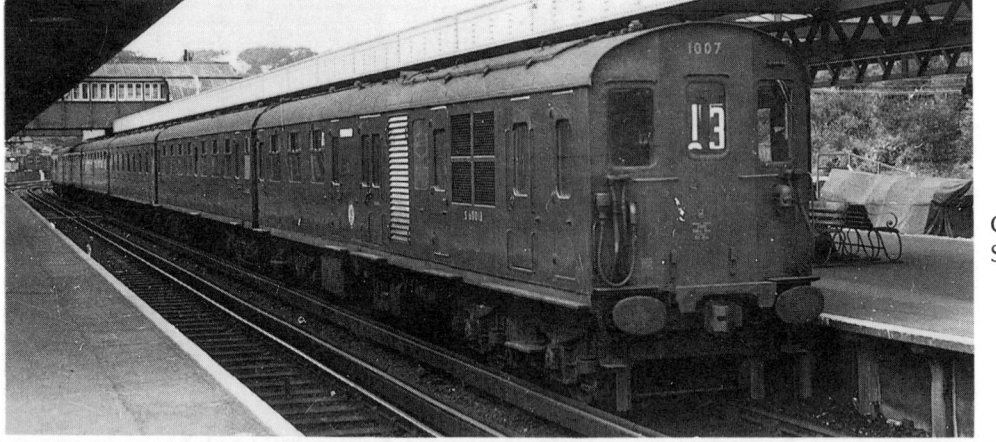

Class 201, set 1007, Hastings 6-car unit with DMBSO No. S60013 nearest the camera. *M.Smith/Kelland collection.*

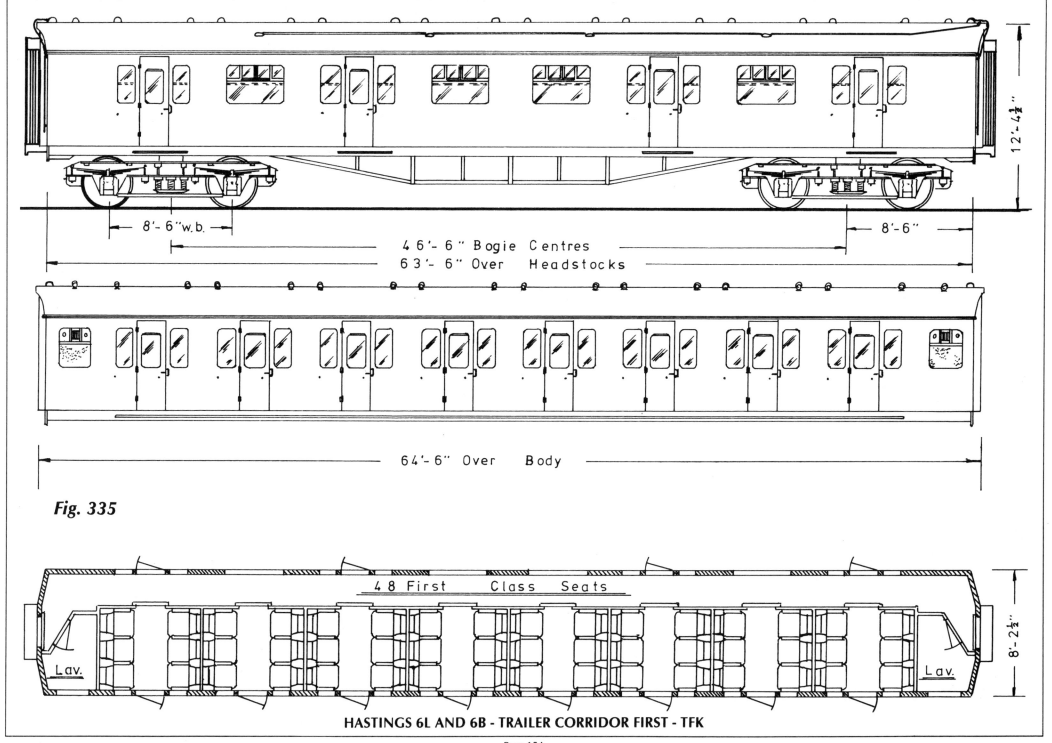

Fig. 335

4 6'- 6" Bogie Centres
6 3'- 6" Over Headstocks
64'- 6" Over Body

12'- 4½"
8'- 6"w.b.
8'- 6"

4 8 First Class Seats

8'- 2½"

Lav.
Lav.

HASTINGS 6L AND 6B - TRAILER CORRIDOR FIRST - TFK

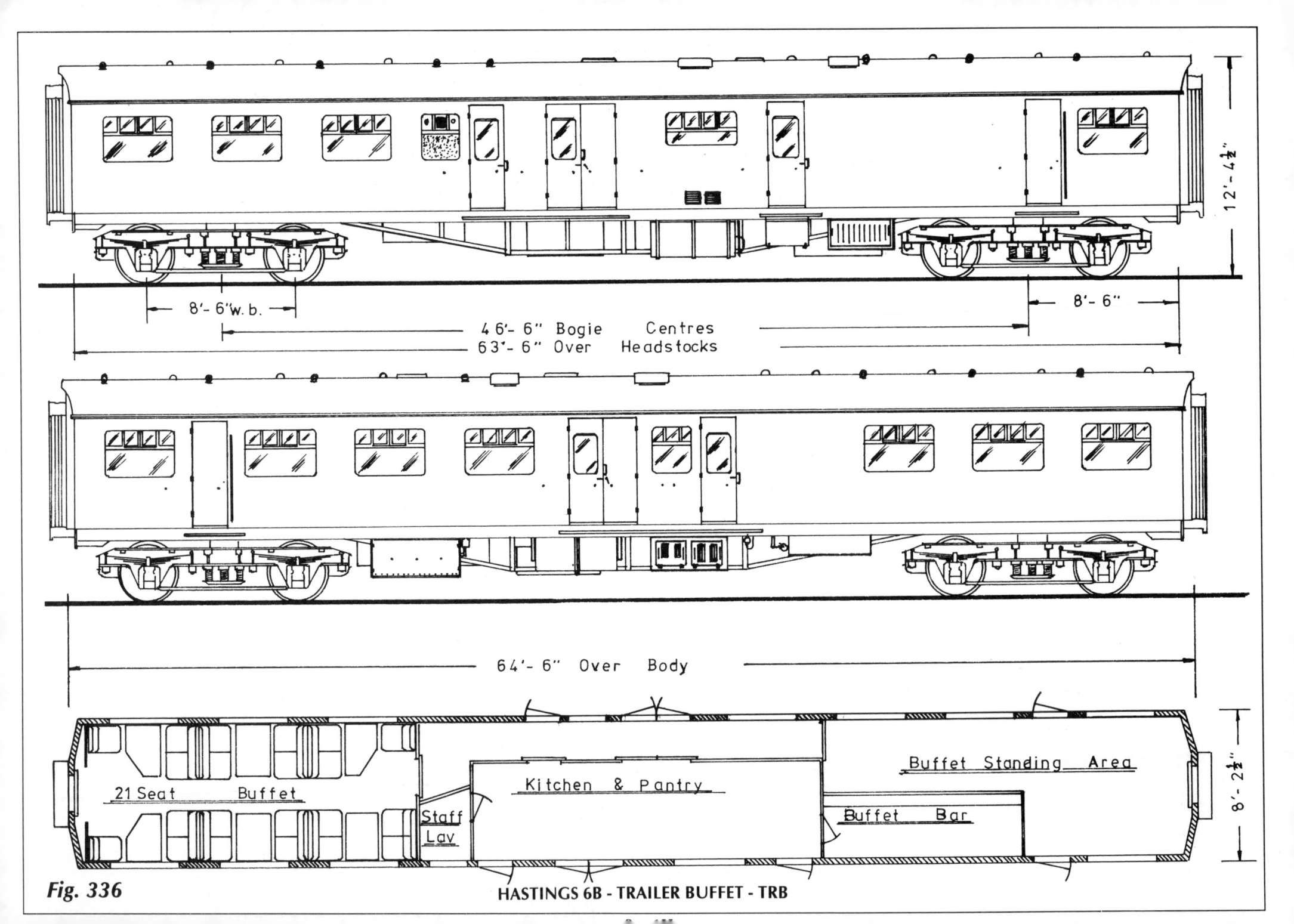

12'-4½"

8'-6" w.b.

8'-6"

46'-6" Bogie Centres
63'-6" Over Headstocks

64'-6" Over Body

8'-2¼"

21 Seat   Buffet

Staff
Lav

Kitchen & Pantry

Buffet Standing Area

Buffet Bar

Fig. 336

HASTINGS 6B - TRAILER BUFFET - TRB

CHAPTER SIXTEEN

Berks & Hants Two and Three car Units

At the same time as the Hastings corridor sets were being produced, Eastleigh Works, Southampton were developing a series of non-corridor sets for use on non-electrified lines on the Southern Region. These were initially turned out as two-car sets comprising a Driving Motor Brake Second and a Driving Trailer Composite, virtually identical to the DTCL cars then being produced for the 2-HAP electric units. The first 18 sets were introduced in 1957 and were allotted set numbers 1101 - 1118. They were classified 2-H (two car Hampshire sets) and later became TOPS Class 204.

There was one difference between the DTCL on these sets and their EMU equivalents in that the compartment next to the driver's cab was second class. this compartment was later converted into luggage space.

Driving Motor Brake Open Second - DMBSO

Seats:	52 second
Nos:	S60100 - 17 (Lot No. 30332)
Weight:	56 tons 0 cwt.
Drawings:	Fig.337 and fig.338. Note: Fig.337 shows the five seating bay layout whilst fig.338 shows the later four bay type. Plan as fig.340. End view as fig.350.

Driving Trailer Composite with Lavatory - DTCL

Seats:	13 first, 62 second (later 50)
Nos:	S60800 - 17 (Lot No. 30333)
Weight:	32 tons 0 cwt.
Drawings:	Fig.341 with plan as fig.342. End view as fig.350.

Four more of these two-car sets (1119 - 1122) were built in 1958 to the same layout as before.

Driving Motor Brake Open Second - DMBSO

Nos:	S60118 - 21 (Lot No. 30398)

Driving Trailer Composite with Lavatory - DTCL

Nos:	S60818 - 21 (Lot No. 30399)

These sets were strengthened to 3-H configuration in 1979 following the reforming of sets with the abandonment of the 'Tadpoles' and the inclusion of a second DTCL.

In 1959 sets 1101 - 1118 were also strengthened to three car sets by the addition of newly built trailer open seconds, having two open saloons similar to those on the contemporary 4-EPB electrics. In this revised form they were reclassified 3-H and became TOPS Class 205.

Trailer Semi Open Second - TSO

Seats:	104 second
Nos:	S60650 - 67 (Lot No. 30542)
Weight:	30 tons 0 cwt.
Drawing :	Fig.343 with plan as fig.344.

At this stage sets 1101 - 18 were allocated to Hampshire services and 1119 - 22 to the Hastings area. Four more sets were built for Hampshire and these were the first to be delivered as three-car units. They were also the first to be delivered with a luggage compartment in the DTCL and identical to the strengthened 3-H Class 205 into which they were incorporated.

Driving Motor Brake Open Second - DMBSO

Nos:	S60122 - 25 (Lot No. 30540)

Trailer Semi-Open Second - TSO

Nos:	S60668 - 71 (Lot No. 30542)

Driving Trailer Composite with Lavatory - DTCL

Nos:	S60822 - 25 (Lot No. 30541)

Considerable remarshalling took place in later years involving many of the sets in both the 204 and 205 classes. Several DTCL cars had the luggage compartment rebuilt as a first, with connection to the side corridor giving the same 19 first class section as their sisters in the 2-HAP sets.

The story of these units is completed by the delivery of seven sets (1127 - 1133) for the Berkshire services in 1962. These three car sets differed from the previous deliveries in recognising the lack of luggage space available resulting from the increased seating capacity effected by the inclusion of the centre trailer cars. In this final batch, the number of seating bays in the DMBSO was reduced from five to four to give a corresponding increase in the size of the luggage van. The leading compartment in the DTCL could thus be used for second class seating. Externally this batch had smaller route indicator blinds and were considered part of the 3-H Class 205 fleet.

Driving Motor Brake Open Second - DMBSO

Seats:	42 second
Nos:	S60145 - 51 (Lot No. 30761)
Weight:	56 tons 0 cwt.
Drawings:	Fig.337 and fig.338 (Note : fig.337 shows the earlier five bay layout). Plan as fig.339 End view as fig.351.

Trailer Semi-Open Second - TSO

Seats:	104 second
Nos:	S60672 - 78 (Lot No. 30672)
Weight:	30 tons 0 cwt.
Drawings:	Fig.343. Plan as fig.344.

Driving Trailer Composite with Lavatory - DTCL

Seats: 13 first, 62 second
Nos: S60826 - 32   (Lot No.30673)
Weight: 32 tons 0 cwt.
Drawings: *Fig.341. Plan as fig.342. End view as fig.351.*

When new these sets carried the darker Malachite green livery with the coaching stock crest on the power cars. First class accommodation was identified by a cream band at cantrail level. A later adornment was a large 'V' in orange-yellow on the leading end of the power car to advise platform staff that the approaching train had no luggage accommodation at the rear. The EMU stock had a small inverted black triangle on the yellow panels for the same purpose. From the late 1960's the cars appeared in all over blue with the yellow ends, later they carried the blue and grey livery and finally the Network South-East liveries.

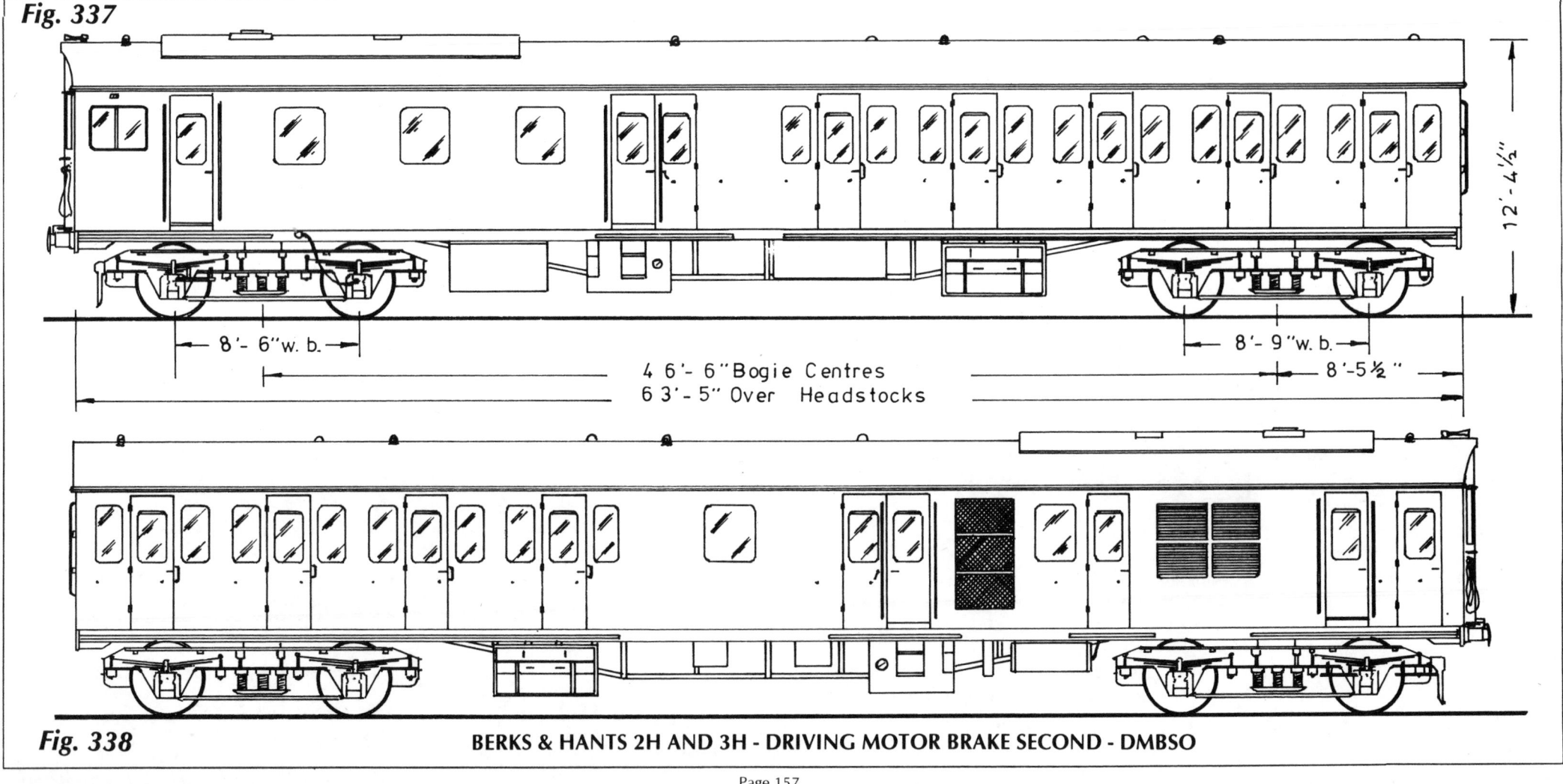

Fig. 337

8'-6" w.b.
46'-6" Bogie Centres
63'-5" Over Headstocks
8'-9" w.b.
8'-5½"
12'-4½"

Fig. 338   BERKS & HANTS 2H AND 3H - DRIVING MOTOR BRAKE SECOND - DMBSO

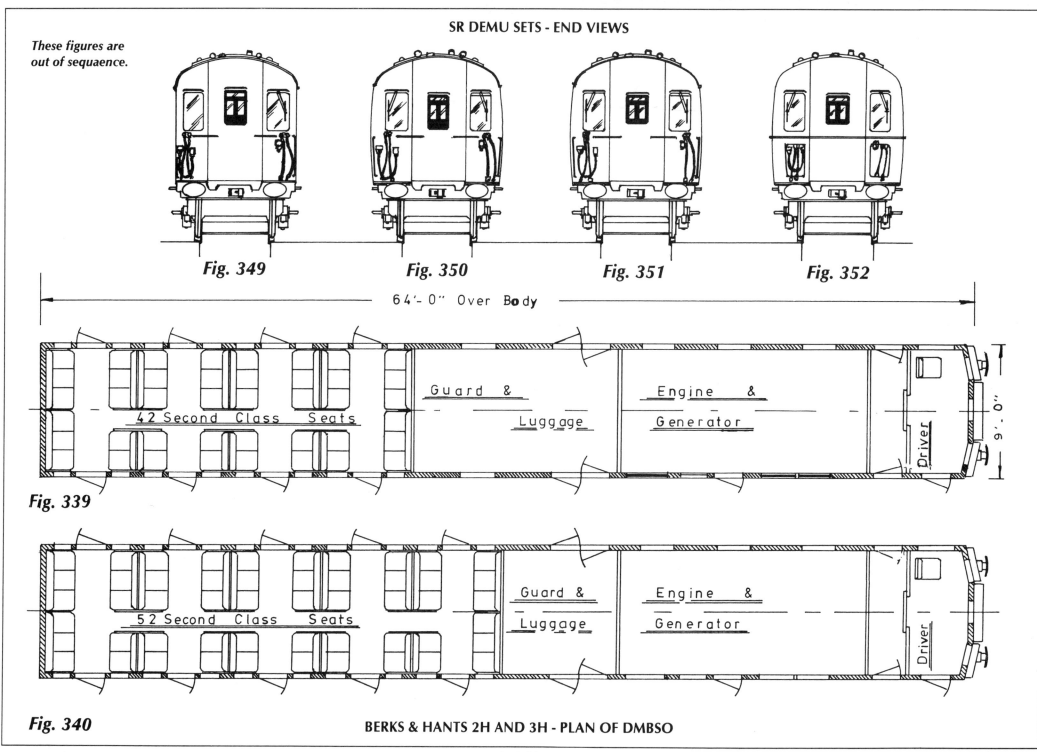

SR DEMU SETS - END VIEWS

These figures are out of sequaence.

Fig. 349　　**Fig. 350**　　**Fig. 351**　　**Fig. 352**

64'-0" Over Body

Guard & Luggage

Engine & Generator

42 Second Class Seats

Driver

9'-0"

Fig. 339

Guard & Luggage

Engine & Generator

52 Second Class Seats

Driver

Fig. 340　　**BERKS & HANTS 2H AND 3H - PLAN OF DMBSO**

Fig. 341

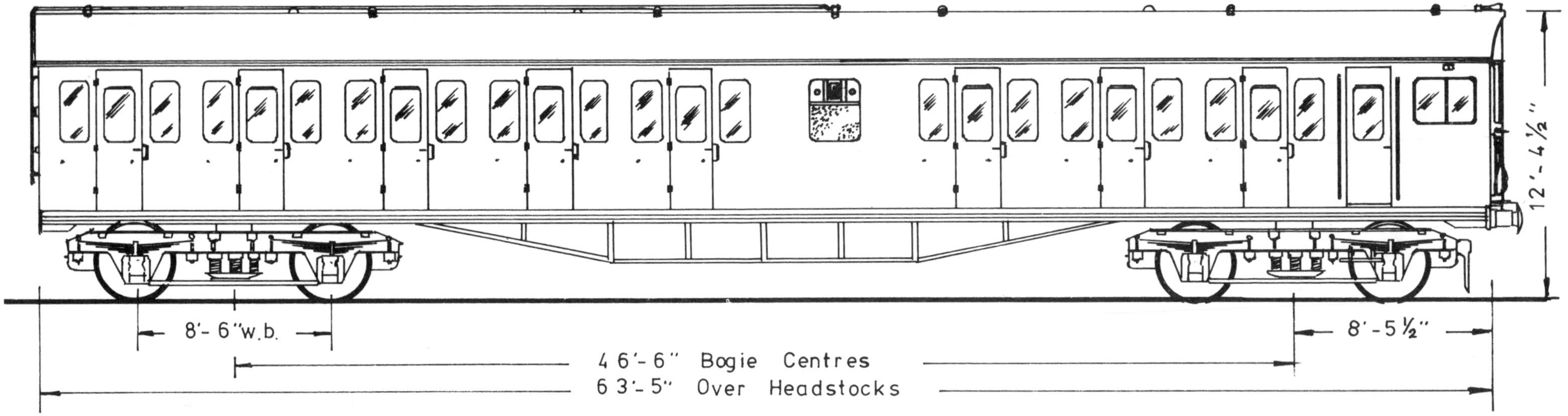

12'-4½"

8'-6" w.b.

8'-5½"

4 6'-6" Bogie Centres

6 3'-5" Over Headstocks

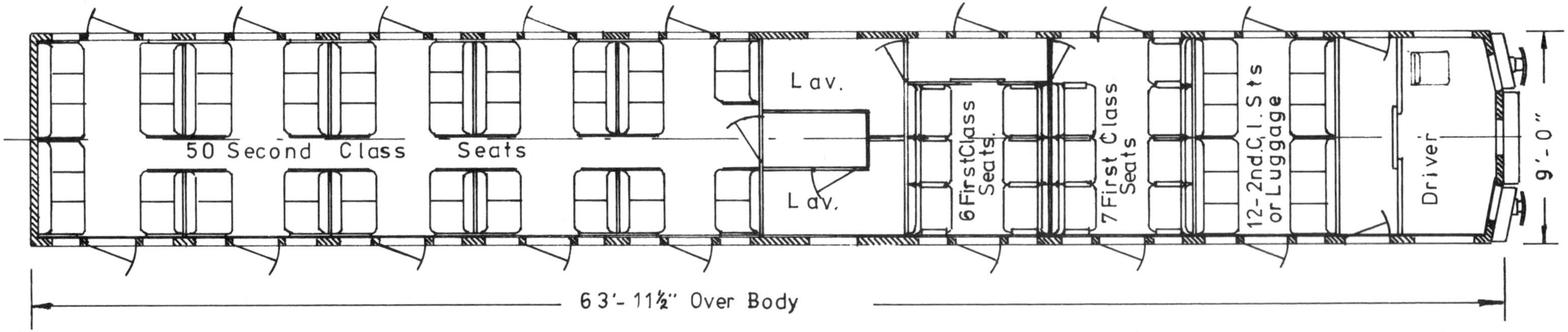

Lav.

50 Second Class Seats

Lav.

6 First Class Seats.

7 First Class Seats

12-2nd.Cl.S†s or Luggage

Driver

9'-0"

6 3'-11½" Over Body

Fig. 342

BERKS & HANTS 2H AND 3H - DRIVING TRAILER COMPOSITE - DTCOL

Class 204 unit No. 1112, with DTCL No. S 60811 nearest the camera, in green livery at Eastleigh, 1959. *R.S.Carpenter.*

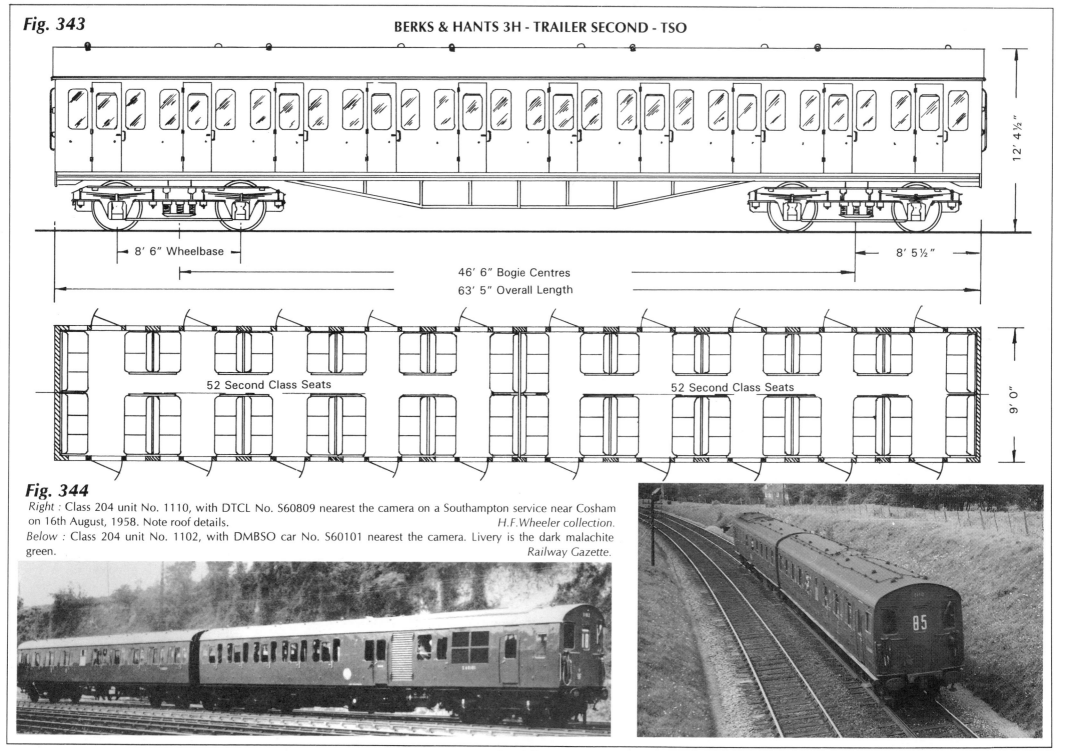

Fig. 343

BERKS & HANTS 3H - TRAILER SECOND - TSO

12' 4½"

8' 6" Wheelbase

8' 5½"

46' 6" Bogie Centres

63' 5" Overall Length

52 Second Class Seats

52 Second Class Seats

9' 0"

Fig. 344

Right : Class 204 unit No. 1110, with DTCL No. S60809 nearest the camera on a Southampton service near Cosham on 16th August, 1958. Note roof details.   *H.F.Wheeler collection.*

Below : Class 204 unit No. 1102, with DMBSO car No. S60101 nearest the camera. Livery is the dark malachite green.   *Railway Gazette.*

CHAPTER SEVENTEEN

East - Sussex three-car units

The East Sussex units, sometimes referred to as the Oxted units, were introduced in 1962 and were to a narrower restriction being only 8' 6" wide - mid way between the Hastings stock and the 2-H and 3-H sets.

Nineteen of these three-car sets were built in 1962 and classified 3-D (TOPS Class 207). Formed as Driving Motor Brake Second, Trailer Composite, Driving Trailer Second their front ends resembled the contemporary Brighton line EMU stock 4-CIG / 4-BIG without gangways.

Driving Motor Brake Second Open - DMBSO

Seats: 42 second
Nos: S60126 - 44   (Lot No. 30625)
Weight: 56 tons 0 cwt.
Drawings: *Fig.345. End view fig.352.*

Trailer composite with Lavatory - TCL

Seats: 24 first, 42 second
Nos: S60600 - 18   (Lot No. 30626)
Weight: 31 tons 0 cwt.
Drawing: *Fig.346.*

Driving Trailer Semi-Open Second - DTSO

Seats: 76 second
Nos: S60900 - 18   (Lot No. 30627)
Weight: 32 tons 0 cwt.
Drawings;   *Fig.347. End view as fig.352*

It will be seen that these sets had a low density seating arrangement with the 2 + 2 configuration in the second class and the three per side in the first class compartments due, in part, to the restricted width.

They followed the same livery changes as the 2- and 3-H sets.

Top right : End view of DTSO No.60901 showing driver's lookout and recesses for jumper and brake connections.   *Railway Gazette.*

Bottom right :
Class 207 East Sussex 3-car unit No. 1318 in green livery with yellow end panel. DTSO car No. S60917 nearest the camera seen at London Bridge, 1968.   *Cheona collection.*

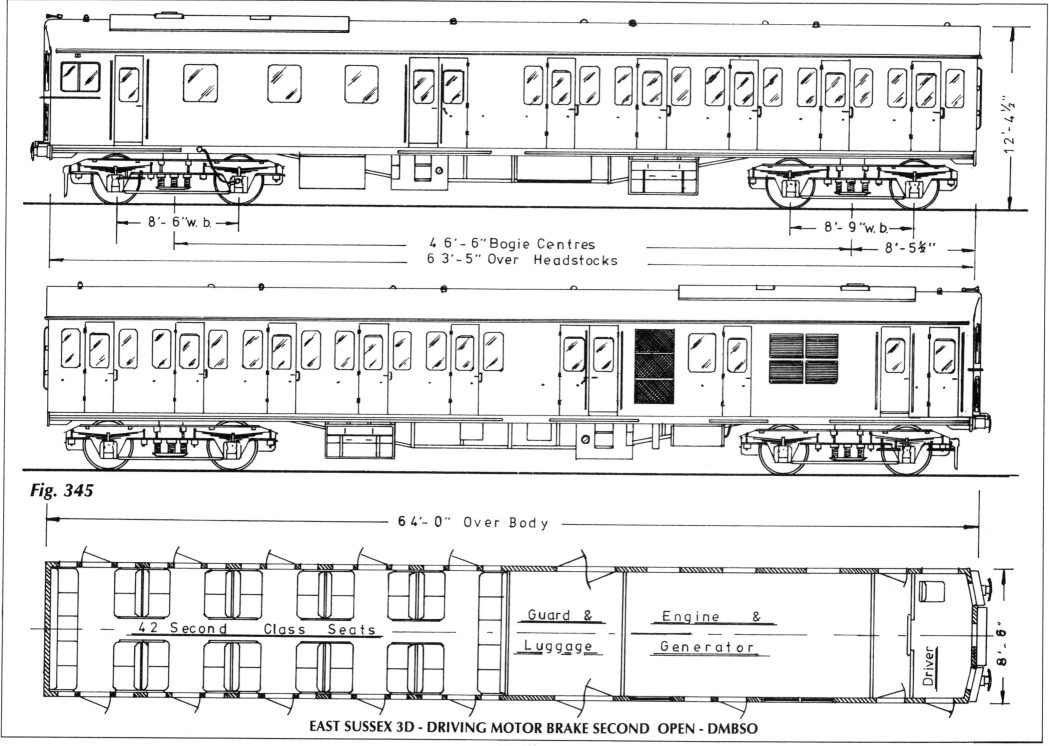

Fig. 345

8'-6" w.b.

4 6'-6" Bogie Centres
6 3'-5" Over Headstocks

8'-9" w.b.

8'-5½"

12'-4½"

64'-0" Over Body

8'-6"

42 Second Class Seats

Guard &
Luggage

Engine &
Generator

Driver

EAST SUSSEX 3D - DRIVING MOTOR BRAKE SECOND OPEN - DMBSO

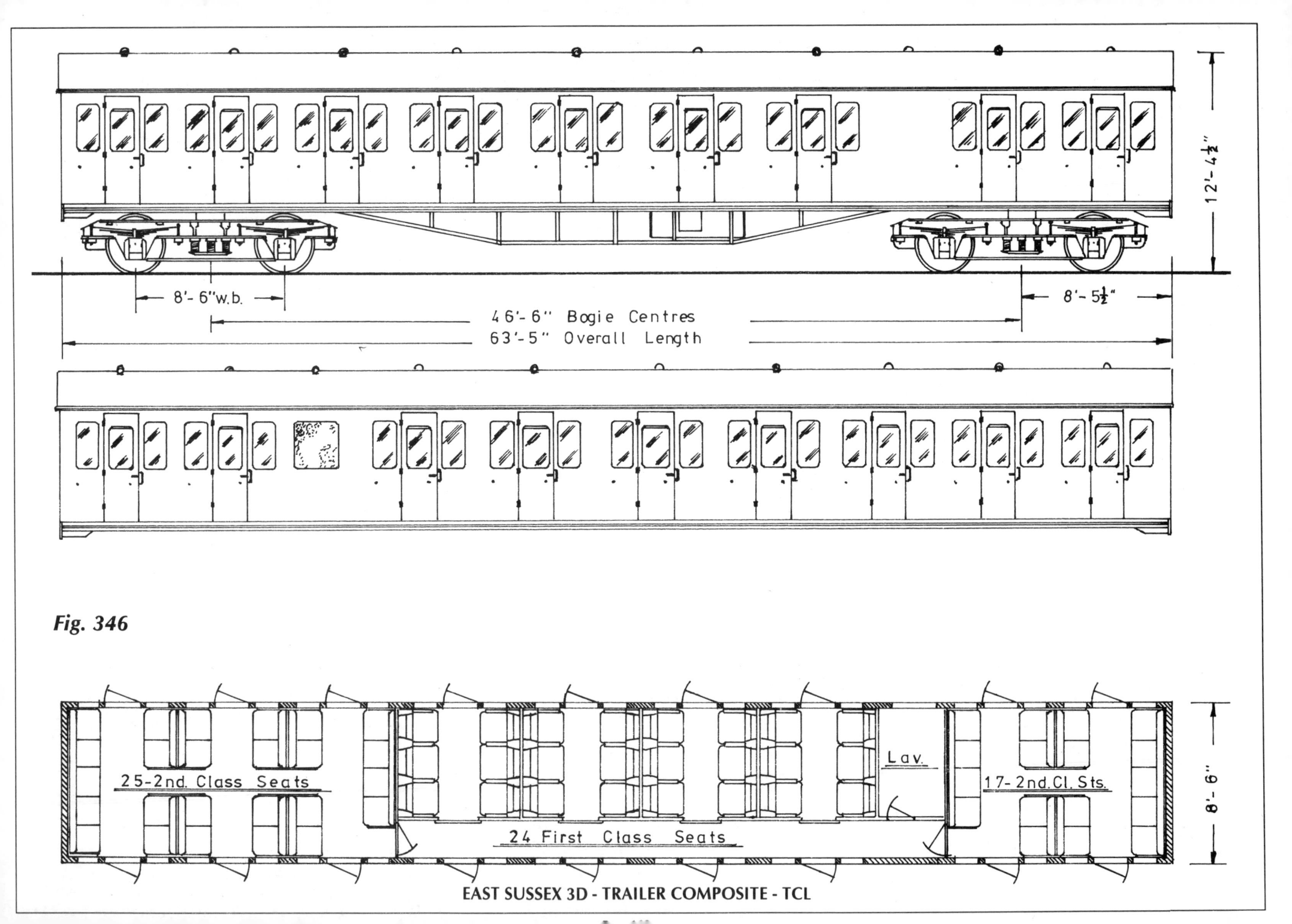

12'-4½"

8'-6" w.b.

46'-6" Bogie Centres
63'-5" Overall Length

8'-5½"

Fig. 346

25-2nd. Class Seats

Lav.

17-2nd. Cl. Sts.

24 First Class Seats

8'-6"

EAST SUSSEX 3D - TRAILER COMPOSITE - TCL

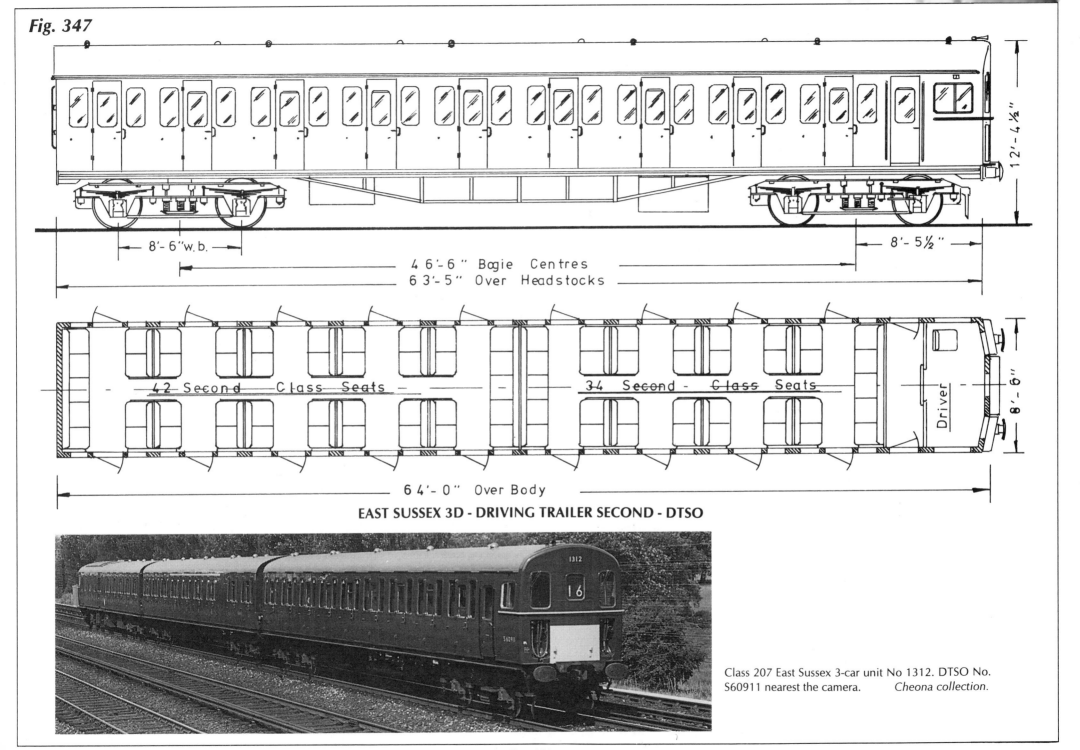

Fig. 347

12'- 4½"

8'- 6" w.b.

8'- 5½"

4 6'- 6" Bogie Centres

6 3'- 5" Over Headstocks

42 Second Class Seats

34 Second Class Seats

Driver

8'- 6"

6 4'- 0" Over Body

EAST SUSSEX 3D - DRIVING TRAILER SECOND - DTSO

Class 207 East Sussex 3-car unit No 1312. DTSO No. S60911 nearest the camera.   *Cheona collection.*

CHAPTER EIGHTEEN

The 'Tadpoles'

Although the Southern kept more rigidly to set formations than the other regions, there were a number of regroupings over the years.

The most startling of these was the 3-R configuration which was produced for the Reading to Redhill service. Six three-car sets were formed in 1965 from the DMBSO and TSOL cars from the disbanded 6-S Hastings sets 1002 - 1004. One of each of these cars was coupled to a Driving Trailer Semi-Open Second which in turn had become surplus to requirements when some 2-EPB electric sets were reformed into 4-EPB. These cars had the seats removed from the last three compartments to provide additional luggage space and the remaining two compartments and four-bay saloon were then locked when the sets operated on the 'pay-train' system The combination of a full-width DTSO and two narrow ex-Hastings cars gave rise to the 'Tadpole' nickname. Officially these were 3-R (TOPS Class 206) sets numbered 1201 - 1206.

Driving Motor Brake Open Second - DMBSO

Seats:	22 second
Nos:	S60002 - 07 (Lot No. 30329)
Weight:	54 tons 0 cwt.
Drawings:	*Fig.330* with end view as *fig.349*.

Trailer Open Second with Lavatory - TSOL

Seats:	52 second
Nos:	S60503 -06/ 09/ 10 (Lot No. 30331)
Weight:	28 tons 10 cwt.
Drawing:	*Fig.331*.

Driving Trailer Semi-Open Second - DTSO

Seats:	66 second (not normally used)
Nos:	S77500/ 03/ 07 -10 (Lot No. 30115)
Weight:	30 tons 0 cwt.
Drawings:	*Fig.348* and end view as *fig.350*.

The Tadpoles were originally in green and followed the various livery changes of the other sets until withdrawn in 1979. After disbandment the Hastings sets 1002 and 1004 were reformed and the remaining cars used as spares. At the same time set 1033 was disbanded and 'Tadpole' set 1206 was reformed carrying the full blue / grey livery as follows:-

Driving Motor Brake Open Second - DMBSO

Seats:	30 second
No:	S60037 (Lot No. 30391)
Weight:	55 tons 0 cwt.
drawings:	*Fig.333* and end view as *fig.349*.

Trailer Corridor Second with Lavatory - TSK

Seats:	42 second
No.	S60702 (Lot No. 30330) This was a downgraded short-framed TFK . At one time it worked in this set as a TCK 6-First and 36-Second.
Weight:	28 tons 0 cwt.
Drawing:	*Fig.332. Note:* This shows the vehicle as built with the seating plan the same except second class.

Driving Trailer Semi-Open Second - DTSO

Seats:	66 second (not normally in use)
No.	S77510 (Lot No. 30115)
Weight:	30 tons 0 cwt.
Drawings:	*Fig.348* and end view as *fig.350*.

This set did not remain in service long.

Class 204 'Tadpole' unit No. 1205 with DTSO nearest the camera and the two narrower ex-Hastings unit cars beyond.   *Cheona collection.*

Fig. 348   TADPOLE 3R SET - DRIVING TRAILER SECOND - DTSO

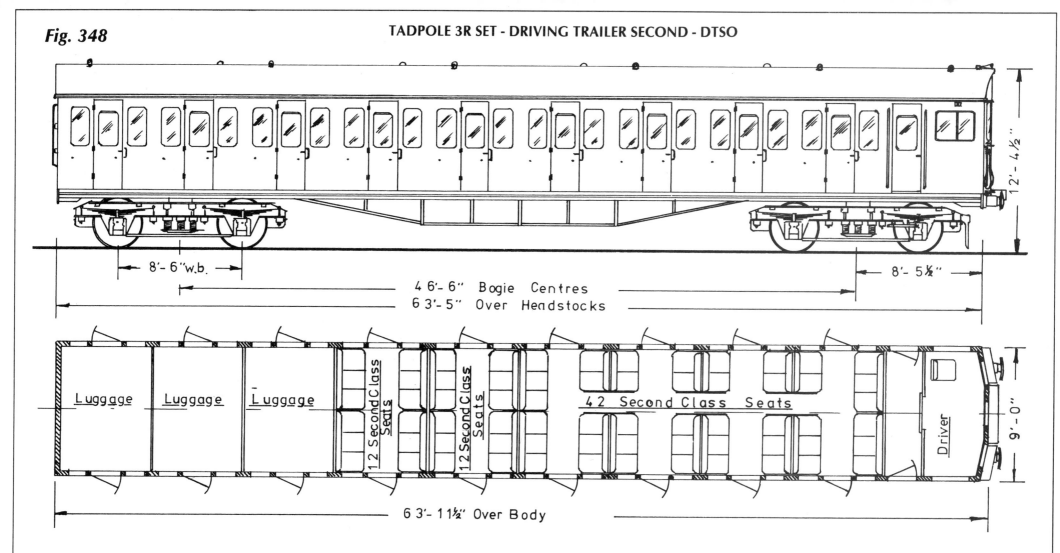

8'-6"w.b.

4 6'- 6" Bogie Centres
6 3'-5" Over Headstocks

8'-5½"

12'-4½"

Luggage   Luggage   Luggage   12 Second Class Seats   12 Second Class Seats   42 Second Class Seats   Driver

9'-0"

6 3'-11½" Over Body

The 'Maggots'

With the introduction of the summer 1995 timetable, some experiments were carried out on the Ashford to Brighton services. These led to the combination of a DMBSO and a DTSO from some remaining East Sussex units, with a spare TSOL from disbanded Class 411/5's (4-CEP units), which provided the lavatory facilities. Three sets were formed in this way :-

Set Number	Name	DMBSO	TSOL	DTSO
207 201	Brighton Royal Pavilion	60126	70286	60903
207 202	Ashford Fayre	60130	70549	60904
207 203	—	60127	70547	60901

These sets are classified as 3DEL 207/2.
One further set (classified 3DEL 205/2) was made by adding an ex 4-CEP trailer to 205101 to give :-

Set Number	Name	DMBSO	TS	DTCL
205 205	—	60110	71634*	60810

*71634 was originally coach 4059

With a wide car between two narrow cars, these 4 sets have been unofficially called 'Maggots'!

CHAPTER NINETEEN

The Blue Pullman Sets

Although not strictly Diesel Multiple Units in the normally accepted sense these super - luxury trains are included since they worked as fixed formation sets and two of them were later modified for multiple working.

The London Midland Region introduced the first two sets in 1959 for the 'Midland Pullman' service from London (St Pancras) to Manchester over the former Midland Railway main line. These two were all - First class six car sets offering the most luxurious accommodation combined with relatively high speed. The formation was :-

Driving Motor Brake first with Lavatory

Engine:	One North British / MAN 1000bhp, twelve cylinder pressured-charged 'V' type L12V18 / 21BS.
Transmission:	Electric. Two 425bhp GEC traction motors driving through Brown-Boveri spring drive.
Body:	66' 5½ x 9' 3". Guard's and luggage compartment, engine room and full width cab at outer end.
Weight:	67 tons 10 cwt.
Seats:	12 first
Nos:	M60090 - 93 (Lot No. 30553)
Drawing:	Fig.353.

Motor Kitchen First with Lavatory (non driving car)

Transmission:	As above
Body:	65' 6" x 9' 3"
Weight:	49 tons 0 cwt.
Seats:	18 first
Nos:	M60730 - 33 (Lot No. 30556)
Drawings:	Fig.354 and fig.356. Note: Fig.354 shows the correct bogie arrangement for this car whereas fig.355 includes two trailer bogies and is correct for the Western Region Trailer Kitchen First.

Trailer Parlour First with Lavatory

Body:	65' 6" x 9' 3"
Weight:	33 tons 0 cwt.
Seats:	36 first
Nos.	M60740 - 43 (Lot No. 30557)
Drawing:	Fig.357.

Trailer Parlour First with Lavatory
Details as above
Motor Kitchen First with Lavatory (non-driving car)
Details as above
Driving Motor Brake First with Lavatory
Details as above

From this it will be seen that the six-car train had just 132 first class seats. In the following year the Western Region introduced three eight-car sets which were similar to the LMR units but included second class accommodation. They were used on Paddington to Birmingham, Paddington to Bristol and Paddington to South Wales services. The formation was :-

Driving Motor Brake Second

Engine:	As fitted to the LMR cars.
Transmission:	As fitted to the LMR cars.
Body:	66' 5½ x 9' 3". Guard's and luggage compartment, engine room and full width cab at outer end. No lavatory was included, instead a third seating bay was fitted.
Weight:	67 tons 10 cwt.
Seats:	18 second
Nos:	W60094 - 99 (Lot No. 30554)
Drawings:	Fig.358 and fig. 359. Note : The two power cars have been drawn showing different sides. Apart from the windows in the passenger sections both types were the same so that both sides are covered between the two drawings.

Motor Parlour Second with Lavatory (non-driving car)

Transmission:	As fitted to the LMR cars
Body:	65' 6" x 9' 3"
Weight:	45 tons 10 cwt.
Seats:	42 second
Nos:	W60644 - 49 (Lot No. 30555)
Drawing:	Fig.360.

Trailer Kitchen First with Lavatory

Body:	65' 6" x 9' 3"
Weight:	36 tons 0 cwt.
Seats:	18 first
Nos:	W60734 - 39 (Lot No. 30557)
Drawings:	Fig.354 and fig.355. Note: Fig.354 shows the Motor Kitchen First as used in the LMR sets. Fig.355 is correct for this car which has two trailer bogies. Plan view as fig.356.

Trailer Parlour First with Lavatory
All details the same as those used in the LMR sets
Nos: W60744 - 49   (Lot No. 30558)
Trailer Parlour First with Lavatory
Details as above
Trailer Kitchen First with Lavatory
Details as above
Motor Parlour Second with Lavatory (non-driving car)
Details as above
Driving Motor Brake Second
Details as above

The total capacity of each of these sets was 108 first and 120 second passengers.

When built the entire Blue Pullman fleet was finished in an attractive livery of Nanking blue approximating to the old Caledonian Railway light blue.

Roofs were painted grey and the area around the passenger windows white. The streamlined cab fronts were also blue with a large Pullman crest placed centrally below the windscreens which were set in a pale grey panel. The effect was very appealing when set against the then standard greens and maroons with the almost universal general grime.

Although, at that time they appeared extremely modern in design and predated the HST by some 17 years, they were overtaken by the march of progress in the Modernisation Plan. The electrification of the West Coast Mainline from Euston, led to the transfer of London to Manchester traffic to the former LNWR line. The Manchester Pullman was replaced by electric locomotive hauled Mk2 Pullman cars and the two Blue Pullman sets made redundant, were stored in 1966/67. The same electrification scheme eventually brought the overhead wires into Birmingham and the bulk of the London to Birmingham traffic was concentrated on the Euston to New Street route at the expense of the Paddington to Snow Hill line. The Birmingham Pullman was withdrawn in 1967 and the Blue Pullman set used as a spare for the other two WR units.

With only around seven years service these units had many more useful miles left in them. The former LMR sets were converted to be able to run in multiple with each other, and had some re-classification of seating to include second class accommodation. They were then used on the Bristol to Paddington service as a twelve car train in the morning peak hour. They then split into two and ran as separate units for one round trip each, one to Bristol and the other to Oxford before re-combining to form one train for the evening peak service back to Bristol. The eight car set displaced from the Bristol run was switched to South Wales to double the number of workings on this route.

In 1968 all the sets were repainted in the new BR colour scheme for Pullman cars as applied to the locomotive hauled West Coast cars. This was mainly rail grey with the window surrounds in Rail Blue. The entire front end as far as the cab doors was then painted yellow. These changes totally destroyed their air of distinction and the magic which had been associated with these units when first launched, was lost. All were finally withdrawn 1973.

In many ways these sets established new standards of service and comfort. This was equally true from a technical standpoint. However, they did not escape their share of problems. One of the most serious and persistent was the 'rough riding' due to the design of the bogies. The Schlieren pattern bogies used were applied to these units without being correctly adapted and developed to suit the particular conditions found on British railways. With a service life of around 14 years, valuable lessons were learned. Later designs including the highly successful HST sets undoubtedly benefited from the experienced gained form the 'Blue Pullman' era.

A Western Blue Pullman unit in first livery but with all yellow end.   *Cheona collection.*

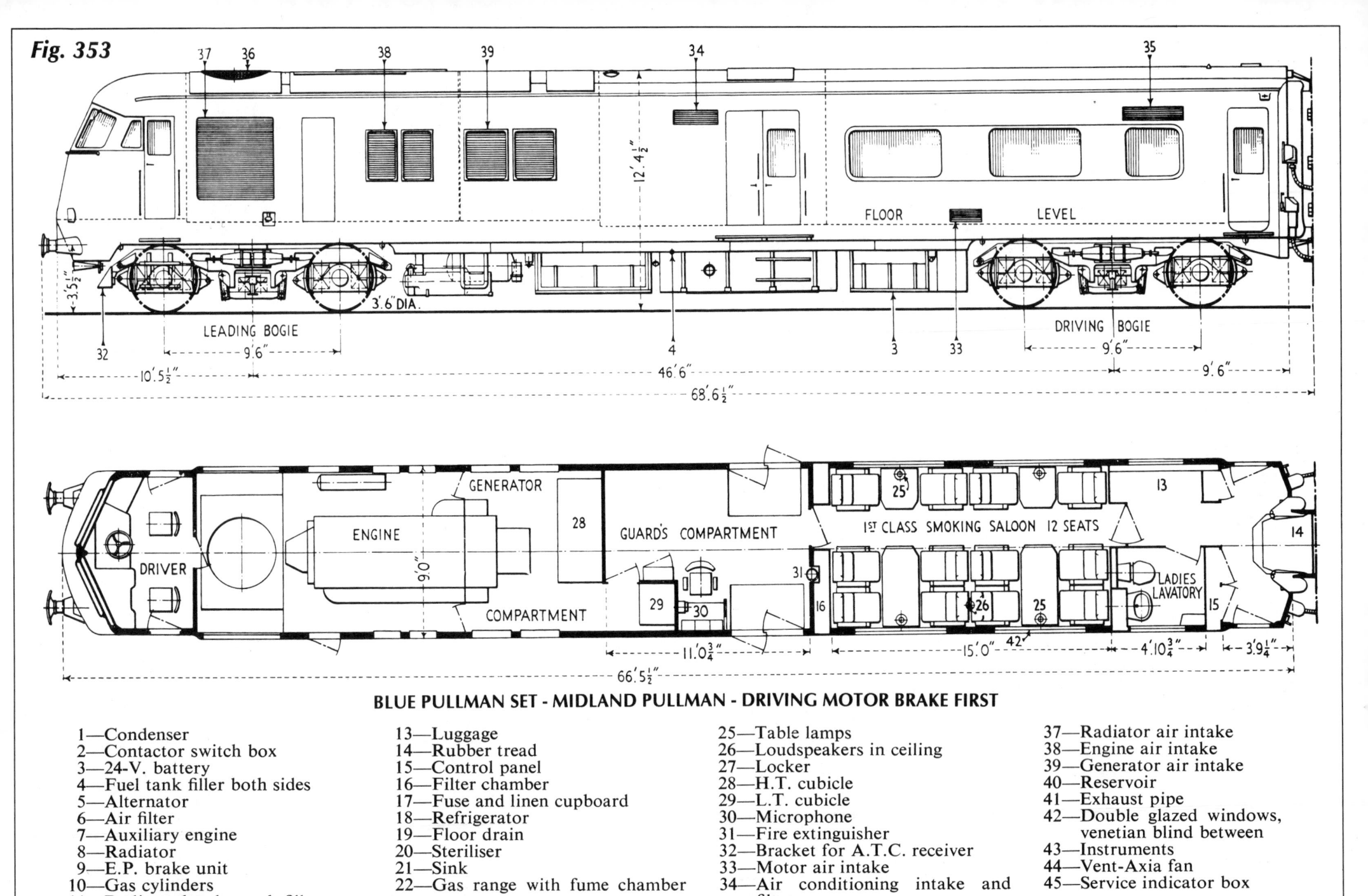

Fig. 353

BLUE PULLMAN SET - MIDLAND PULLMAN - DRIVING MOTOR BRAKE FIRST

1—Condenser
2—Contactor switch box
3—24-V. battery
4—Fuel tank filler both sides
5—Alternator
6—Air filter
7—Auxiliary engine
8—Radiator
9—E.P. brake unit
10—Gas cylinders
11—Radiator header tank filler
12—Air conditioning exhaust and air intake filter on opposite sides

13—Luggage
14—Rubber tread
15—Control panel
16—Filter chamber
17—Fuse and linen cupboard
18—Refrigerator
19—Floor drain
20—Steriliser
21—Sink
22—Gas range with fume chamber over
23—Silencer
24—Tank filler

25—Table lamps
26—Loudspeakers in ceiling
27—Locker
28—H.T. cubicle
29—L.T. cubicle
30—Microphone
31—Fire extinguisher
32—Bracket for A.T.C. receiver
33—Motor air intake
34—Air conditioning intake and filters
35—Air conditioning exhaust
36—Radiator exhaust fan

37—Radiator air intake
38—Engine air intake
39—Generator air intake
40—Reservoir
41—Exhaust pipe
42—Double glazed windows, venetian blind between
43—Instruments
44—Vent-Axia fan
45—Service indicator box

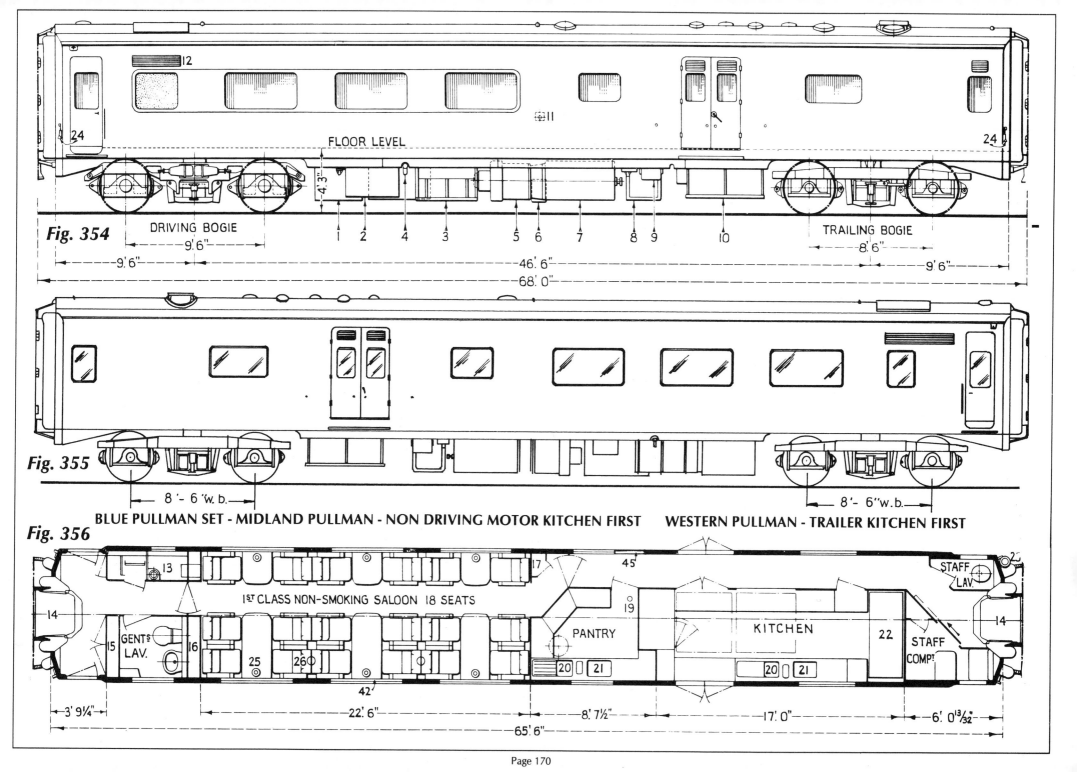

Fig. 354

DRIVING BOGIE
9'6"

FLOOR LEVEL
4' 3"

1 2 4 3   5 6   7   8 9   10

9' 6"

TRAILING BOGIE
8' 6"

46' 6"
68' 0"

9' 6"

Fig. 355

8'- 6" w.b.

8'- 6" w.b.

BLUE PULLMAN SET - MIDLAND PULLMAN - NON DRIVING MOTOR KITCHEN FIRST   WESTERN PULLMAN - TRAILER KITCHEN FIRST

Fig. 356

STAFF LAV.

13   17   45

1ST CLASS NON-SMOKING SALOON 18 SEATS

14   PANTRY   KITCHEN   22   STAFF COMPt   14

GENTS LAV.

15   16   25   26   19   20 21   20 21

42

3' 9¼"   22' 6"   8' 7½"   17' 0"   6' 0 13⁄32"
65' 6"

Fig. 357

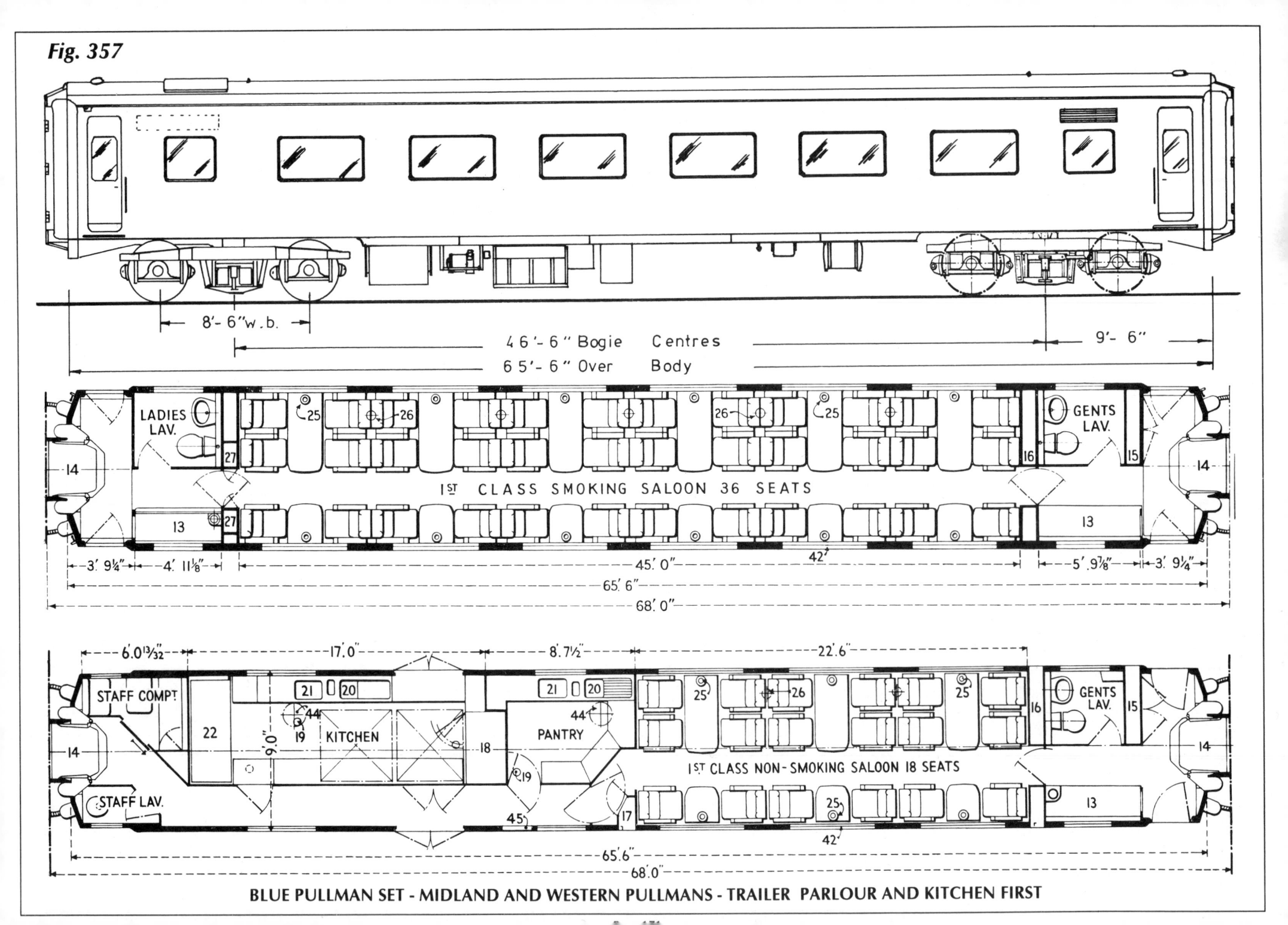

BLUE PULLMAN SET - MIDLAND AND WESTERN PULLMANS - TRAILER PARLOUR AND KITCHEN FIRST

Fig. 358

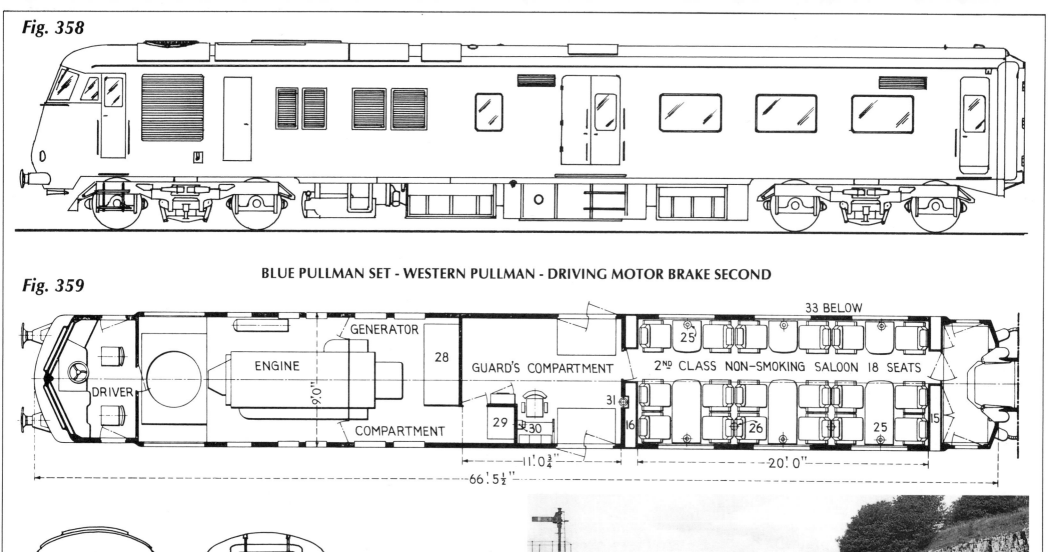

BLUE PULLMAN SET - WESTERN PULLMAN - DRIVING MOTOR BRAKE SECOND

Fig. 359

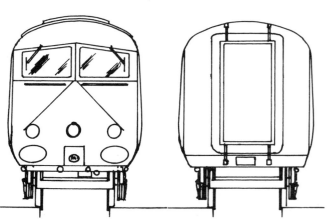

The 'Midland Pullman' passing through Millers Dale on an up service. First livery with Pullman crest on the front. *J.R.Morten.*

Fig. 360

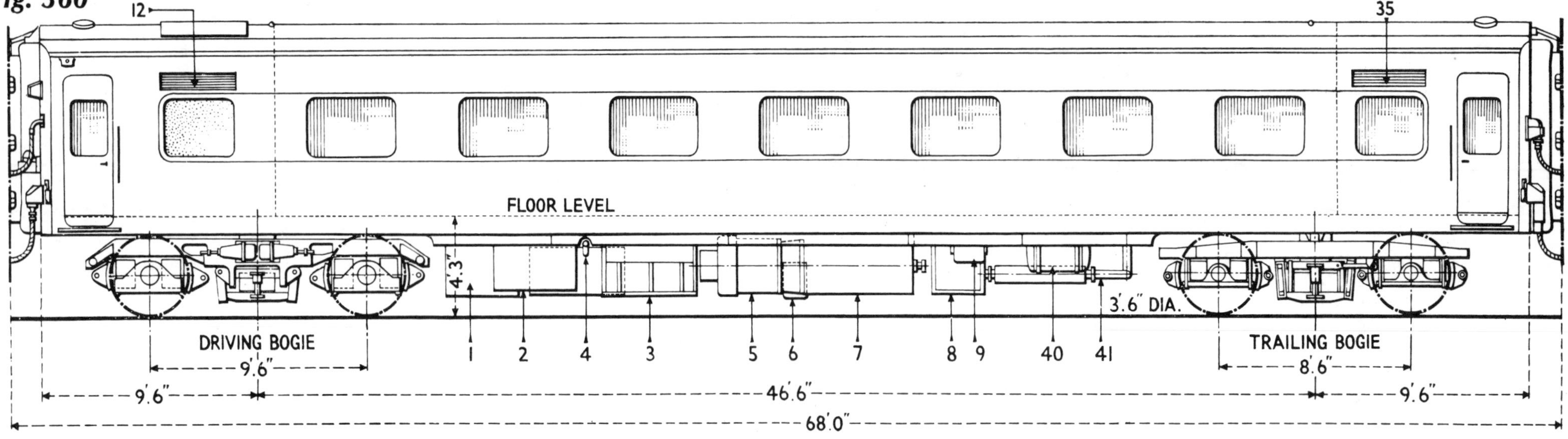

12
35
FLOOR LEVEL
4.3"
3.6" DIA.
DRIVING BOGIE
9.6"
TRAILING BOGIE
8.6"
1 2 4 3 5 6 7 8 9 40 41
9.6"
46.6"
9.6"
68.0"

BLUE PULLMAN SET - WESTERN PULLMAN - NON-DRIVING MOTOR PARLOUR SECOND

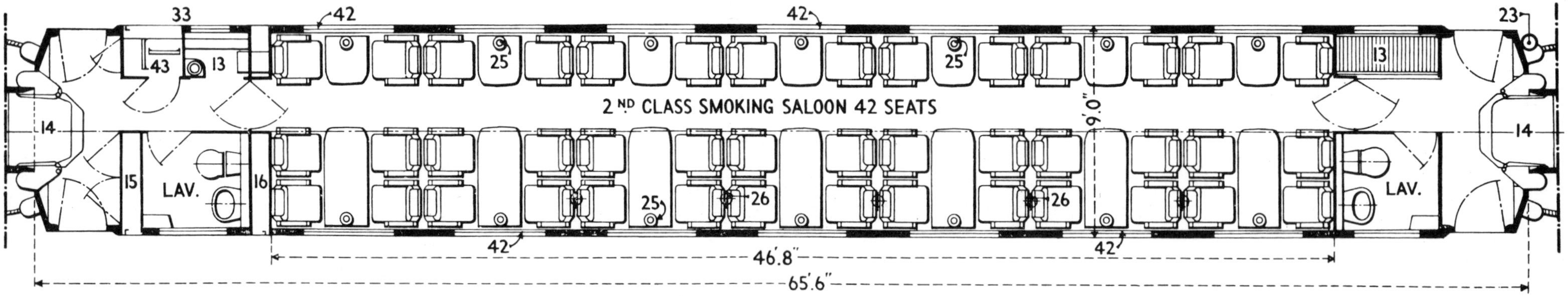

33
42
42
23
43
13
25
25
13
2 ND CLASS SMOKING SALOON 42 SEATS
9.0"
14
14
15
LAV.
16
25
26
26
LAV.
42
42
46.8"
65.6"

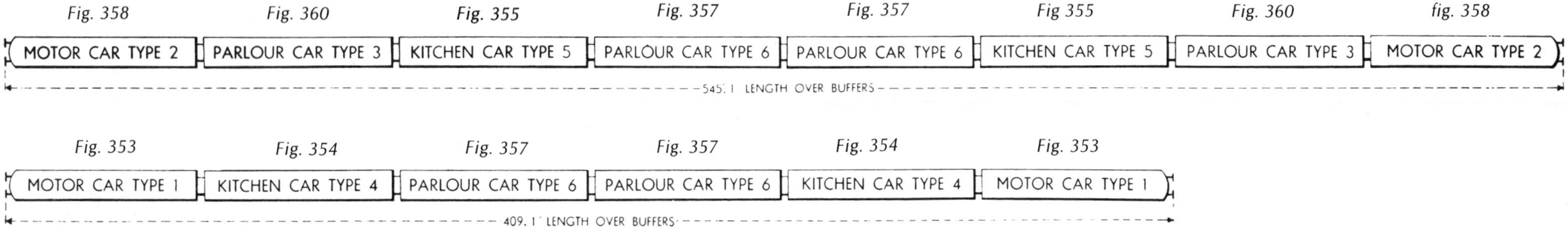

Fig. 358
Fig. 360
Fig. 355
Fig. 357
Fig. 357
Fig 355
Fig. 360
fig. 358
MOTOR CAR TYPE 2
PARLOUR CAR TYPE 3
KITCHEN CAR TYPE 5
PARLOUR CAR TYPE 6
PARLOUR CAR TYPE 6
KITCHEN CAR TYPE 5
PARLOUR CAR TYPE 3
MOTOR CAR TYPE 2
545.1 LENGTH OVER BUFFERS
Fig. 353
Fig. 354
Fig. 357
Fig. 357
Fig. 354
Fig. 353
MOTOR CAR TYPE 1
KITCHEN CAR TYPE 4
PARLOUR CAR TYPE 6
PARLOUR CAR TYPE 6
KITCHEN CAR TYPE 4
MOTOR CAR TYPE 1
409.1' LENGTH OVER BUFFERS

Block diagrams showing formation of complete double-end six- and eight-car trains

Models of Heritage Diesel Multiple and Diesel Electric Multiple Units

The number of different types of units produced in 'ready-to-run' form has been relatively small although variety has been achieved by marketing them in different liveries.

The following section details the major ready-to-run units which have been produced to date.

Class	Year	Maker	Cars	Liveries	Scale	Notes
101	1958	Triang	2	G	00	An intermediate car was made later
101*	1982	Grafar	2 & 3	G, B, BG R,NSE,RR	N	
104	1963	Triang	3	G	TT	Announced in 1961
110*	1982	Hornby	2	G,B,BG,R	00	
117*	1981	Lima	3	G,B,BG,R NSE,RR	00	
124	1966	Br.Trix	2	G	3.8mm to 1ft.	A 6-car set could be produced by converting other BR Mk.1 coaches
124	1974	Liliput	2	G,BG	3.8mm to 1ft.	Liliput took over production from Trix
124*	1994	Dapol	2	G	3.8mm to 1ft.	Trix unit produced by its third owner. Unit raised on bogies to be more compatible with 00 models
Blue Pullman	1963	Triang	3	Blue & White Silver roof	00	Continued by Triang Hornby used incorrect bogies. Power Bogie from SR EMU.Other bogies BR B1 coach.
Blue Pullman	1964	Triang Hornby	3	Reversed BG	00	Livery grey mainbody with blue panels around windows and extended along the power cars to radiator at rear of cab door.

Key :   G = BR Green : B = BR Blue : BG = BR Blue-Grey : R = BR Refurbished colours : NSE = Network South East : RR = Regional Railways   * Still currently available

Anbrico

This company produced batches of some units in BR green livery as well as constructing 'specials' to customers specifications. All models were in 00 gauge. Units were produced in batches and included :-

Class 105 Cravens 2-car, Class 108 Derby 2-car and Class 128 Gloucester single unit parcel cars.

The units were of all-metal construction and had seats and controls as standard fittings.

KITS
00 / 4mm Scale

Kitmaster

In 1961 this company produced all-plastic kits of the Midland Pullman. No power bogie was available, but motorisation could be achieved using the power bogie from Triang EMU or DMU cars. Three vehicles were produced ie. Motor Brake First, Motor Kitchen First and Trailer Parlour First. Two of each of these vehicles would give the prototypical six-car set.

Kits Available (as at August 1995)

N / 2mm Scale

B.H.Enterprises

These kits are obtainable direct or at Model railway exhibitions.

They consist of plastic body sides to correct profile, plastic roofs and floors, plastic underframe mouldings, plastic bogies with additional white metal castings where appropriate, cast white metal ends and etched brass sides. Full instructions are included together with practical suggestions for motorising. *Units available.*

Classes : *105, 108, 114, 116, 117, 118, 119, 120, 121, 122, 123, 128, 129, 205 and 207*

The company sells a complete catalogue of all its N gauge products.

00 / 4mm Scale

D.C. Kits

Precision plastic kits for a two-car Class 101 unit with two different centre car conversion kits. Cast white metal underframe fittings. Bogies are plastic. May be powered using Lima or Hornby DMU power bogie or by D.C.Kits own power bogie kit.

Modern Traction Kits Ltd (MTK Ltd)

These kits are obtainable direct or at Model Railway Exhibitions.

Units consist of an aluminium metal shell with windows, rainstrips and solebars pressed out and the shell pre-formed to shape. Included are all cast parts, ends, underfloor engine details, vents, bogie sides. Interiors and wheels are not included. *The following list is available :*

Company Code	Type
DMU 1	SCR 6-car Intercity unit (2 x 3 units)
DMU 2*	Cravens 2-car Class 105 Standard Series
DMU 3	Cravens 2-car Hydraulic set. Large Headcode type
DMU 4	Derby short 2-car Class 108
DMU 5	BRCW 2-car Class 104
DMU 6	BRCW 3-car Class 104
DMU 7*	Gloucester 3-car Cross Country Class 119
DMU 8	Pressed Steel Single unit Class 121/2
DMU 9	As above plus Driving Trailer
DMU 10	Derby High Density 3-car Class 116
DMU 11	Derby Marylebone 4-car Class 115
DMU 12	Derby Original Single Unit M77990
DMU 13	Derby Original Single Unit M77991
DMU 14*	Derby Original 2-car unit
DMU 15	Park Royal 2-car Class 103
DMU 16	Swindon 4-car Inter City Class 123
DMU 17	Trans Pennine 5-car Inter City Class 124
DMU 18	Mixed 4-car Swindon / Trans Pennine Class 123/4
DMU 19	Swindon 3-car SCR Inter City Class126
DMU 20	Swindon 3-car Cross Country Class 120
DMU 21	Gloucester Cross Country 2-car Class 100
DMU 22	Derby long Cross Country 2-car Class 114
DMU 23	Derby SCR Cross Country short 3-car Class 107
DMU 24	Wickham Cross Country 2-car set
DMU 25	Swindon 2-car Class 120 (MU81) extra large guards van.
DMU 26	Buffet Coach for trans-Pennine sets
DMU 27(B)	Metro Cammell 2-car Class 101
DMU 28(B)	Metro Cammell 3-car Class 101

Diesel Parcels Units

DPU 1	Gloucester gangway Parcels unit Class 128
DPU 2	Gloucester non-gangway Parcels unit Class 128
DPU 3	Gloucester gangway-removed (Red Star) Class 128
DPU 4	Class 127 2-car unit
DPU 5	Class 120 2-car unit
DPU 6	Class 114 2-car unit
DPU 7	Cravens single unit

Diesel Units (Railbuses)

RB 6 (B)	Waggon und Maschinenbau Railbus (Wagonbasher)
RB 7 (B)	Bristol / ECW Railbus

Diesel Electric Multiple Units

DEMU 1	Hampshire 2H Class 205 2-car set
DEMU 2	Hampshire 3H Class 205 3-car set
DEMU 3	Berkshire 3H Class 205 3-car large brake van.
DEMU 4	Hybrid 3T Class 205 3-car set
DEMU 5	Oxted 3D Class 207 3-car set
DEMU 6 (B)	Tadpole 3R Class 206 3-car set
DEMU 7 (B)	Hastings 6S Class 210 6-car Short set
DEMU 8 (B)	Hastings 6L Class 201 6-car Long set
DEMU 9 (B)	Hastings 6B Class 201 6-car Buffet
DEMU 10 (B)	Hastings 4L Class 201 4-car Long

Note : (B) indicates available in brass (etched) only (body shells)
 * indicates available in etched brass or aluminium (body shells)
 No symbol indicates available in aluminium only (body shells)

Airfix / Dapol

Airfix produced a green plastic kit for the four-wheeled Park Royal Railbus in 1960, complete with plastic wheels, clear plastic moulded windows and transfers. When the Airfix range was taken over by Dapol Model Railways Ltd., the kit continued in production, the only differences being the use of grey instead of green plastic and the plastic wheels were replaced by Dapol 3-hole disc coach wheels on metal pinpoint axles. The kit is still in production. Motorizing kits for this vehicle have been introduced by D.C. Kits and Branch Lines. The latter company can supply a complete package for this railbus ie. Dapol kit, motorizing kit and interior detailing kit.

0/7mm Scale

MTK Ltd

A range of kits as listed in 00 section is produced in etched brass where the bodies fold up with the floor, and the ends are produced etched also. A separate extruded roof is provided. Underframe details, bogies and other fittings are in cast white metal, but no wheels, gears, motors or interiors are included. ODMU 6 is produced as a punched aluminium bodyshell formed up with solebars and rainstrips already in place. Fittings etc. are as for the etched brass kits in this scale. The units can be powered by using TRACTOPAK power bogies available from Slater's Plastikard.

British Rail DMU's

ODMU 1 (B)	Cravens 2-car Class 105
ODMU 2 (B)	BRCW 2-car Class 104
ODMU 3 (B)	Calder Valley 3-car set
ODMU 4 (B)	Gloucester 3-car Cross Country Class 119
ODMU 5 (B)	Swindon 3-car Cross Country Class 120
ODMU 6	Gloucester Parcels Class 128 DPU single unit
ODMU 7 (B)	Derby 2-car short Class 108
ODMU 8 (B)	Metro Cammell 2-car Class 101
ODMU 9 (B)	Pressed Steel single unit Class 121
ODMU 10 (B)	'Wagonbasher' Railbus
ODMU 11 (B)	Swindon 4-car Inter City Class 123

Southern Region DEMU

ODEMU 1 (B)	3H Class 205 2 coach set
ODEMU 2 (B)	3H Class 205 3 coach set
ODEMU 3 (B)	3D Class 207 3 coach set
ODEMU 4 (B)	6S